Research in Urban Educational Settings

Lessons Learned and Implications for Future Practice

Research in Urban Educational Settings

Lessons Learned and Implications for Future Practice

edited by

Kimberly A. Scott
Arizona State University

and

Wanda J. Blanchett
University of Missouri-Kansas City

Information Age Publishing, Inc.
Charlotte, North Carolina • www.infoagepub.com

Library of Congress Cataloging-in-Publication Data

Research in urban educational settings : lessons learned and implications
for future practice / edited by Kimberly A. Scott and Wanda J. Blanchett.
    p. cm.
  Includes bibliographical references.
  ISBN 978-1-61735-206-5 (pbk.) -- ISBN 978-1-61735-207-2 (hardcover) --
ISBN 978-1-61735-208-9 (e-book)
  1. Education, Urban--Research--United States. I. Scott, Kimberly A. II.
Blanchett, Wanda J.
  LC5131.R465 2011
  370.9173'2--dc22   2011010592

Printed in the United States of America

CONTENTS

FOREWORD

Carol D. Lee

The year 2009 marks a historic shift in U.S. politics with the election of Barack Obama as the first African American president. I was lucky and honored to be present at the inauguration to experience not only the official swearing in of the president, but the outpouring of affection of more than a million people who came from across the country and the world to bear witness to the dream. President Obama's election carried forward and indeed embodied the narrative of America as a land of hope and equal opportunity. However, as Dr. Martin Luther King proclaimed on that same mall in Washington, DC in 1964, for too many Americans have written a check with insufficient funds, one that has persistently challenged those historically underserved: the descendants of Africans who were enslaved from the founding of the country, ripped from their homelands to face a 200-year holocaust on these shores (including their more recent Black brethren immigrating from the Caribbean, South America and Africa); the indigenous populations of American Indians who were the first inhabitants of this American continent, whose lands and bodies were usurped through war; the descendants of those from across Latin America, many of whom immigrated to the United States, either because their lands had been annexed through war or U.S. economic policies deflated the economies of their countries of origin; Asian Americans who immigrated in large numbers in the nineteenth century from China and more recently from central Asia and historically faced constraints codified in law, and poor Whites, especially those who experience persistent intergenerational poverty in areas like Appalachia and the Mississippi Delta, from a tradition which also included White indentured servitude in the early days of the republic. Part of the promise of America has been the upward mobility from poverty to middle-class status across these populations, achieved largely through the opportunities that education has provided. At the same time, the check with insufficient funds has also meant that education has often served to reinforce second-class citizenship and opportunity. This, unfortunately, is the case in too many urban school districts where the majority of students are indeed Black, Brown, and poor.

Donald Stokes (1997) describes what he calls "Pasteur's Quadrant" in describing the focus and function of research. Stokes wrestles with the distinctions that have been made in scientific research between basic and applied research. This distinction has often been used to situate applied research as not as rigorous. However, Stokes argues that Pasteur's research addressed fundamental scientific questions about the role of germs in disease while at the same time focusing on a compelling problem of practice (e.g., public policy around the delivery of safe milk to the population). The argument has been made that educational research falls into this category of Pasteur's Quadrant that is, research that seeks to address fundamental problems of knowledge and practice. New fields like the Learning Sciences have sought to address the dual foci directly (Sawyer, 2008). The challenge had been to conceptualize this dual focus in ways that build upon the fundamental cultural foundations of all learning (Lee, 2008).

In part because the problems of education, particularly in our urban centers, are so pervasive and dire, a significant amount of attention is paid to these problems across fields of educational research. However, there have been persistent challenges in presumed hierarchies, where researchers working out of traditions like critical race theory, multiculturalism, and activist scholarship—often carried out by scholars of color—have been sidelined in mainstream research media and not well represented in funding venues. Dr. Joyce King has used the term "data plantations" to describe how urban school settings, populated predominantly by students of color and students from low income communities, have become ubiquitous sites for the privileged to analyze the needs and produce solutions for the under privileged. It is this context of educational research in urban school settings that makes this volume so important and necessary.

One of the most exciting aspects of the campaign of Barack Obama for the presidency of the United States was the outpouring of political activism among the young and across communities of color. President Obama's campaign has continued to call for grass roots organizing around the issues of equity that were addressed during the campaign. Indeed, in 2009 we face unparalleled economic perils that affect the middle class and the poor, and that undoubtedly constrain efforts to transform our schools. This means we need to articulate a knowledge base, based on an on-the-ground track record of that has proven effective, that facilitates the efforts of researchers and community activists (including researchers who are themselves community activists) to forge alliances with those working with their feet on the plough (e.g., teachers, parents, administrators, students). This is work that can require deep and humble reflection on stereotypes and deficit assumptions that many of us bring to our work in these urban settings, often unconscious but no less virulent. Learning to build collaborations and shared vision is not easy work. Learning to navigate between the academy and the community involves tricky waters.

The authors in this volume represent a stellar array of scholars, junior and senior, who have built partnerships in urban school settings, who have investigated both questions of foundational knowledge and practice, and who have wrestled personally with the dilemmas of navigating the academy and the community. These chapters are not simple testimonies, but rather they articulate the challenges of articulating meaningful questions for inquiry, establishing productive relationships with institutional and community players in the field, collecting data in what are often the messy waters of practice, analyzing data in ways that include community and school partners, communicating findings in ways that empower constituencies and extend beyond the walls of the academy.

Our President Barack Obama has said, "we are the ones we have been waiting for." These include a new generation of scholars with a passion for helping to create change, change not only in the educational outcomes for youth who have historically been underserved in our schools, but change in the conduct of research that seeks to align itself with community interests and needs as co-workers in the struggle for educational equity. This volume represents an important part of the methodological arsenal that will be required for this important and timely work.

Carol D. Lee, PhD
January 2009
Northwestern University
President, American Educational Research Association
(April 2009–April 2010)

REFERENCES

Lee, C. D. (2008). The centrality of culture to the scientific study of learning and development: How an ecological framework in educational research facilitates civic responsibility. *Educational Researcher, 37*(5), 267–279.

Sawyer, K. (Ed.). (2008). *Cambridge handbook of the learning sciences.* New York: Cambridge University Press.

Stokes, D. (1997). *Pasteur's quadrant: Basic science and technological innovation.* Washington, DC: Brookings Institution Press.

ACKNOWLEDGMENTS

It was considerable support, patience, and guidance that made this publication possible. A sincere thanks to Gene Glass for introducing us to Information Age Publishing. We are grateful to each author, particularly Carol Lee, for their persistence along the way. A special mention of gratitude to Ann Sanders (Wanda's exceptional assistant during critical phases of this project) for her keen eye and patience with us and all of the contributors. Thanks to George Johnson for not giving up on us or this labor of love—we are exceptionally grateful for your patience. Kim wants to particularly thank William Tate and Sarane Boocock for reviewing and providing critical feedback. And thanks to Zuri for allowing her mother the much-needed time to collaborate with Aunt Wanda and see this project to fruition.

INTRODUCTION

In the early 1990s, we (Scott & Blanchett) attended one of our first American Educational Research Association Conferences. Like most graduate students, we were "star-gazed," looking in awe at people whose work we had read in a multitude of classes. In our eagerness, we attempted to attend every session and warily approached scholars in hopes that we could gain some insight without publicizing our self-perceived minimal knowledge. As we navigated the program, we had the good fortune of hearing Jacqueline Jordon Irvine speak. Her words helped to shape both our research agendas, personal commitments, and to refine our intent as scholars with a desire to conduct research that positively impacts often marginalized children, families, and communities.

Dr. Irvine instructed us to be mindful of how we conduct research in urban areas. Too often, she explained, researchers treat urban sites as plantations. After they gather data, they leave these spaces with eyes too focused on how the newly acquired information will benefit their careers than on how their presence affected the communities and its people, for better or worse. In the end, the urban communities often receive very little, if any, benefits from the researcher's presence and from having been studied. Equally disturbing, the researcher too often fails to consider her effect at multiple levels. Upon hearing this warning, the need to work with urban school and communities contexts in different ways than even some of the very same individuals we idolized became apparent. Foremost in our minds were questions such as why should we conduct a research project if it only makes a positive impact on our own academic careers? To whose end should our work serve?

As our professional lives matured and we began to move from graduate students to faculty members and beyond, our vision of ourselves and the communities in which we prefer to research crystallized. Clearly, we wanted to develop culturally sensitive research approaches (Johnson-Bailey, 1998, 1999, 2003; Tillman, 2002, 2006) and construct methodological processes that are empowering for both the participants and us as researchers (Dillard, 2000; Ladson-Billings, 2000, 2004; Milner, 2006). We also understood these goals required a heightened sensitivity to three key elements: (1) Intersecting sociocultural features such as race, gender, social class, immigration status, and/or perceived ability as influences on our engagements with urban communities, schools, and our colleagues; (2) Understanding how these features shape our interactions with participants; and (3) Articulating appreciation and demonstration of how interactions are often circumscribed by relevant issues of power and privilege. The only logical means to maintain these commitments were to center the voices and epistemologies of peoples and communities by rejecting dominant paradigms that often cast them as "pathological" and "deficient" (Ladson-Billings, 2000). We were not interested in simply "giving voice" to urban communities as is often mentioned in the literature which is another manifestation of power and privilege. Rather, we sought to provide spaces in which their voices were heard. Like so many efforts that go against the grain, our aspirations posed challenges.

Presenting to the best extent possible the authentic perspectives and lived experiences of oppressed urban communities requires us to be responsible and accountable to the children and families that reside in such settings. Our duty includes deconstructing ourselves as cultural beings who cannot escape our own values and worldviews even while conducting research (Banks, 1998; Lather, 2004). In this volume, authors argue how they engage in this self-reflective process when conducting culturally responsive research. To this end, we challenge the notion that the most *valid* research is *objective* research void of subjectivity. Our subjectivities, we believe, emerge from our multiplicitous identities shaped by socially constructed features. Authors provide various anecdotes illustrating how our decision to *subjectify* ourselves and our research plays out within various settings. In general, the consequences of our heightened sensitivities place us in precarious positions.

For those of us who dare place race, ethnicity, ability, language, immigration and other sociocultural elements as important variables within education research we counter the commonly held belief that these features are unimportant (Nasir & Hand, 2006) and inappropriate units of analyses. Not too surprisingly, our counternormative efforts often result in our work and our identity as researchers being devalued, dismissed (Delgado Bernal & Villalpando, 2002), and "acknowledged as worthwhile only to the degree to which the research moves both the researcher and the population studied from the margins to the center" (Welch & Pollard, 2009, p. 3). To do anything else, would allow for greater misinterpretation of data, conflation of terms, and the posing of misguided questions that further fail our methodologies, urban communities, and participants. This book provides counterstories to the dominant discourse of what is required to conduct research—that is, culturally responsive, empowering research—with urban settings. As educators and policy makers take a closer examination at schools in general, and urban schools in particular, our responsibility to spotlight how these characteristics shape situated identities thereby our research and understanding of urban communities increases in importance.

Although this work was started by others long before we arrived on the scene, our commitments to marginalized communities and its inhabitants have allowed us to create a network of like-minded scholars. Importantly, our relationships with each other represent cross-gender, interracial conversations that have allowed us to vent our frustrations, celebrate our successes, and share lessons learned on how to further our methodological engagements and transactions with participants in meaningful, empowering ways. As in any fluid, interpersonal experience, questions arose. What are some of the critically important issues researchers should consider when working with urban schools and communities? What should be researchers' commitment to the urban communities in which they conduct research? How can researchers develop a trusting relationship in an environment justifiably distrustful of outsiders? How can researchers develop a broader understanding of urban students and communities and maintain the authenticity of their subjects' experiences and of the research questions and subsequent data? What are some of the ways researchers can work within urban settings to produce research that can influence policymakers and improve the conditions of those living in urban settings? Pondering these questions and utilizing our diverse, but collective, experiences as educational researchers to improve the life experiences of urban communities through urban education research is the foundation of this volume.

Hence, courageously and without apology, authors in this compilation describe how their work with marginalized, urban communities attempts to expand methodological conversations and what it means to conduct research in urban contexts. By providing practical accounts of what has and has not worked for them as scholars, authors demonstrate the (dis)connect between classroom discussions of urban education and real-life field experiences of researchers working in urban settings. To this end, the authors aim to broaden discussions of reflexivity by expanding its meaning to include how our culturally responsive methods depend on contextualized engagements within urban settings.

In sum, these chapters are meant to encourage a dose of hope and realism to all readers. They also serve as a reminder that the road towards a new way of thinking, particularly one that requires deconstruction and reconstruction may be lonely at times, but we are never all alone.

OVERVIEW OF THE BOOK

There are three sections of this text. The first part, *Transitions* includes chapters that discuss how researchers cross various divides separating discussions of and about urban schools from other educational spheres. In chapter one the authors, Scott and Solyom, "focus on how education leadership programs—particularly for urban educators—can use various tenets from critical race theory as praxis within their courses of study." In chapter two, Blanchett and Zion, "address four questions: (1) What constitutes educational research?; (2) What are the prevailing educational research paradigms?; (3) What is the role of power and privilege in educational research?; and (4) How can educational researchers ask questions of the themselves and the field of educational research that transforms current research, practice, and educational policy in ways that improves the life chances of often marginal children, families, and in urban communities?" Beverly Cross, the author of chapter three, analyzes how "two strategies of power—knowledge production and representation—[are] enacted thorough research that reproduces marginalization." Cross uses an intersectional framework that demonstrates how "these strategies of control are employed through research as White professors knowingly and knowingly participate in marginalization of racial, ethnic, cultural and linguistic minority groups." In Chapter 4, Jody Polleck furthers the conversation about privilege as she describes her struggle "as a White female researcher working with participants of color; and to simultaneously work to become what Banks (1998) calls a 'transformative scholar.'"

The chapters in Part II, "Lessons Learned," provide specific examples of how researchers have purposefully designed research projects in culturally responsive ways. In Chapter 5, author Andrew Brantlinger, writes "about my experiences as a practitioner researcher who studied critical pedagogy in my mathematics classroom with the goal of positively contributing to the lives of urban you and communities." The importance of relationships shape the narrative Kimberly Woo creates in Chapter 6: "This chapter considers how one second-grade teacher tailored her classroom curriculum to meet her students' interests and needs, while also actively involving their parents in the learning process." In Chapter 7, writers Monika Shealey,

Liana Rodrguez, and Delsue Frankson present "an argument for a cohesive and comprehensive urban special education research agenda, which acknowledges the inflexibility of traditional mainstream special education research and offers alternate epistemologies and methodologies in examining the intersection of race, culture and disability."

In the final section of the book, titled "Negotiations and Collaborations," the chapters provide specific accounts of and recommendations for researchers aiming to gain insider status in urban settings.

Chapter 8 author, Raquel Farmer-Hinton, examines the possibilities of scholar service as a "potential avenue in which scholars gain greater cultural knowledge of school communities of color." Chapter 9's author, Jamie Lew draws on pragmatic realism (Roberts & Sanders, 2005) to describe how her research "before, during, [and] after fieldwork activated mechanisms of reflexivity and intersubjectivity" that led to "a meaningful ethnographic study." In Chapter 10, Eustace Thompson provides "a dual critique of urban school leadership and the academy's educational leadership program with a focus on educational leadership program improvement." Authors of Chapter 11, Amina Jones, Na'ilah Suah Nasir, and Tryphenia B. Peele-Eady, draw on their experiences researching in three urban sites "to explore some of the features of urban settings that make them complex research sites within which to negotiate methodology and researcher positionality." In this final chapter, the authors describe how challenges "were negotiated in partnership with participants, and the nuances of these interactions."

REFERENCES

Banks, J. A. (1998). The lives and values of researchers: Implications for educating citizens in a multicultural society. *Educational Researcher, 27*(7), 417.

Delgado Bernal, D., & Villalpando, O. (2002). The apartheid of knowledge in the academy: The struggle over "legitimate" knowledge for faculty of color [Special issue]. *Journal of Equity and Excellence in Education, 35,* 169–180.

Dillard, C. B. (2000). The substance of things hoped for, the evidence of things not seen: Examining an endarkened feminist epistemology in educational research and leadership. *International Journal of Qualitative Studies in Education, 13*(6), 661–681.

Johnson-Bailey, J. (1998). Black reentry women in the academy: Making a way out of no way. *Initiatives, 58*(4), 37–48.

Johnson-Bailey, J. (1999). The ties that bind and the shackles that separate: Race, gender, class, and color in a research process. *Qualitative Studies in Education, 12*(6), 659–670.

Johnson-Bailey, J. (2003). Everyday perspectives on feminism: African-American women speak out. *Race, Gender & Class, 10*(3), 82–99.

Ladson-Billings, G. (2000). Racialized discourses and ethnic epistemologies. In N. Denzin & Y. Lincoln (Eds.), *The SAGE handbook of qualitative research* (2nd ed., pp. 257–277). Thousand Oaks, CA: SAGE.

Ladson-Billings, G. (2004). Landing on the wrong note: The price we paid for Brown. *Educational Researcher, 33*(7), 3–13.

Lather, P. (2004). This is your father's paradigm: Government Intrusion and the Case of Qualitative Research in Education. *Qualitative Inquiry, 10*(1), 15–34.

Milner, H. R. (2006). Culture, race and spirit: A reflective model for the study of African-Americans. *International Journal of Qualitative Studies in Education, 19*, 367–385.

Nasir, N., & Hand, V. (2006). Exploring sociocultural perspectives on race, culture, and learning. *Review of Educational Research, 76*, 449–475.

Roberts, J. M., & Sanders, T. (2005). Before, during, and after: realism, reflexivity, and ethnography. *The Sociological Review*, 294–313.

Tillman, L.C. (2002) . Culturally Sensitive Research Approaches: An African-American Perspective. *Educational Researcher, 31*(9), 3–12.

Tillman, L.C. (2006). Researching and writing from an African-American perspective: Reflective Notes on Three Research Studies. *International Journal of Qualitative Studies in Education, 19*(3), 265–287.

Welch, O. M., & Pollard, D. S. (2006). Introduction. In D. S. Pollard & O. M. Welch (Eds.), *From center to margins: The importance of self-definition in research* (pp. 1–6). Albany, NY: State University of New York Press.

PART I

TRANSITIONS

CHAPTER 1

STORIES FOR EDUCATIONAL LEADERSHIP PROGRAMS

Research at its Best

Kimberly A. Scott and Jessica A. Solyom

INTRODUCTION

If current and future educational leaders are to foster successful, equitable, and socially responsible learning and accountability practices for all students, then substantive changes in educational leadership preparation and professional development programs are required.

—Brown (2004, p. 80).

Unfortunately, attempts to revise preparatory experiences for educational leaders and seriously consider the above issues rarely encourage prospective school administrators to deconstruct and/or understand race and racism (Henze, Katz, Norte, Sather, & Walker, 2002; Lopez, 2003). At best, the word multicultural and/or diversity may be affixed to one of the required graduate courses in an educational leadership program's course

Research in Urban Educational Settings: Lessons Learned and Implications for Future Practice, pp. 3–20
Copyright © 2011 by Information Age Publishing

of study. Research indicates, however, that such efforts barely require critical examination of how schools reproduce the race-, social class-, gender-hierarchies (see Jay, 2003). For educational leaders charged to lead urban schools, not understanding these concepts and how they intersect with social class, ethnicity, language, agency, and equity can cause even the best intentioned leaders to fail at fulfilling any social justice agenda. Race, social class, and gender, among other sociocultural features, shape the unique social, political, and historical context of urban schools causing America's schools to persist as an apartheid system (Kozol, 2005). How educational leadership programs can prepare urban administrators to disrupt this system requires a more complex analysis than typically espoused. While some researchers have highlighted the importance of critical race analyses to administrators' practices and policies[1] we, like others (e.g., Lopez, 2003; Stovall, 2004), argue that for urban school improvement, efforts must include leadership preparation programs encouraging administrators to critique and create stories about race, racism, marginalization, exploitation, and urban communities.

Non-education-related research has done better than education sources in illustrating a story's potency. Kristof and Wudunn's (2009) powerful book, for example, relates how stories will move people toward action and advocacy more than statistics (pp. 99–100). Unfortunately, education research has yet to provide comparable reports. The examples that do exist tend to center stories by education faculty (Perry et al., 2009), students of color (Knaus, 2009), and teachers of color as a means to illuminate the systemic isms persisting in our schools. While these accounts are both instructive and necessary, how narratives can be used as an instructional strategy with education leaders—that is, with individuals most likely to spearhead reform—is narrowly understood. Instead, greater emphasis has been placed on how other classroom practices, such as problem-based learning (e.g., *Journal of Cases in Educational Leadership*), learning communities (Doolittle, Stanwood, & Simmerman, 2006) or action research (Ringler, 2007) can motivate administrators to orchestrate school change. In short, the possibility of storytelling may sound promising, but little attention has been paid to how and to what end it can be implemented within an education leadership program. Since storytelling is integral to critical race theory, we use this heuristic as a basis for our argument.

In this chapter, we focus on how education leadership programs—particularly for urban educators—can use various tenets from critical race theory as praxis within their courses of study. We initiate our argument in the racial realism of our times. In the end, we make specific recommendations, while accounting for some barriers, of how leadership programs can integrate critical race theory as praxis whereas more urban educational leaders can locate stories as both units of analysis and points of departure for urban school administrators.

EDUCATIONAL LEADERS AND RACIAL REALISM

African American and Hispanic children are three times more likely than Whites to attend an impoverished urban school (Orfield & Lee, 2005). Within these majority-poor-minority settings (Frankenberg, Lee, & Orfield, 2003) rest educational leaders and teachers who rarely share the same racial, ethnic, and/or socioeconomic categories as the students. In Arizona—where we both work and study—the majority of principals are White (80.5%) with only 11.8% of Hispanic descent, 2.8% African American, and 7.9% American Indian. These statistics stand in contrast to the growing number of Arizona K–12 students of color these principals lead: American Indian/AK Native, 5.6%; Black, non-Hispanic, 5.3%; White, non-Hispanic, 45%; Hispanic, 41%; and Asian, 2.6% (National Center for Education Statistics, 2007). Sadly, these percentages are often assumed as the "natural order" in Arizona. Many of Scott's graduate students—those acting administrators or teacher leaders pursuing a doctorate of education--admit that she is the first African American who "has [ever had] some power over me." Since Scott is the only Black faculty member teaching in our university's graduate school of education, their student-professor interactions may be the one and only instance that the "normal" power dynamic is upset for the graduate students/practicing leaders.

Not that race and/or ethnicity are automatic proxies for behaviors, but the cultural mismatch among teachers, education leaders, students, and communities often prevent greater academic and social advancement for the urban settings and its inhabitants (see Parker & Villalpando, 2007). With minimal understanding of how race and racism appear in the everyday lives of students and their parents, many urban leaders enact policies that exacerbate racial tensions (Larson & Ovando, 2001). These practices and policies originate from majoritarian stories shaped by isms (e.g., racism, classism). Integral to these responses is how administrators learn about the schools they must lead.

Stories about low-income students and communities of color continue to be oppressed, dismissed, distorted, ignored, silenced, destroyed, appropriated, and/or commodified (Bell, 1995; Bonilla-Silva, 1997). Dominant society dismisses critiques of these biased tales as "unhelpful, un-American, or even racist" (Bonilla-Silva, Forman, Lewis, & Embrick, 2003). Little attention is paid to how these one-dimensional, racist concepts influence the everyday thoughts, behaviors, and interactions of educators in urban contexts (Yamamoto, 1997).

Many preservice teachers adopt preconceived, erroneous notions about inner-city schools from popular films (Grant, 2002; Trier, 2005), Scott finds school administrators engage in the same process. In her 10 years of teaching school administrators in both the Northeast and Southwest, an overwhelming majority list the following films as their favorite stories about urban school: *Dangerous Minds, Lean on Me, Stand and Deliver,* and *Freedom Writers.* Without a critical examination of this media, Scott has seen students discuss Michelle Pfeiffer's character in *Dangerous Minds* as an example of an instructor using culturally responsive methods. While we find images of a White female threatening physical force to engage her Black and Brown students far from reflecting any aim of culturally responsive pedagogy (see Gay 2000, 2002; Howard, 2001, 2003; Lee, 2007; Villegas & Lucas, 2007), we recognize this false connection as a result of the urban school administrators' reactions to trying to understand a "buzz word" (Stovall, 2004)—that is culturally responsive pedagogy—and the lack of critical analysis in their preparation programs.

Educators who work in urban schools do not automatically have a greater sensitivity to urban issues. Their presence in these contexts does not endow them with a knowledge set that positions them as insiders. Over the years, Scott has noted that some of the most vociferous protests for urban educational reform come from those graduate students working in urban contexts. As one African American male student indicated,

> I have been working in urban schools for 10-years now, even attended an urban school as a child, and most of these kids are simply dumb. There is no way around it and theories that say their stupidity is a result of something else besides their dumbness are false.

In several chapters contained in this volume (e.g., Jodey Polleck and Blanchett & Zion), Banks' (1998) insider-outsider typology and its transformative potential appear. We agree with these authors that identities are dynamic and multifaceted, positioning individuals at various times as both insider and outsider. The insider-outsider dichotomy is too simplistic to encompass who we are (Merriam et al., 2001). Suburban educators are sometimes no less able to understand urban education than their urban correlates. Nevertheless, the cultural isolation between the communities from which the leader typically hails and the one where they work does make a significant impact on how education leaders understand and interact with the multiple ingredients shaping the urban context.

Recalling Banks' work, being a geographic-outsider does not preclude an individual from gaining insider knowledge or nurturing a culturally sensitive praxis. Unfortunately, without diverse images of urban communities, it is little wonder that many inner-city education leaders have problems (re)conditioning their minds to normalize non-pathological, culturally-enriched counterstories. Without administrators critiquing the "normal" stories how can we expect them to nurture teachers that encourage, seek, and nurture counterstories of success for all children?

Drawing on CRT as praxis, we agree with Stovall (2004) that such a heuristic has considerable potential for broadening urban education leaders. However, we appreciate the work done by scholars in different disciplines. Consequentially, we draw on Stovall's suggestions for mapping CRT as Praxis onto education administrators' training and expand it to include more preservice experiences for administrators.

CRITICAL RACE THEORY AS PRAXIS—ONE RESPONSE

Originating in the field of legal studies, critical race theory (CRT) questions the "neutrality" of law and challenges mainstream notions of race, racism and racial power in U.S. society (Crenshaw, Gotanda, Peller, & Thomas, 1995; Delgado & Stefancic, 2000; Donnor, 2005; Matsuda, 1987). CRT arose in the mid-1970s as a response to critical legal studies (CLS) which argues that the law must focus on how it is applied to specific groups in particular circumstances. Critical race theorists claimed that CLS scholars not only failed to address issues of racial inequality directly, but also overlooked and underplayed the role that race and racism assumed in the very construction of the legal foundations upon which our society rests (Crenshaw, 1998; Delgado & Stefancic, 2000; Harris, 1994; Parker & Lynn, 2002). Thus, CRT is an intellectual perspective that theorizes the potential of grounding a study in the particulars of social reality based on an individual's lived experiences and his or her racial group's collective historical experiences within the United States (Donnor, 2005). For this reason, CRT places a heavy emphasis on honoring, respecting, including and examining the stories of people of color. Despite this suggestion, few CRT educational works use stories (for notable exceptions, see the work of Patricia J. Williams and Richard Delgado). That said, the theory comprises six major tenets:

1. Recognition that racism is endemic to society (Bell, 1995) and its intercentricity with other forms of subordination including oppression based on gender, class, immigration status, surname, phenotype, accent and sexuality (Solórzano & Yosso, 2002).
2. Employment of a variety of theoretical traditions including Marxism, feminism, post-structuralism, and critical legal studies (Matsuda, Lawrence, Delgado, & Crenshaw, 1993).

3. An emphasis on the absolute centrality of history and context (Crenshaw et al., 1995).

4. A challenge to dominant ideology including notions of objectivity, meritocracy, color-blindness, equal opportunity and race neutrality (Dixson & Rousseau, 2005).

5. Placing value on experiential knowledge in order to posit that "reality" is situational and socially constructed (Ladson-Billings, 1998).

6. A call toward activism and actively working toward the elimination of racial oppression, with the goal of ending all forms of oppression (Bell, 1995; Brayboy, 2005; Donnor, 2005; Matsuda et al., 1993).

CRT has expanded beyond theoretical discussions of justice and equity to include practical methods to challenge the traditional research paradigms, texts, and theories used to explain the experiences of students of color. Not surprisingly, the theory has been applied to the field of education. Solórzano and Yosso (2002) explain that CRT in education is a framework or set of basic insights, perspectives, methods, and pedagogy to understand the inequitable educational experiences of students of color. Similar to its progenitor, critical race theory in education maintains an activist approach as it also seeks to identify, analyze, and transform structural and cultural aspects of education that maintain subordinate and dominant racial positions in and out of the classroom (Ladson-Billings & Tate, 1995). CRT scholars in education encourage teachers and school leaders to place the stories of students and communities of color in historical and social context (Stovall, 2004). When the ideology of racism is examined and racist injuries are named, victims of racism can find their voice (Solórzano & Yosso, 2002). Counterstories serve as a tool to understand how race influences educational and legal policy in ways that are felt and experienced daily for members within the community. CRT in education serves as a lens to unpack and address issues of internal and external race and racism in the school setting (Stovall, 2004). How to effectively use the heuristic in practical ways is best understood through its progeny, CRT as Praxis.

CRT as Praxis allows scholarship to reach beyond the theoretical and the academy in order to offer practical applications of the theory to community concerns. Yamamoto (1997) challenges CRT legal scholars to engage in a praxis that bridges theoretical concepts to everyday practice and produce tangible results (Lawson, 1995). Stovall (2004) outlines a CRT "race-praxis" in education that involves forging relationships with parents, students, community organizations, student-teachers, and first-year and veteran teachers. School leaders often find themselves listening and collecting stories of students, teachers, parents, and concerned community members (what ethnographic researchers might consider "data collection"). The stories, compacted with empirical data, are crucial in making cases for educational policy to the school's central office. In this way, experiential knowledge serves as an informing agent for school leaders who make challenging educational decisions. Additionally, "the use of an interdisciplinary perspective enables the teacher to use non-conventional approaches to address issues of race in school" (Stovall, 2004, p. 10).

Unfortunately not all institutions of higher education subscribe to this notion—that is, linking theory to practice in a structured course; reading texts that center the experiences and knowledge of subordinated populations; recognizing the individual as part of a collective whole; and providing a framework that encourages and inspires collective activism. As Stovall (2004) reminds us, "It is one thing to know and analyze the functions of race; it is yet another to engage in the practice of developing and maintaining a school with an anti-oppressive, anti-racist agenda in an age of conservative educational policy" (Stoval, 2004). We offer the following three recommendations, not as an exhaustive list of possibilities, but suggestions to better prepare urban leaders to fostering a more socially just school environment.

RECOMMENDATION #1: MEDIA ANALYSES ANALYSIS SHOULD DRAW FROM OTHER DISCIPLINES

We agree with Ladson-Billings' (2009) method of using film stories of urban schools and communities to initiate discussion of how these movies distort images of urban life. Drawing on CRT, we believe that encouraging leaders to consider how films deliberately demoralize Black and/or Brown students' and parents concerns' can challenge their own habits of mind. Concomitantly, students/leaders need to compare their own beliefs with those portrayed in films. Many education leaders (from both urban and suburban contexts) believe as truth popular culture's stories of urban life. Without careful analysis of these beliefs and a disruption of their synergistic relationship, leaders and films maintain three myths of urban communities, schools, and people:

1. Urban communities have little interest in urban school improvement. Films cast urban school community leaders as either disinterested in youngsters' educational lives or actively working to prevent their achievement. In the end, the idea that urban communities and its inhabitants are anti-intellectual and depraved pre-

vails. For example: In the film *Coach Carter*, the coach is depicted as believing that the predominantly low-income Black students are not achieving adequately and the only way to motivate them is through physical containment—he locks them in a gym. Very similar to Joe Clark's character in *Lean on Me*, the community revolts against such draconian measures. In both instances, overworked, underpaid, angry African American women represent the community's distrust of the African American man/savior. With great bravado, these women protest the man's efforts to improve the academic livelihood of their children. These films present the Black female characters as caring more about their children's participation in sports or other non-academic subjects than their child's scholastic future.

2. Change in an urban school or community is a result of a community-outsider working in isolation and with minimal results. Even if the "savior" belongs to the same racial or ethnic category as the students, the films portray these characters as *indigenous-outsiders* (Banks, 1998). For example: Most often the leading character in these films is the White individual who eventually overcomes all odds and adversaries (see *Freedom Writers*, *Dangerous Minds*, and *Blackboard Jungle*). More recent films portray African American males in this savior role, but typically their "saving" translates into physically punishing the students' as the only means to control them (e.g., *Lean on Me* and *Akeelah and the Bee*). At times, the only recourse for interacting with the savage urban students is justifiable murder (e.g., *187*). Except for *The Marva Collins Story*, which was released as a television movie, African American female saviors are conspicuously absent from these stories of who can improve inner-city life.

3. Students or individuals from urban areas succeed once they leave the community and gain support from an outsider—typically individuals who represent the dominant culture. For example: Chris Gardner's character in *The Pursuit of Happyness* does not succeed until the bosses at the stockbroker firm understand his brilliance. They experience this epiphany after Chris interns for 6 months without pay and his distrustful, unsupportive African American wife abandons him and their only son. The film suggests that Chris' success was a result of a colorblind meritocratic system in which the only source of benevolence and understanding comes from rich, White males.

Inevitably, the acting-administrators/graduate students express their shock and chagrin once we discuss these themes. Comments such as the following consume a considerable portion of class time: "I will never be able to look at that film the same!" or "I thought it was an upbeat movie, but now I see it really is biased" or "I can see how this may be pejorative now but if we hadn't discussed it, I would never see how it maintains any one group's agenda." Identifying these myths serves as one step toward encouraging leaders to produce a counter-narrative, which is a story which challenges the normed images described above (Solórzano & Yosso, 2001). To this end, leaders must study and learn about themselves as beings influenced by and influencing the creation and maintenance of a master narrative. What do their unexamined reflections mean about their own status in the world? How can these notions influence their professional interactions and decision making along race and social class divides? Without analyzing these images and beliefs, we fear their unexamined praxis will reinforce deficit thinking that the films they watch normalize. Importantly, analysis needs to draw on more non-educational texts. Education leadership programs would do well to assign works from Douglas Massey or economists like Ronald Ferguson or historian VP Franklin to provide leaders with a more holistic understanding of how majoritarian stories evolved and persist.

RECOMMENDATION #2 PROVIDE MODEL STORIES

Education leaders enrolled in a leadership program tend to be extremely busy people often working full-time while pursuing their degrees. Scott recalls how one graduate student worked during the day as an assistant principal then drove at least 3 times a week, 3-hours one-way to attend a 4:30 P.M. class. Despite the time-demands, many students are willing to fulfill the academic expectations. As invigorated as they may be, graduate students in leadership programs seem to prefer narrative texts or explicit discussions that explain how theory links to practice rather than literature syntheses or theoretical pieces. Assigning even the most interesting empirical article and/or book that presents a counter-narrative still requires unpacking of racialized believes.

Just recently, Scott assigned her doctoral class of education leaders Kozol's (2005) book *Shame of a Nation*. Coincidentally, Jonathan Kozol conducted a private lecture at our campus to which Scott's students attended. Immediately following his presentation, the class discussed their impressions of his work. Several of the White students articulated their suspicions of Kozol's descriptions: "I have never heard that these conditions exist in this country. This is America for God's sake! When I read this, I thought he was some crazy radical liberal that was spinning a tale." While Scott appreciated the authenticity of these statements, how students explained the shift in their attitudes became troubling. Upon attending the lecture, one White female (prospective administrator) student stated, "Once I saw and heard him, I started thinking that maybe it was my problem. Just because I never saw it before doesn't mean it doesn't exist. It just means I live in a different America than what he described." Clearly, Kozol's White maleness provided legitimacy to his story. Without seeing his race and gender, the student suggests his descriptions were too "radical" [*counter-narrative*]. His telling of the Others' story becomes valid. This incident intimates that if Kozol was a Black female, for instance, his story would have lost credibility.

The above demonstrates the need to incorporate more narratives into education leadership programs and center the voices of people of color. Milner (2008) demonstrates how counter-narratives can change the discourse of urban schools to include more hopeful images of success than typically provided. To accomplish this goal requires a greater influx of ethnographic texts. Given the current tenor of the times, this may be difficult.

David Tyack's 1974 book describing the history of urban schools seems to have ushered in the first wave of academic publications on urban education. Drawing on his work as a beginning marker, we reviewed the most notable manuscripts on urban education and leadership published between 1975 and 2008 for unifying themes. Using the keywords "urban education" in ERIC's database reveals 168 books published during this time period. As Table 1.1 presents, the majority of texts seem to fall within one of three categories with many overlapping between two areas: (1) ethnography; (2) pedagogy and/or; (3) organizational reform.

In the next section, we analyze the three primary categories using a CRT as Praxis lens. To this end, we transition to detail what is conspicuously absent from these groupings and enumerate what we believe is needed to enhance the educational and research experiences of school leaders interested in urban education.

Ethnography and Urban Education

Ethnographies artfully tell the story of a culture-sharing group when a good ethnographer balances his voice (e.g., etic) with that of the participants' (emic). For ethnographies recounting the lives of urban school life, the rough realities of the students, teachers, and administrators texturize what statistical data reveal. Works such as Kozol's, Anyon's (1997) *Ghetto Schooling*, Valdes' *(1996) Con Respecto*, describe both the painful realities and hopeful examples of what is and can be in urban communities.

Although ethnographies maintain an important position in methodological approaches, a relative few capture the lives and the voices of

Table 1.1.   Urban Education Books 1975–2008

	Ethnography	Pedagogy	Organizational Change	Total
Ethnography	14	15	1	30
Pedagogy		71	9	80
Organizational Change			57	57
Total				**168**

urban students. The reasons for this paucity cannot automatically tether to publishers' lack of interest in this area. Granted, conducting a credible ethnography consumes an incredible amount of time and effort. The implication that researchers do not have nor want to spend the time using this methodology does not negate Bell's (1995) point that storytelling is rarely valued among scholars:

> critics ... will critique critical race theory ... with their standards of excellence and find this new work seriously inadequate. Many of these critics are steeped in theory and are deathly afraid of experience. They seek meaning by dissecting portions of this writing—the autobiographical quality of some work, and the allegorical, storytelling characteristic in others. (p. 910)

Moreover including the stories of urban students signals an attempt to confront unjust social arrangements (Ladson-Billings, 2003). Yet the over-reliance on positivist epistemologies that diminishes the import of subjectivities prevails. To include the words of urban children, to paint in both broad and detailed strokes their situated lives, communities, and childhoods would suggest their humanity. Highlighting the every day lived experiences of urban schools would open the educational system to the type of critique CRT encourages—that is, both an analysis and meta-analysis of how our schools (post-secondary included) subordinate students of color (Solórzano & Yosso, 2000). Equally important, telling the stories of urban students would uphold CRTs aim to "unapologetically challenge the scholarship that would dehumanize and depersonalize us" (Ladson-Billings, 2000, p. 270).

Pedagogy and Urban Education

The lack of ethnographic accounts of urban school life stand in contrast to the much larger number of publications on teaching in urban schools. Central to these texts is culture. How teachers need to understand their cultural biases and appreciate their students' cultures tends to be a popular theme.

Publications on culturally relevant teaching took hold in education conversations when authors such as Gay (2000), Ladson-Billings (1994), Irvine (2000), Hollins and Oliver (1999), Irvine et al. (2001), to name a few, produced practical answers to the question of how to conjoin critical pedagogy with culture-centered teaching (Lynn, 2004). According to Ladson-Billings (2002), culturally responsive teaching centers "students' achievement," "supports students' cultural competence" and "promotes students' social political consciousness" (p. 111). These texts often appeared in multicultural or diversity series rather than urban education categories. Carol Lee's (2007) recent work on culturally responsive modeling continues the discussion of culture's salience in the classroom, in general, and urban contexts, in particular.

For authors outlining culturally relevant pedagogies, urban students and their teachers enter a space where cultures clash. In this sense, culture is more than an individual's race, ethnicity, and/or gender. Socio-economic differences intersecting with race, ethnicity, and gender can foster a lack of understanding between educational leaders and students (Stovall, 2004). Unfortunately, many districts focus on one unit of analysis and assume a race-as-culture framework—particularly for African American low-income students (O'Connor, Lewis, & Mueller, 2007). In such contexts, the students' race/culture becomes the feature to be transformed rather than the teaching. And even less attention is paid to why race/culture is the unit of analysis. Sadly, Ruby Payne's (1996) popularity serves as an example of how some urban areas desperately align themselves with frameworks that make devastating reference to culture based on the income and racial demographics of students' communities.

Organizational Reform and Urban Education

Almost equally popular with pedagogical practices are books on organizational change in urban schools. Variation appears as to what part of the organization should be the target of the reform. For some scholars, curriculum needs to be deconstructed and sometimes deleted to allow for academic and psychosocial success of urban students. Afrocentric curriculum, first developed by Molefi Asante (1987, 1988, 1991) serves as a prime example.

Between 2004 and 2008, the majority of texts focuses on identifying the "problems" plaguing urban schools and how individuals within these contexts can work to ameliorate these issues. The implicit message coursing through the manuscripts remains constant: "educational reform groups do not typically work with community organizations to create or link to programs providing external student and family support" (Anyon, 2005, p. 185). The emphasis on the individual making change rather than the collective prevails. And as CRT states, to understand the hierarchical power structure in which some groups of individuals benefit (e.g., non-urban schools) while others suffer (e.g., urban schools and people), we need to refine our research efforts and publications to consider not just one's successes or failures, but the collective's subjectivity bounded by oppression (Ladson-Billings & Tate, 1995; Delgado, 1990).

The discussion above does not account for the many substantive journal articles that do not yield a book manuscript or the many notable journals dedicated to publishing articles exclusively on urban schools, communities, or people navigating these interconnected spaces (e.g., *Urban Education, Urban Review, Education and Urban Society, Urban Affairs Review*). Yet, our analysis suggests that urban education publications may do well if greater emphasis is spent on describing lived experiences as models from which educational leaders can regard and analyze.

RECOMMENDATION #3 STORYTELLING AS A COLLECTIVE

Finally, education leaders interact with multiple individuals in any given day. These associations help shape the experiences of the students, teacher morale, perceptions of the parents, and community trust toward the administrator. It is during these interactions that multiple stories emerge. As one leader/graduate student who works in an urban Phoenix district explained, "When I talk with parents they are reading me just like I am reading them. Our conversations help to determine how supportive the parents will be." These "reads" are rarely analyzed or documented by the social actors. We suggest that education leadership programs attempt to change this tide and prepare future leaders to provide collective-counternarratives using a multi-step, combined approach.

Cultivating prospective administrators' understanding of the master narrative (Recommendation #1) and providing model ethnographic examples (Recommendation #2), can invigorate leaders' *activism*. Not that these steps are part of a linear process, but guiding students/leaders on how to access community voices while assuming an "asset building approach" (Akom, 2008) can and should be part of their preparation programs. It is insufficient and antithetical to critical race theory as praxis to cease preparation at the awareness stage. Infusing both qualitative and quantitative methodology courses with a combination of research approaches that ultimately leads to the centering of community voices seems integral to the process. How to work with the community that media has disempowered through pejorative images of depravity to tell a counter-story in all its complexities is a learned set of skills. We encourage leadership preparation programs—particularly those for urban school administrators—to assume this responsibility. Offering methods classes often focuses on how school administrators can manipulate the data in their own contexts. Greater emphasis could be spent on how to forge partnerships with community members to create a collective story.

For some, participatory action research accomplishes this goal. Typically used for urban youth empowerment programs (see, e.g., Ginwright, Noguera, & Cammarota, 2006), youngsters learn how to research and voice social and/or community issues on their own terms. While powerful, there are few empirical examples of participatory action youth projects crossing age, geographic and/or racial/ethnic barriers toward a common, more global goal. If integrated in leadership programs' methods classes, administrators, many of whom are already crossing these divides, school leaders could model what urban youth should also do—collaborating with others to demonstrate through collectively created stories the complexity of a lived experience in their own words.

By challenging the *dominant ideology of objectivity* and documenting our subjectivities we describe our situated identities. Rather than the one-dimensional media portraits of city dwellers, typically told by one voice, our suggestion invites greater attention to the intersecting variables that texturize our stories and our selves. In practical terms, the administrators' program of study would teach how to produce a multi-voiced, counternarrative highlighting interactants' meaning-making of various features (e.g., race, gender, social class, agency, spirituality, etc.).

LAST WORDS

We recognize that our recommendations are not easy—it requires dedication, time, and resources, but it is necessary. Importantly, they also require a preparation program to take seriously the importance of race and racism and how these constructs influence a multitude of factors informing the myths and realities shaping urban schools. Additionally we realize that our suggestions require faculty members committed to these notions of equity and equality as a collective group and not one or two professors teaching one or two "diversity" classes. For some readers, our argument is a reminder that change is possible. We must move beyond our comfort spaces, engage each other, share our knowledge and talents, and create new stories that include multiple voices. Education leadership programs can facilitate this process by incorporating critical race theory as praxis into their curricula.

NOTE

1. The *Education Administration Quarterly* published a special edition on this topic (Volume, 43, No. 5 December 2007).

REFERENCES

Akom, A. (2008). Black metropolis and mental life: Beyond the "burden of 'acting white' " toward a third wave of critical race studies. *Anthropology and Education Quarterly, 39*(3), 247–265.

Anyon, J. (1997). *Ghetto schooling: A political economy of urban education reform.* New York: Teachers College Press.

Anyon, J. (2005). Radical possibilities: Public policy, urban education, and a new social movement. New York: Routledge.

Asante, M. K. (1987). *The Afrocentric Idea.* Philadelphia, PA: Temple University Press.

Asante, M. K. (1988). *Afrocentricity.* Trenton, NJ: Africa World Press.

Asante, M. K. (1991). The Afrocentric idea in education. *Journal of Negro Education, 60*(2), 170–180.

Banks, J. A. (1998). The lives and values of researchers: Implications for educating citizens in a multicultural society. *Educational Researcher, 27*(7), 417.

Bell, D. (1995). Who's afraid of critical race theory? *University of Illinois Law Review,* 893–910.

Bonilla-Silva, E. (1997). Rethinking racism: Toward a structural interpretation. *American Sociological Review, 62*(3), 465–480.

Bonilla-Silva, E., Forman, T. A., Lewis, A. E., & Embrick, D. G. (2003). "It wasn't me!": How will race and racism work in 21st century America. *Research in Political Sociology, 12.* 111–134.

Brayboy, B. M. J. (2005). Toward a tribal critical race theory in education. *The Urban Review, 37*(5), 425–446.

Brown, K. M. (2004). Leadership for social justice and equity: Weaving a transformative framework and pedagogy. *Educational Administration Quarterly, 40*(1), 77–108.

Crenshaw, K., Gotanda, N., Peller, G., & Thomas, K. (1995). *Critical race theory: The key writings that formed the movement.* New York: The New Press.

Crenshaw, K. (1998). Playing race cards: Constructing a pro-active defense of affirmative action. *National Black Law Journal, 16,* 196–214.

Delgado, R. (1990). When a story is just a story: Does voice really matter? *Virginia Law Review, 76*(1), 95–111.

Delgado, R., & Stefancic, J. (2000). Introduction. In R. Delgado & J. Stefancic (Eds.), *Critical race theory: The cutting edge* (2nd ed., pp. xv–xix). Philadelphia, PA: Temple University Press.

Dixson, A. D., & Rousseau, C. K. (2005). And we are still not saved: Critical race theory in education ten years later. *Race, Ethnicity and Education, 8*(1), 727.

Donnor, J. K. (2005). Towards an interest-convergence in the education of African-American football student athletes in major college sports. *Race Ethnicity and Education, 8*(1), 45–67.

Doolittle, G., Stanwood, H. M., & Simmerman, H. (2006). Creating professional learning communities in a traditional educational leadership preparation program. *Educational Considerations, 33*(2), 10–16.

Frankenberg, E., Lee, C., & Orfield, J. (2003). *A multiracial society with segregated schools: Are we losing the dream?* Cambridge, MA: The Civil Rights Project at Harvard University.

Gay, G. (2000). *Culturally responsive teaching: Theory, research, and practice.* New York: Teachers College Press.

Gay, G. (2002). Preparing for culturally responsive teaching. *Journal of Teacher Education, 53*(2), 106–116.

Ginwright, S., Noguera, P., & Cammarota, J. (Eds.). (2006). *Beyond resistance: Youth activism and community change.* New York: Routledge.

Grant, P. A. (2002). Using popular films to challenge preservice teachers' beliefs about teaching in urban schools. *Urban Education, 37*, 77–95.

Harris, A.P. (1994). Forward: The jurisprudence of reconstruction. *California Law Review, 82*, 741–785.

Henze, R., Katz, A., Norte, E., Sather, S. E., & Walker, E. (2002). *Leading for diversity: How school leaders promote positive interethnic relations.* Thousand Oaks, CA: SAGE.

Hollins, E. R., & Oliver, E. I. (1999). *Pathways to success in school: Culturally responsive teaching.* London: Routledge.

Howard, T. C. (2001). Telling their side of the story: African-American students' perceptions of culturally relevant teaching. *Urban Review, 33*(2), 131–149.

Howard, T. C. (2003). Culturally relevant pedagogy: Ingredients for critical teacher reflection. *Theory into Practice, 42*(3), 195–202.

Irvine, J. J. (2000). Afrocentric education: critical questions for further considerations. In D. S. Pollard & C. S. Ajirotutu (Eds.). *African-centered schooling in theory and practice* (pp. 199–210). Westport, CT: Bergin & Garvey.

Irvine, J. J., Armento, B. J., Causey, V. E., Jones, J. C., Frasher, R. S. & Weinburgh, M. H. (2001). *Culturally responsive teaching: Lesson planning for elementary and middle grades.* New York: McGraw-Hill.

Jay, M. (2003). Critical race theory, multicultural education, and the hidden curriculum of hegemony. *Multicultural Perspectives, 5*, 39.

Knaus, C. B. (2009). Shut up and listen: Applies critical race theory in the classroom. *Race, Ethnicity, and Education, 12*(2), 133–154.

Kozol, J. (2005). *The shame of a nation.* New York: Crown.

Kristof, N. D., & WuDunn, S. (2009). *Half the sky: Turning oppression into opportunity for women worldwide.* New York: Alfred Knopf.

Ladson-Billings, G. (1994). *The dreamkeepers: Successful teachers of African American children.* San Francisco: Jossey-Bass.

Ladson-Billings, G. (1998). Just what is critical race theory and what's it doing in a nice field like education? *International Journal of Qualitative Studies in Education, 11*(1), 724.

Ladson-Billings, G. (2000). Racialized discourses and ethnic epistemologies. In N. Denzin & Y. Lincoln (Eds.), *The SAGE handbook of qualitative research* (2nd ed., pp. 257–277). Thousand Oaks, CA: SAGE.

Ladson-Billings, G. (2002). I ain't writing nutting: Permissions to fail and demands to succeed in urban classrooms. In L. D. Delpit & J. Dowds (Eds.), *The skin that we speak: Thoughts on language and culture in the classroom* (pp. 107–120). New York: New press.

Ladson-Billings, G. (Ed.). (2003). *Critical race theory perspectives on the social studies: The profession, policies, and curriculum.* Greenwich, CT: Information Age Publishers.

Ladson-Billings, G. (2009). "Who you callin' nappy-headed?" A critical race theory look at the construction of black women. *Race, Ethnicity, & Education, 12*(1), 87–99.

Ladson-Billings, G., & Tate, W. F., IV (1995). Toward a critical race theory of education. *Teachers College Record, 97*(1), 47–68.

Larson, C. L., & Ovando, C. J. (2001). *The color of bureaucracy: The politics of equity in multicultural school communities.* Belmont, CA: Wadsworth.

Lawson, R. (1995). Critical race theory as praxis: A view from outside the outside. *Howard Law Journal, 38,* 353–370.

Lee, C. D. (2007). *The role of culture in academic literacies: Conducting our blooming in the midst of the whirlwind.* New York: Teachers College Press.

Lopez, G. R. (2003). The (racially neutral) politics of education: A critical race theory perspective. *Education Administration Quarterly, 39,* 68–94.

Lynn, M. (2004). Inserting the "race" into critical pedagogy: An analysis of "race-based epistemologies." *Educational Philosophy and Theory, 36*(2), 153–165.

Matsuda, M. J. (1987). Looking to the bottom: Critical legal studies and reparations. *Harvard Civil Rights-Civil Liberties Review, 72,* 30–164.

Matsuda, M., Lawrence, C., Delgado, R., & Crenshaw, K. (Eds.). (1993). *Words that wound: Critical race theory, assualative speech and the first amendment.* Boulder, CO: Westview Press.

Merriam, S. B., Johnson-Bailey, J., Lee, M., Kee, Y., Ntseane, G., & Muhamad, M. (2001). Power and positionality: Negotiating insider/outsider status within and across cultures. *International Journal of Lifelong Education, 20*(5), 405–416.

Milner, H. R., IV. (2008). Disrupting deficit notions of difference: Counter-narratives of teachers and community in urban education. *Teaching and Teacher Education: An International Journal of Research and Studies, 24*(6), 1573–1598.

National Center for Education Statistics. (2007). *Elementary & secondary education characteristics, state education data profiles.* Retrieved January 26, 2010, from http://nces.ed.gov/programs/stateprofiles/sresult.asp?mode=full&displaycat=1&s1=04

O'Connor, C., Lewis, A., & Mueller, J. (2007). Researching "Black" educational experiences and outcomes: Theoretical and methodological considerations. *Educational Researcher, 36*(9), 541–552.

Orfield, G., & Lee, C. (2005). *Why segregation matters: Poverty and educational inequality.* Cambridge, MA: Harvard University, The Civil Rights Project. Retrieved September 3, 2009, from http://www.civilrightsproject.ucla.edu

Parker, L., & Lynn, M. (2002). What's race got to do with it? Critical race theory's conflicts with and connections to qualitative research methodology and epistemology. *Qualitative Inquiry, 8*(1), 7–22.

Parker, L., & Villalpando, O. (2007). A race(cialized) perspective on education leadership: Critical race theory in educational administration. *Educational Administration Quarterly, 43*(5), 519–524.

Payne, R. (1996). *A framework for understanding poverty.* Highlands, TX: aha! Process, Inc.

Perry, G., Moore, H., Edwards, C.,Acosta, K., & Frey,C. (2009).Maintaining credibility and authority as an instructor of color in diversity-education classrooms. *Journal of Higher Education, 80*(1), 80–105.

Ringler, M. C. (2007). Action research an effective instructional leadership skill for future public school leaders. *AASA Journal of Scholarship & Practice, 4*(1), 27–42.

Solórzano, D. G., & Yosso, T. J. (2000). Toward a critical race theory of Chicana and Chicano education. In, C. Tejeda, C. Martinez, & Z. Leonardo (Eds.), *Charting new terrains of Chicana(o), Latina(o) education* (pp. 35–65). Cresskill, NJ: Hampton Press.

Solórzano, D. G., & Yosso, T. J. (2001). Critical race and latcrit theory and method: Counterstorytelling Chicana and Chicano graduate school experiences. *International Journal of Qualitative Studies in Education, 14*(4), 371–395.

Solórzano, D. G., & Yosso, T. J. (2002). Critical race methodology: Counter-storytelling as an analytical framework for education research. *Qualitative Inquiry, 8*(1), 23–44.

Stovall, D. (2004). School leader as negotiator. *Multicultural Education, 12*(2), 8–12.

Trier, J. (2005). "Sordid fantasies": Reading popular "inner-city" school films as racialized texts with pre-service teachers. *Race Ethnicity and Education, 8*, 171–189.

Tyack, D. (1974). *A history of American urban education.* Cambridge, MA: Harvard University Press.

Valdés, G. (1996). *Con respeto: Bridging the difference between culturally diverse families and schools: An ethnographic portrait.* New York: Teachers College Press.

Villegas, A. M., & Lucas, T. (2007). The culturally responsive teacher. *Educational Leadership, 64*(6), 28–33.

Yamamoto, E. (1997). Critical race praxis: Race theory and political lawyering practice in post civil-rights America. *Michigan Law Review, 95*(7), 821–900.

CHAPTER 2

ASKING THE RIGHT QUESTIONS IN URBAN EDUCATION RESEARCH

The Role of Privilege

Wanda J. Blanchett and Shelley D. Zion

If you have come to help me, you are wasting your time. But if you have come because your liberation is tied up with mine, then let us work together. (Lily Watson, Aboriginal activist)

INTRODUCTION

The biographical journeys of researchers and scholars impact their research values, beliefs and assumptions, creating a research identity bound up in histories of privilege or marginality that influences the research questions they ask, methodologies they employ, the lens they bring to their analysis, and ultimately their policy and practice recommendations and implications (Banks, 1998). As a doctoral student at The Pennsylvania State University in the early 1990s, I (Wanda) entered my program extremely excited about the possibility of being able to conduct

Research in Urban Educational Settings: Lessons Learned and
Implications for Future Practice, pp. 21–37
Copyright © 2011 by Information Age Publishing
All rights of reproduction in any form reserved.

and disseminate research that would positively impact the African American and other marginalized communities. The faculty in my department were all accomplished researchers consisting of only two African American females both of whom were untenured, three White females (one full professor, one associate professor, and one untenured assistant professor), and a host of White males, all but one of whom were tenured full professors. As new doctoral students, we were expected to identify our research interests and to secure graduate assistantships with faculty who were conducting research in areas of interest to us. Idealistic, I set out to find a faculty member whose interests accorded with my own. As I literally went from office to office speaking with faculty, I soon realized that none of the faculty was conducting research that, in my opinion, would improve the educational opportunities and life chances of my people (African Americans) or other marginalized groups. Even when I approached the two untenured African American females whose research activities were far more interesting and nontraditional than the others, I quickly realized that while they were interested in topics such as multicultural education and early childhood interventions that targeted children affected by crack cocaine and fetal alcohol syndrome, these researchers also used very traditional research approaches. More important, although they were wonderful teachers and brought insights to their teaching that were clearly missing in the other faculty members' teaching in terms of cultural perspectives, they were not considered "real" researchers by those with the most power in the department—the White males. In fact, several males commented to us doctoral students that these women were great teachers and contributed a lot to service but their research lacked the rigor needed to succeed at a large research institution, because they conducted research in the "soft" versus "academic" areas. On more than one occasion when we doctoral students asked why we were rarely exposed to empirical studies that included race/ethnicity and social class as variables, we were simply told that good educational research is generalizable. Even when we identified the research of scholars of color, we were cautioned that this body of work often did not meet the high and rigorous standards for inclusion in our research activities. This was my first introduction to the notions and assumptions of purity and perceived objectivity in educational research. I would later learn that the faculty in my doctoral program were not, as I suspected at the time, insane and out of step with widely accepted and often uncontested conceptualizations of what constitutes valid educational research. In fact, I have now come to the conclusion that they were in effect "Good Stewards" of the widely held but fallible assumptions that educational research when held to the highest standards and certainly when conducted by top researchers in their fields is at a minimum objective, rigorous, and void of a researcher's value, beliefs, and assumptions. Make no mistake about it, the faculty that I had the privilege to work with in my doctoral program were really good people, great scholars, and worked with me tirelessly to ensure that I was successful and well prepared for the academy. I owe them all a great debt of gratitude. However, with a few exceptions, they had also bought into the prevailing notions of what constitutes research and they were seemingly unaware of biographical and cultural underpinnings associated with educational research in general and specifically related to special education research. Since for the most part research was presented to me as objective and culture-free and those scholars who conducted research on marginalized communities were at that time marginalized themselves, I was really confused. However, my conceptualization and understanding of educational research broadened and changed significantly after being exposed to researchers (e.g., Banks, Foster, Gay, Hollins, Irvine, & Ladson-Billings) who infused Black feminist literature into their work. These scholars of color were outside of my special education discipline, but they were addressing issues that I yearned to address and they were doing it in ways that challenged and expanded the then current conceptualizations of educational research by approaching their work from a biographical and cultural perspective. What made these scholars unique was the fact that they openly acknowledged that who they were as African Americans in terms of their life experiences did influence the research questions they asked, methodology employed, analysis applied to data, and ultimately their policy and practice implications. They not only shattered the notion that good research is unfiltered, they advocated for research in urban and diverse settings and with often marginalized populations to acknowledge and be responsive to the sociocultural context of the individuals and environments being studied. Additionally, these scholars called for researchers conducting research with diverse and often marginalized communities to disclose their own biographical and cultural selves.

Needless to say, in spite of the prevailing efforts to present research as objective, all research is subjective as it is filtered through the lenses we bring to our studies. Who the researcher is, their personal and professional journeys, values, beliefs, and assumptions always impact their work including the questions asked, methods employed to answer her questions, and ultimately the lens through the findings are sifted to arrive at results and subsequent research, policy, and practice recommendations. To be clear, we recognize the importance of these steps in constructing new knowledge and extending existing understanding. However, we also recognize the need to analyze educational research from the perspective of who is privileged in the research process, and whose knowledge really counts. As history has shown (i.e., Tuskegee Experiment), many marginalized populations and communities have experienced great harm at the hands of researchers and in instances where physical and other direct forms of harm did not result, many in these communities have been exploited by and further marginalized by educators and scholars (e.g., Payne's culture of poverty and Ogbu's theory of involuntary minorities) whose work has perpetuated stereotypes and lowered expectations. Educational research is no different and is not exempt from causing harm to children and families when research is conducted on/with children, families, and communities—especially those in urban settings. Thus, the purpose of this chapter is to address four questions: (1) What constitutes educational research?; (2) What are the prevailing educational research paradigms?; (3) What is the role of power and privilege in educational research?; and (4) How can educational researchers ask questions of the themselves and the field of educational research that transforms current research, practice, and educational policy in ways that improve the life chances of often marginalized children, families, and urban communities?

OLD WINE NEW BOTTLES: THE DEBATE ON WHAT CONSTITUTES EDUCATIONAL RESEARCH

Over the last decade, we have witnessed the re-emergence of the seemingly never ending debate in the field of education over widely held assumptions about what constitutes educational research and which methodologies and researcher characteristics are likely to yield the most objective results. The debate seems to be heavily influenced by politically motivated policies that privilege some social science research methodologies while marginalizing others and has received much attention in all of the major education journals and resulted in a number of books and/or chapters (Atkinson 2004; Cook & Payne 2002; Lather, 2004; National Research Council, 2002; Shaker & Ruitenberg, 2007). Among the educational research assumptions that have been the subject of debate and challenge are the beliefs that undergird a recent national push toward "evidenced-based research" methodologies. Some researchers (Eisenhart & Towne 2003; Nasir & Hand, 2006) have challenged the whole notion of "evidenced-based research" because the operational definition of what constitutes evidenced-based research methodologies and interventions is very narrow and privileges experimental research designs, touting them as the most likely to yield objective and generalizable results (Lather, 2004). Additionally, quantitative evidence-based research methodologies often fail to acknowledge the cultural assumptions that undergird the methodologies employed and to address critically important social contextual variables and nuances that are important to the research including the acknowledgment of the researcher's cultural values and beliefs. Consequently, these methodologies are purported to be culture-free and neutral. Lather (2004), however, refuted this assumption by illustrating that NO research is value and culture free, meaning that ALL research is grounded in someone's cultural values and worldview (Banks, 1998; Lather, 2004; Smith, 1999). In fact, even before the most recent rounds of debate, researchers agreed that the goal with regard to rigorous research should be to achieve greater levels of objectivity in social science research but they also maintain that most research rarely approaches objectivity. To ensure that we are moving toward greater levels of objectivity, it is critically important for researchers to be honest with themselves and with their audiences about their own personal and professional assumptions and biases that might influence their methodologies.

The assertion that evidence-based research will result in higher quality research and consequently higher quality practice has also been the subject of debate in the professional literature (Lather, 2004; Shaker & Ruitenberg, 2007). Surprisingly, this debate has been fueled by a lack of evidence supporting the notion that evidence-based or research-based practices do in fact result in better quality educational practices for anyone, let alone for culturally and linguistically diverse learners who are often the focus of discussions pertaining to the "academic achievement and learning gap" (Lather, 2004). More important, in their attempts to move toward objectivity, many quantitative educational researchers have adopted a stance that the sociocultural contextual issues of race, class, and culture *do not* matter in educational research (Nasir & Hand, 2006). Yet, because many of these researchers do not fully understand the individuals, communities, and cultures of the individuals they study, they have actually misinterpreted their data and in some instances have caused harm to African American and poor children and families through the practice and policy recommendations they have made (Banks, 1998).

PREVAILING EDUCATIONAL RESEARCH ASSUMPTIONS

No aspect of social reality can be understood without presuppositions--we rely on cultural values to provide those presuppositions, Ain every case only a *part* of concrete reality is interesting and *significant* to us, because only it is related to the *cultural values* with which we approach reality. (Weber as cited in Heckman, 2004, p. 236, emphasis in the original)

Educational research that adheres to hegemonic positivistic and post-positivistic paradigms often ignores the contexts in which research occurs, excludes the meaning and purposes that humans attach to activity, presupposes that outsider perspectives can be brought to bear on the experiences of insiders, and focuses on generalizability, ignoring the importance of specific instances of individual experience (Guba & Lincoln, 2004). Researchers who bring a positivistic lens to their research believe that there is a truth, and that it can be known, and so focus on verifying or falsifying hypothesis without critique of the structures in which knowledge claims are based. As Harding (2004, p. 128) states, "it is a delusion to think that human thought could completely erase the fingerprints that reveal its production process" when in fact, those efforts at objectivity allow no process for identifying the values and beliefs that are held by all of the members of the scientific community, and the lack of inclusion of researchers whose beliefs differ ensures that "culturewide assumptions *that have not been criticized within the scientific research process* are transported into the results of research." Therefore, as Harding illustrates, objectivity in educational research may be a goal but it is just that—a goal that is rarely obtainable. More important, when we privilege some research methodologies and some researchers over others while pretending to be objective, we fail to create spaces where diverse and differing perspectives can be included and heard. As a result, we miss opportunities to obtain the greatest level of understanding of the subjects or phenomena being studied.

In fact, the ways in which our society is structured has epistemological consequences. Harding (2004) identifies some social structures that influence our epistemology and research methodologies as:

- the link between knowledge and power,
- the interactions of people with others and social systems,
- the dominant narratives that are instantiated within social structures,
- hegemonic meaning making which ensures that both oppressor and oppressed accept the bounds of current social structures, and
- the location of politics of power that support supposedly value neutral conceptual frameworks.

These social structures, and specifically the ways that dominant narratives and the systems of power and privilege are instantiated, constrain the ability of marginalized groups to participate in the construction of knowledge. Knowledge and power are conferred or denied based on the social positions of people in the world, creating and eliminating opportunity to act and to learn. Limitations are also created by the narratives of the power hierarchy, by which all members of society come to understand, participate, and reinforce social structures that privilege some and marginalize others. In short, efforts to understand the lives of marginalized communities cannot hide behind efforts at objectivity or neutrality, but must grapple head on with the structures in our social systems that privilege particular forms of knowledge, inform our epistemological stances, influence the questions we ask, and define roles we play in the communities we research.

A critical question to be explored in relationship to the tension between positions of objectivity and subjectivity is the values that drive these assumptions and the attendant impacts on marginalized communities that urban education researchers purport to serve. James Banks (1998) called us out, naming claims of neutrality as a means to relieve the researcher of responsibility to the studied community and to continue to maintain and support the status quo. As long as we continue to devise our questions, conduct our research, and make meaning of our findings using "neutral" claims, we continue to privilege mainstream, dominant culture norms and to further marginalize the students, families, and communities on whom we conduct our research. Freire (2005) names the importance of including the perspectives of the researched alongside the researchers to make powerful meaning that accurately depicts the systems studied.

> It is not our role to speak to the people about our own view of the world, nor attempt to impose that view on them but rather to dialogue with the people about their view and ours. We must realize that their view of the world, manifested variously in their actions, reflects their situation in the world. (p. 77)

Guba and Lincoln (2004) have developed this idea further, in support of the importance of bringing a critical/constructivist lens to our research, in which we leave behind the debate regarding the relative strengths of insider or outsider perspectives are best, but how to bring the critical lens of the outsider to bear in construction of meaning regarding the questions asked, lived experience of, and interpretation of our research. Feminist Standpoint theory as posited by Harding provides another potential framework for naming the values that might guide urban education researchers, by assuming that incorporating the perspectives of marginalized groups to create more objective accounts of the world (strong objectivity). Standpoint theory names the place from which individuals view the world, how they make meaning (socially construct) their world, acknowledges the influences of social group membership and of the inequalities of different social groups (privilege some ways of knowing over others), and makes clear that any given standpoint is partial; multiple standpoints coexist in any given person. In this stance, no idea is reflective of the whole of reality, as it will be situated in a particular context, the standpoint of the research, and dictated by the interests of the investigator.

While standpoint theory gives us a way to think about the influences that an individual researcher brings to a question, critical perspectives add an additional layer, via the central value of critical theory—a commitment to "penetrate the world of objective appearances and to expose the underlying social relationships they often conceal" (Giroux, 1983, p. 7). This requires an exploration of the dynamics of power and privilege that are instantiated in our institutions and systems. Using a critical theory approach to designing, conducting, and making meaning of our research requires us to look at and uncover instances of hegemony, domination and oppression, explore the role of power and privilege, and understand how the hidden curriculum and reproductive nature of our school system conspire to perpetuate inequities between members of dominant and marginalized groups.

The concepts of cultural and social reproduction note that groups of people reproduce their social structures and patterns over time, which results in the transfer of systemic inequalities, such that marginalized groups find themselves unable to acquire the knowledge afforded to members of the dominant culture via educational and other social systems, ensuring that they remain at a disadvantage (Passeron & Bourdieu, 1990). Recognizing our own self-interest in the issues on which we choose to work, challenges us to work side by side with people who are less fortunate, rather than seeing ourselves as benevolent outsiders working to help others. Without intentional efforts to both recognize that our education system in a political site that "represents arenas of contestation and struggle among differentially empowered cultural and economic groups" (Giroux, 1983, p. 3) and that our own values and assumptions can either disrupt or reify the status quo, we will continue, through our research, to reproduce current structures of power and privilege.

POWER AND PRIVILEGE IN EDUCATIONAL RESEARCH

> Many researchers, academics, and project workers may see the benefits of their particular research projects as serving a "greater good" for mankind, or serving a specific emancipator goal for an oppressed community. But belief in the ideal that benefitting mankind is indeed a primary outcome of scientific research is as much a reflection of ideology as it is academic training. It becomes so taken for granted that many researchers simply assume that they as individuals embody this ideal and are natural representatives of it when they work with other communities. (Smith, 2002, p. 3)

The research traditions that form the foundation of educational research serves in many ways to perpetuate the values of the dominant culture, resulting in undervaluing or unawareness of the knowledge and perspectives of marginalized groups, and the implication that marginalized groups are inferior and unable to participate in the solutions to the challenges they face. These practices have "perpetuated an ideology of cultural superiority that precludes the development of power sharing processes and the legitimization of diverse cultural epistemologies and cosmologies" (Bishop, 1998, p. 201). The focus on objectivity and neutrality as criteria for validity serves to legitimize the perspectives of the researcher, and to preclude the subject of the research from participation in the creation, validation, and dissemination of knowledge. Some authors have begun to explore the power and privilege dynamics of research through and examination of the experience of indigenous people as research subjects (Bishop, 1998; Smith, 2002), and named traditional research approaches as those in which the primary benefit of the research is to advance the interests and methods of the researcher, and instead advocate for a research approach that is collectivistic, intended to benefit all research participants (researcher and researched), and is mutually designed from the development of research questions through the methodology, meaning making, and dissemination of results. This approach assumes the legitimacy of the social, political, historical, cultural and intellectual experiences of the researched and is committed to an exploration of the differential levels of power present in social interactions. Bishop (1998) advocates for an "enhanced research relationship" in which the researcher and researched form a long term, reciprocal relationship focused on a mutually developed purpose. This requires that the researcher know themselves, understand their own cultural values and lenses, and commit to a shared development of research agendas—working with, rather than for, the researched.

Many researchers have begun to raise questions about whose perspectives are privileged and whose are marginalized in educational research (Bishop, 1998; Foster, 1999; Guba & Lincoln, 2004; Harding, 2004; Hill Collins, 1986; Smith, 2002), and to point out the importance of engaging with the community that is the object of the research, leading to an assumption that research validity will be improved by the inclusion of researchers from the same cultural background as the object of the research. However, the assumption that an indigenous community member will hold the values and beliefs that honor the community is often erroneous, and outsiders to the community may bring a strong connection (see Table 2.1). Banks first named a typology of cross-cultural researchers in 1998, identifying four typologies—the indigenous-insider, indigenous-outsider, external-insider, and external outsider. This conceptualization allows us to more accurately understand the specific role and impact a researcher may bring to the subject, and to critique the privilege and influence that are assumed.

The four typologies in Table 2.1 give us a place to start as individual researchers looking at how who we are impacts what we do in education

Table 2.1. Banks' Typology

	Insider	*Outsider*
Indigenous	Is a member of the community/culture	Was socialized within the cultural community but has left the original community and become part of another.
	Endorses, understands, and sustains the unique values, perspectives, behaviors, beliefs, and knowledge of the group.	Has adopted the values, beliefs, perspectives, and knowledge of the outside culture or community.
		Is not only regarded as an outsider by indigenous members of the cultural community and is considered to have "sold out" to the outside community.
	Is perceived by the community as a legitimate member	Is often chosen by leaders of the mainstream community as their spokesperson for issues related to his or her original community
		Is viewed as legitimate by the mainstream but not by the indigenous community.
External	Is not a member of the community/culture.	Is not a member of the community/culture in which he or she is doing research.
	Has rejected many of the values and beliefs of their original group.	May have a partial, inaccurate, or negative understanding of the values, perspectives, and knowledge of the community he or she is studying.
	Has adopted the values and beliefs of the new culture/community.	Likely to misunderstand and misinterpret the behaviors within the community, and describe the studied community as pathological or deviant.
	Is viewed by the new community as an "adopted" member and is often negatively perceived and sanctioned by his or her first community.	Believes that he or she is the best and most legitimate researcher to study the subject community because he or she has a more objective view of the community than researchers who live within it.
		Is criticized by members of the studied community but is often praised and highly rewarded by the outside community, which is often more powerful and influential than the studied community.
		May violate the integrity of the communities, may contribute to the disempowerment and oppression of these communities, and may be used by policymakers to justify the marginalized positions of the indigenous people in the studied community.

research. Using this model, a researcher might strive to identify the ways in which the cultural community in which she/he was raised has influenced the beliefs and values held, and how that set of values and beliefs might sit in contrast to the lived experience and understandings of the communities to be studied. The acknowledgment that our communities of origin influence our understanding of the world is critical, and paves the way for reflection and understanding of the ways that background benefits or hinders our work. As shown in the typologies, however, it is also of critical importance to understand the complexity of individual identity development, the ways we interpret and make meaning of our experiences lies in the complex interactions between race and class, gender and family status, region and generation, political and religious experiences. Our ideological and epistemological stances are not automatic, based on group memberships (as seen in the categories of indigenous-outsider and external-insider), but are developed over time, and may endorse or oppose the communities in which we originate (Banks, 1998, p. 5).

So how do we navigate the tensions between the need for a degree of objectivity and the need to capture the reality of the lived experiences of those we research? How do we value the perspective of the participants, while naming the institutional structures of power and privilege of which our participants may be unaware? And, how do we keep ourselves "in check" to ensure that we are not allowing our own ideas of the value of our research to overshadow our commitment to the co-construction of knowledge with the communities we hope to empower? It is in the understanding of our individual stances that provides the place to stand, and from which to begin a critique of the field of urban education research and of specific research agendas.

ASKING THE RIGHT QUESTIONS IN URBAN EDUCATION RESEARCH

> For the master's tools will never dismantle the master's house. They may allow us to temporarily beat him at his own game, but they will never enable us to bring about genuine change. (Lourde, 1984, p. 112)

Asking the right questions in educational research as a whole and especially when conducting and participating in urban education research has to start with us as individual educational researchers. It is our belief that we need to ask the right questions on at least three levels: (1) we must ask questions of ourselves; (2) then of the field or discipline of education as a whole; (3) and finally of our specific research agendas. We must distribute our eagerness and commitment to asking these questions equally.

As individual educational researchers who are engaged, or potentially interested, in educational research in the urban context, there are a number of important questions that we could ask of ourselves that would greatly improve urban education research. Among the most significant are three: (1) Who are we as individuals?; (2) How might we value and accurately portray the perspectives of our participants and also name institutional and social structures of power and privilege of which our participants may not be aware?; and (3) How might we keep ourselves "in check" to ensure that we are not allowing our own ideas of the value of our research to overshadow our commitment to the co-construction of knowledge with the communities we hope to empower through our work?

Then, as educational researchers, instead of primarily looking outside of the academy to ask research questions, it would behoove us to turn our gaze inward to some critical questions of ourselves as a collective community of educational researchers. These questions should seek to garner greater understanding of why we find it necessary to hold on to narrowly constructed conceptualizations of educational research and notions of what constitutes valid research even when we know that many of these methodologies do not allow the authentic voices of often marginalized urban education communities to be heard. Further, we also know that many of these conceptualizations and assumptions emerged during a period of this country's history when women and people of color were rarely given access to discussions and forums that formed much of the knowledge base that guides educational research today. Undoubtedly, had our educational research foundation been built with diverse and heterogeneous perspectives factored prominently into the conceptualizations of educational research, educational research would likely have evolved quite different. Instead, as discussed previously, though there is a significant literature base illustrating that constructive and critical approaches to educational research are more inclusive and authentic in terms of creating spaces for diverse perspectives than positivist and post-positivist research, we continue debates in which the illusion of objectivity is still privileged. Hence, we often fail to ask questions that would advance the deconstruction of illusions of objectivity and the role of privilege in educational research in terms of the questions that we ask.

More important, we are not asking questions of our field of education that would, if indeed answered, improve the life circumstances of some of our most underserved and marginalized communities. Instead, we as educational researchers seem content to continue to conducting research using the "master's tools." By this, we mean, using research tools that we know were developed to objectively study subjects and phenomena rather than to alter or transform the situation. However, it is indeed our argument that the ultimate purpose of urban education research is to create change in conjunction with answering some of the most challenging questions that continue to not be answered. If we can meet these conditions, we will improve the educational conditions of poor children and their families, children of color, and children labeled as having disabilities. However, this is the distinction between constructive and critical research as positivistic and post-positivistic research is merely focused on naming and explaining these issues and phenomena without any sense of obligation to act, alter, or transform.

CASE IN POINT: RE-FRAMING THE
ACADEMIC ACHIEVEMENT GAP RESEARCH QUESTION

Despite the awareness that measuring the academic achievement of African American and other students of color in urban settings by comparing their test scores to those of their White suburban peers without examining critical social contextual variables has not advanced our ability to better educate poor or children of color, we still continue to play this comparative game. Although in recent years more attention has been given to trying to control for issues of race, class, and gender or the interaction of all or some combination of these variables, it is not apparent that we have stopped and said maybe it is not appropriate to continue to compare these two groups of students as though they are equal in terms of access. It is surprising that as a community of educational researchers, we have not consistently or collectively questioned the assumptions associated with pursuing academic achievement as a goal. This might include questioning the fundamental purpose of schooling in America, the definition of achievement and the measures we use, and how we measure achievement. Additionally, we have not come to grips with the fact that measuring academic achievement is not the same as measuring student learning. However, we continue to equate these two constructs as one and the same or we assume that if we measure students' academic achievement it can become a proxy for what they have or have not learned. It also seems to have occurred to only a few educational researchers that comparing African American and other students of color to their White middle- and upper-class peers is like comparing apples to oranges and doing so does not inform us of what either group of students really knows. Rather, such comparisons simply tell us how two contextually unmatched groups perform relative to each other. When it comes to highlighting how inappropriate it is to compare the test scores of poor students and students of color to those of their White middle class peers when we know that social context matters, the educational research community has been largely silent. As a result, we have not forced our field to ask meaningful and deep questions pertaining to opportunities to access the educational system, participate fully within it, and to achieve. When we have addressed or developed research questions on this topic, it has been to identify solutions to closing the "achievement gap" and rarely to actually questioning the framing of the issue of the failure of the American educational system to take responsibility for all of its children by continuing to promote White privilege by comparing the performance of various disaggregated groups of students of color to that of the aggregate of their White peers. For example, the recurring question that is asked in educational research is: How are African American, Asian, Hispanic, and Native American students doing academically as measured by standardized test (or dropout rates, or college completion) when compared to their White peers? Although the answer has been consistently that students of color lag behind their White peers on the standardized measures, the research questions have not changed very much.

The "achievement gap" is rarely framed applying a critical social context lens whereby we examine both perceptions of students achievement as measured by test scores as well as issues of educational access and opportunities to learn on the basis of the intersection of race, class, language, and perceived disability. To do so would require a paradigm shift from the acknowledgment that some schools are better resourced and staffed than others and as a result creates inequitable opportunities and access to a realization that the paradigms need to shift to ensure that ALL students really do have equitable educational opportunities and access. Continuing to frame "academic achievement" or the "achievement gap" by comparing students of color to White students without considering social contextual is inappropriate and supports research findings that result in the reproduction of hegemony. In discussing how hegemony and privilege plays out in educational research especially as it relates to marginalized children and families, Asa G. Hilliard (2007) stated that,

> If we understand the structures of power, and the uses of those power structures for hegemony, including the schooling part of it, we will note several things. Commonly accepted educational research methods may be applied "correctly," then as now, but to the wrong questions, then as now. The right questions simply may never be raised, from the point of view of a centered people, now as in the past. Methods, tools and theories, the "master's methods, tools, and theories," themselves also require critique and change. (Hilliard, 2007)

We contend that educational researchers who are indeed concerned with the educational inequities that exist in urban education and urban communities must be willing to push our field of education to ask questions of ourselves and our field that seek to unearth "the right questions," the "right methodologies." Most importantly we must critique, and where needed, change "the master's methods, tools, and theories."

CONCLUSION

Some might say that the solution to bridging the gap between educational researchers and the participants and phenomena they study in urban settings is simply a disconnect between the investigator and urban communities. However, as illustrated by Banks' typology of researchers, even when the researcher originates from a particular non-dominant community, it is not automatic that she is able to authentically represent the community in her research. More important, the illustration highlights the need for research knowledge, methodology, questions, and analysis and interpretation to be constructed with marginalized and oppressed communities and not on them. Therefore, to move toward conducting socially responsible educational research requires a shift from the current dominant, hegemonic, positivistic and post-positivistic educational research paradigms to a standard that acknowledges and embraces the need to bring the critical lens of the outsider into all aspects of research. If we as a community of educational researchers who are concerned about and want to represent to the best extent possible the authentic perspectives and lived experiences of marginalized and oppressed communities including the children and families that reside in urban settings, we have to be willing to do the following:

1. Question the narrowing of what constitutes rigorous and valid research to a few research methodologies.
2. Question prevailing notions and assumptions of research and researcher objectivity.
3. Question the exclusion or omission of social/cultural context as critically important variables.
4. Question the exclusion or omission of the researcher's background, beliefs, values, and lived experience when discussing research findings and implications.

In summary, as educational researchers we have to be willing to flip the switch on ourselves and to really come to grips with what we are or are not asking with regard to research questions. James Banks is one of few educational researchers that have called upon all scholars, and particularly those in education, to question our practice with a specific focus on whose questions are we asking. Whom do they benefit? Whose values and beliefs do they reflect? We extend Banks' questions to include: Why is the American educational system continuing to fail poor children, students of color and their families, particularly those in urban settings? What is our individual and collective role and responsibility as educational researchers to transform ourselves, tools, and methodologies to benefit the marginalized communities that we say we care about and that we study?

REFERENCES

Atkinson, E. (2004). Thinking outside the box: An exercise in heresy, *Qualitative Inquiry, 10(1)*, 111–129.

Banks, J. (1998). The lives and values of researchers: Implications for educating citizens in a multicultural society. *Educational Researcher, 27*(4), 417.

Bishop, R. (1998). Freeing ourselves from neo-colonial domination in research: A Maori approach to creating knowledge. *Qualitative Studies in Education, 11*(2), 199–219.

Cook, T. D., & Payne, M. R. (2002). Objecting to the objections to using random assignment in educational research. In F. Mosteller & R. Boruch (Eds.), *Evidence matters* (pp. 150–178). Washington, DC: The Brookings Institute.

Eisenhart, M., & Towne, L. (2003). Contestation and change in national policy on "scientifically based" education research. *Educational Researcher, 32*(7), 31–38.

Freire, P. (2005). *Education for critical consciousness.* New York: Continuum International Publishing Group.

Foster, M. (1999). Race, class, and gender in education research: Surveying the political terrain. *Educational Policy, 13*, 77–85.

Giroux, H. (1983). *Theory & resistance in education: A pedagogy for the opposition.* New York: Bergin & Garvey.

Guba, E., & Lincoln, Y. (2004). Competing paradigms in qualitative research. In S. Hesse-Biber & P. Leavy (Eds.), *Approaches to qualitative research: A reader on theory and practice* (pp. 17–38). New York: Oxford University Press.

Harding, S. (Ed.). (2004). *The feminist standpoint theory reader: Intellectual and political controversies.* Routledge: New York.

Heckman, S. (2004). Truth and method: Feminist standpoint theory revisited. In S. Harding (Ed.), *The feminist standpoint theory reader: Intellectual and political controversies.* Routledge: New York.

Hill Collins, P. (1986). Learning from the outsider within: The sociological significance of black feminist thought. *Social Problems, 33*(6), S14–S32.

Hilliard, A. (2007, April). *Shaping research for global african educational excellence: It is now or never.* Paper presented at the American Educational Research Association W.E.B. DuBois Lecutre, Chicago, IL.

Lather, P. (2004). Scientific research in education. *Journal of Curriculum and Supervision, 20*(1), 14–30. [Joint publication with *British Educational Research Journal, 30*(6), 759–772].

Lourde, A. (1984). *Sister outsider.* Berkeley, CA: Crossing Press.

Nasir, N., & Hand, V. (2006). Exploring sociocultural perspectives on race, culture, and learning. *Review of Educational Research, 76*, 449–475.

National Research Council. (2002). *Scientific research in education.* Committee on Scientific Principles for Education Research (J. Shavelson & L. Towne, Eds.) Washington, DC: National Academy Press.

Passeron, J., & Bourdieu, P. (1990). *Reproduction in education, society, and culture.* London: Sage.

Shaker, P., & Ruitenberg, C. (2007). Scientifically-based research: The art of politics and the distortion of science. *International Journal of Research & Method in Education, 30*(2), 207–219.

Smith, L. T. (1999). *Decolonizing methodologies: Research and indigenous peoples.* New York: Zed.

Smith, L. (2002). *Decolonizing methodologies: Research and Indigenous peoples.* New York: Zed Books.

CHAPTER 3

RESEARCH AS AN EPISTEMOLOGICAL ARCHITECT OF MARGINALIZING POWER IN THE INTELLECTUAL ENTERPRISE

Beverly E. Cross

INTRODUCTION

Five years ago I casually browsed a catalog that arrived in my campus mailbox from a well-known academic publisher. The centerfold of the catalog was a splashy layout announcing and featuring new titles available for course adoptions. I noticed that the centerfold advertised approximately a dozen books that featured recent research on racial, ethnic, linguistic or cultural minority groups (e.g., Mexicans, African Americans, Puerto Ricans, and American Indians). I became excited to see what I thought was a feature on authentic voices from the margins of U.S. society and also mostly from its marginalizing contextual equivalent, urban

Research in Urban Educational Settings: Lessons Learned and Implications for Future Practice, pp. 39–58
Copyright © 2011 by Information Age Publishing

schools. Soon, however, I further observed that all of the researchers were White, including a colleague in my department. I was startled by what I perceived to be a centerfold that promoted and celebrated research that others. The centerfold seemed to have an invisible header or billboard that flashed "The center speaks for the margin." I went to my colleague and asked if she was disappointed to be included in the proud display of White scholars enacting privileged forms of knowing, representing, and controlling the identities and representation of marginalized, minority groups. She seemed simultaneously annoyed by and dismissive of my question and asked me "Are you saying that White scholars do not have the right to study other groups. Don't I have the right to study anyone I want?" I stated possibly, but do you have a concern about the image that this centerfold produces and that you are included in it. She stated, "No." I asked, "Isn't it a little disturbing in its blatant message about the state of educational research as a power strategy to marginalize." I attempted to initiate a conversation about research, power, representation and the researchers' stance. She did not want to engage with me in this dialogue. We seemed at an impasse as she turned and walked away.

I have never forgotten this exchange and the feeling I had that we interpreted this centerfold so differently and that our different interpretations had everything to do with our ideological stance toward research, our positionalities in the academy, and moreover, our experiences as racial, ethnic and cultural beings. We both conduct research in urban educational settings. She seemed to view research as her professional obligation with unlimited privilege regardless of her own identities and experiences. She denied the unseen, unacknowledged, denied subtleties in the eyes and ears of privilege (Dei, Karumanchery, & Karamanchery-Luik, 2007). I view research as a professional obligation that carries immense considerations about my identities and experiences, particularly my racial, cultural, and urban identities. I constantly worry about research as form of power that carries epistemological, representational, and cultural considerations. She did not appear to be bothered by such concerns because she had the right and privilege to study "anyone" she wants. I have subsequently thought seriously about the role of research in terms of the power relations that it embodies. Thinking about how I should be guided as a scholar by my identities and experiences does not appear an option to me. Rather, it is an ethical requirement. I do not feel that I have the right to study whomever I want without giving deep consideration to whom I am and my positionality in relationship to them. I understand the "structures, processes, and belief systems that maintain unequal power relations in academe and educational research" (Sleeter, 2006, p. ix). My White colleague seemed unencumbered by such considerations. I conversely am encumbered by my subjectivities, the power relations inherent in research, and my relationship to marginalized groups, particularly those in urban contexts. I was reminded of how much I shared (e.g., minority status, urban resident) with the marginalized groups in our city and how I worried about my relationship to them as a scholar and how she was so extremely estranged (she is White and from an area suburb) from them yet felt completely privileged to view them as othered research subjects.

In this chapter, I will examine the way in which this brief but powerful tête-à-tête is emblematic of research as operationalization of power when it is conducted under the ideology of privilege and othering in urban contexts. I suggest that research is an epistemological architect of marginalizing power in the intellectual enterprise. Marginalization is defined by Young (1990) as groups who suffer severe material deprivation and are expelled from useful participation in social life. They further are racially marked and often positioned by the dominant culture to relations of dependency where they are excluded from equal citizenship and rights. In addition, the severe and strict spatial isolation and segregation in urban communities, interact to produce a context in which the operationalization of power and marginalization play out in insidious, deleterious ways largely around the social axes of racial, ethnic, linguistic and cultural lines. It is the intersectionality of marginalization and urban spatial and social isolation along social axes that sets the framework for this chapter.

I will analyze two strategies of power—knowledge production and representation—enacted thorough research that reproduces marginalization. I will then describe how knowledge production and representation produce power and domination. These two power strategies work silently and invisibly through research and constitute one way in which researchers maintain the hegemonic relations of the status quo that advantages those involved who are privileged by their roles as researchers. These strategies of control are employed through research as White professors knowingly and unknowingly participate in marginalization of racial, ethnic, cultural and linguistic minority groups. Each of the two components will be examined as power strategies that result in research operating as a tool of domination—an invisible tool to sustain inequity.

PRODUCING KNOWLEDGE: EXAMINING THE OTHER

Research is not, of course, objective or benign. The epistemology that frames research considers the rules and standards by which knowledge about the world is formed (Popkewitz, 1991, p. 218). Further, theories about research are underpinned by a cultural system of classification and representation, by views about human nature, and human morality and virtue (Smith, 2001). The rules of science embody visions of social order as well as conceptual distinctions that define power relations (Popkewtiz, 1991, p. 15), and these can either marginalize or suppress the diversity of human worldviews (Rains, 2006, p. 24). Thus the production of knowledge carries immense importance and implications since it drives our society's identity, values, culture and even our economic viability. We often hear that the U.S. produces ideas and other societies produce the products that come from those ideas. If this perspective holds any merit, then "Knowledge as a technology of power" (Popkewitz, 1991, p. 37) is of critical importance in producing ideas about groups around the world and marginalized groups within U.S. urban communities.

Producing knowledge about the world has been largely the uncontested sole proprietary charge of research communities. Virtually every U.S. institution (e.g., economic, cultural, political and social), has relied on or summoned the research community to fuel its operation. I am reminded of the role of researchers in the eugenics movement, for example. In today's context, the United States is frequently viewed worldwide as knowledge-producing and information-producing. Paradoxically, when knowledge is produced, controlled and distributed by the dominant group, then power and inequities result at the same time that the world becomes more and more diverse in terms of knowledges, values, cultures, and identities. For example, Rains (2006, p. 23) explains how research has

> cut across my body; slashed my identity, worked to destroy in subtle ways, the power of Indigenous knowledge and my sense of self. I witnessed how research and theories were used to erase, marginalize, objectify, and ignore Native Peoples and our histories and relationships with the lands. I felt the power of the Western colonizing knowledge production enterprise.

She makes clear the need to recognize knowledge as a social construction that is based in dominant ideologies, epistemologies and axiologies that oppress and denies the voices from the margin and validates the dominant voice to speak for the margins. It follows then, as urban schools become increasingly racially, ethnically, culturally and linguistically diverse, research communities step up to thwart the Other from rewriting and rerighting their own histories (Smith, 2001). It reinscribes its power to produce knowledge of the other through classification and representation. They control how they are known in the world.

The colloquial phrase, "Knowledge is Power," has always seemed to me to be incomplete and in need of amendment due to the disparity in control over the production and role of knowledge within the sociocultural context of U.S. society. Since research is tied to new and old ways of exploration, discovery, conquest, exploitation, distribution and appropriation (Smith, 2001), it seems more accurate to state that the power to produce knowledge is power not clear since it encompasses producing knowledge of others. Welch and Pollard (2006) capture the importance of the power to produce knowledge when they state:

> Thus, for many years, the preponderance of research focusing on people of color has been done by White, middle class investigators, with the result that much of the research focusing on populations defined as marginal takes a deficit approach to its subjects: it raises questions that focus on the pathologies and problems presumed to reside within those under study. (p. 2)

Education research has served a key role in pathologizing urban communities and the marginalized groups within them. Even well intentioned researchers operating under the perception that they are "giving voice" to others, have unwillingly focused on problems that contribute to approach. Research allocates the power to define and represent the truths and realities of Others under its regime of "truth." "It is important to understand the manner in which oppressive 'truths' are produced in order to examine how they become hegemonic through practices, techniques and technologies of power that run through racial discourse" (Dei et al., 2007, p. 48) or other marginalizing discourses. Groups that are subordinated without this power may not feel that knowledge is power but that knowledge is the product of the power that defines, produces, and represents them to the larger world. "Foucault reverses the traditional belief that knowledge is power and defines power as embodied in the manner in which people gain knowledge and use the knowledge to intervene in social affairs" (Popkewitz, 1991, p. 30). Sleeter (2006, p. viii) reflects on this when she states as a White researcher, "I have power and authority to shape which perspectives count as legitimate, to support some perspectives and ignore or marginalize others, and to position my work in a way that will ensure my continued power and authority." Rains continues with

> Research has played an instrumental role in devaluing Indigenous knowledge in this privileging process. Urban communities and marginalized groups, too, are devalued through this same privileging process. An irony, to be sure, given that research is the pursuit of knowledge. (Sleeter, 2006, p. 24)

The privileging process refers to the advantaging of Western epistemology and knowledge while not only disadvantaging other knowledges and epistemologies but actually controlling them to further marginalize non-dominant groups.

Educational researchers remain overwhelmingly White, with only about 16.5% of university faculty representing racial minority groups (Gose, 2007). These voices from the margins have not shifted the center in terms of its epistemological hold on what is truth. Doing so can create intellectual space that "offers the academy the opportunity to pull back its heavy curtains on the broader landscape of epistemologies adding vibrancy to the intellectual enterprise and the quest for knowledge" (Rains, 2006, p. 22). Instead of pulling back the curtain, research is still dominated by White researchers and knowledge of the world is still controlled by them. Therefore, this mix of science, cultural arrogance and political power continues to present a serious threat to the Othered (Smith, 2001). Such dominance positions research as the architect of power in the intellect enterprise to shape and control equity, voice and representation and to silence and marginalize some groups. It assures that research will remain a tool of oppression rather than liberation because the curtain has not been pulled back to expose a battle of intellectuals "to challenge the regimes of truth and world-making images, including that of the intellectual" (Popkewitz, 1991, p. 242). It has not created space for multiple voices from their colleagues from the margins. As Welch and Pollard (2006, p. 3) state, "The work of marginalized researchers is unique precisely because it is embedded with the cultural and social perspectives of those researchers." They suggest this is critical to creating space and place where different questions, issues and interpretations of research can surface. This does not suggest a monolithic voice or perspective from marginalized researchers, but rather it suggests the critical need for diversity emanating from various experiences, ideologies, and contexts rather than the dominant strong hold that currently exists. There is rich diversity in race, class, language and culture within marginalized groups. And as their 16.5% increases, more drill down of voice and perspective will continue to be of more importance from within the margins itself.

Too infrequently is research critiqued for what it means when the researchers are predominantly White, middle class and privileged while their subjects/participants are racial, ethnic, cultural, linguistic minority groups from urban communities. An overwhelming number of researchers do not come primarily from urban communities and have not had extensive, authentic experiences of any kind there. They have not engaged with those who live and attend school there, yet researchers have increased their gaze on marginalized communities. They have not experienced the marginalization that they feel confident and competent to represent, create and recreate. This is more than a demographic mismatch: a cultural, racial, linguistic and class gap exists between researchers and those that are the objects of their inquiry. It is problematic to generalize White privilege, but as Hilliard (1999) stated, any considerations of race [and marginalization] is useless unless it also considers racism and White privilege—and considers them as a hegemonic system. Too little emphasis is given to the researchers own ideologies, prejudices, and misconceptions while they create images of marginalized groups, even when they are well intentioned and disclose themselves, power relationships are not eliminated or diminished. Researchers decide what to disclose, how to disclose it, as they self-disclose their objects of study. "There is a vast array of competing interests, tensions, and contradictions in thinking through the power relations of knowledge production in the broader context of anti-racism" (Dei & Johal, 2005, p. 3) and other marginalizing research.

Researchers are positioned to reinscribe their power positions to carry out their White privileged status to observe others. Observation is an act of power and facilitates control and domination of others from marginalized subordinated groups. In today's sociopolitical context, control and domination do not operate through outright physical force but rather than institutions. It works through numerous invisible strategies that reinscribe power and domination such as conducting research on the Other through privileged positions to do so. Fiske (1993, p. 72) describes one such strategy as surveillance [read research] as a "system of knowledge and power that is practically achieved through institutions developed to monitor and control behavior." The researchers are allowed to see and not be seen, to know but not be known. Power and control is unidirectional through this process. For illustrative purposes here, I will describe how surveillance works as a research strategy. Researchers operate under the authority of knowledge producers without much critique of their work as an act of power. They utilize their position (of power) to place others under their watchful eye for the purpose of their academic gain. They are empowered to monitor others, document others, examine others, evaluate others, and rank others as part of their work as cultural and political agents (although this element of their work may not be acknowledged or analyzed). Fiske (1993) argues that such examination, surveillance, and monitoring is essential to assure that the subordinates (marginalized groups) submit to the power of those in power positions (White researchers) to observe, monitor, document and even control them. Marginalized groups become objects of power of a White system of hegemonic research.

For sure, the discourse of research describes these acts in very different terms. Researchers assert that observation and surveillance occurs for the sake of learning and studying others in order to produce knowledge about them so that the world knows more about them and will appreciate them. For example, education scholars have been deployed to urban communities and schools to study them for the sake of learning about them and illuminating them to the remainder of the world. Instead, the implicit message in observation and surveillance is that White scholars are cultural actors who monitor others for their own benefit and advantage to control social order. This is problematic because researchers, as the producers and legitimators of culture, are the group most closely aligned to the colonizers in terms of their class interests, their values and their ways of thinking (Smith, 2001). Such practices are often quite extreme in monitoring and surveillance. For example, I know of some education researchers who proposed to equip urban schools with video cameras with the expectation that they would not even have to physically enter these environments to conduct their work. They can ultimately see and not be seen. The tapes produced by the hidden cameras are invisible and sustain the invisibility of the researcher whose tentacles of monitoring and surveillance operate in the virtual extreme. Researchers could benefit from the investigative work to examine the Other for their own professional understanding, needs and eventual intended or unintended control and domination, further distancing Others and subjugating them to the needs, whims and power of dominant White researchers.

Researchers often do this without first understanding or critiquing this process as a form of surveillance, monitoring and domination that marginalizes. They are not required to examine their own ideologies, lenses, positions before they do the same to others. Their own lives are protected and unexamined, while those they choose to gaze upon (an act of power) are supposed to be open to them because they desire it and can benefit from it. Their identities are constructed around a politics of difference that allows Whites to be viewed as neutral and objective, while the lives of others are reduced to subjects and commodities for their use. Haymes (1995) explicates that this occurs:

> By making nonwhite cultures markers for racial difference … results in whites being deracialized and nonwhites racialized … makes race the problem of nonwhites and not whites … constructs nonwhites as either exotic or dangerous. (p. 107)

Being White becomes the invisible, unspoken norm. The privileges, interests, and power of this invisible norm often are not examined and even if they are, the acts of surveillance occur anyway. For example, "When considered as research subjects, women of color are routinely marginalized when their behavior, attitudes, and emotions are analyzed solely from the perspectives of White middle class researchers." Many times this results in interpretations that describe women of color as deviant or exotic (Pollard, 2006, p. 7) or inferior (Rains, 2006). The same is true for other marginalized groups.

Urban contexts frequently are observed and monitored as a geographical intact pool of the other. Therefore, it is increasingly gazed upon to determine what is aberrant or abnormal. This strategy involves the process of what Fiske (1993) calls individuation, another act of power. Here those granted the power to observe, monitor, document, evaluate and control the individuality and social relations of the Othered and so place them in the required social order that advantages the dominant society while disadvantaging marginalizing groups. Fiske states, "individuation identifies the individual but cannot produce identity: Indeed it is threatened by identity, so works to evacuate it" (p. 68). Research does not reinforce the values, actions, customs, culture, and identity of others (Smith, 2001). Therefore, research sets up the stage to individuate, other, categorize and generalize rather than to see different identities, histories, and experiences. Fine describes social research that:

> constructs, legitimates, and distances others, banishing them to the margins of the culture ... always to rob them of whole, complex, humanity.... These Others are represented as unworthy, dangerous, and immoral, or as pitiable, victimized, and damaged. (p. 139)

Othering is achieved first by applying a meaning of aberrant to marginalized groups put under surveillance while simultaneously inscribing superiority to those who other.

Othering is secondly achieved by representing those othered as the appropriate terrain where the power of White researchers is properly exercised (Fiske, 1993). In the first step, this plays out when educational research pathologizes urban communities and marginalized groups and creates negative and fearful images of them, their schools, their neighborhoods and their families. In the second step, because of the articulated, research-based pathology, then urban communities become the terrain where further examination and correction punitive measures need to be applied. Clearly, producing knowledge about the other is more than objective research being carried out.

Another example will illustrate this practice. Some researchers now feel they should have access to all parts of urban communities, including homes. The public discourse to support this practice is that such observation [read surveillance] is essential for researchers to do their work well. Again, this extends the White researchers' tentacles of surveillance and power to own and represent. I have frequently asked what right does a White university researcher have to ask to enter the homes of families with whom they have no real relationship. When did the rights to privacy for racial minority families become sacrificial for the sake of researchers. There often seems to be no end to the expectation that racial minority groups are at the disposal of Whites as subjects to study. bell hooks (1994) warns against this as a new form of slavery where racial minority groups are to teach Whites about them for their own use and advantage—likely for control and domination.

The act of surveillance enables the next power strategy to be possible. The above examples of power strategies help to maintain the social order that advantages those who participate in these strategies, the dominant society. Through surveillance, they are able to write the world for their benefit and to perpetuate control over those whom they do not see as worthy of that same benefit and who may be unaware of the invisible mechanisms that assure they do not, and will not, have access to those privileges and advantages. Marginalized groups become "reduced to the imagery [and description/representation] of the colonizer" (Giroux, 1991, p. 7)—that is researchers. In an attempt to produce knowledge about diverse groups, it is odd that the researchers will likely become intolerant, shallow, narcissistic and uninformed through their acts of surveillance and the application of their power. This paradoxical context—the desire to understand others while simultaneously enacting power upon them—is one of the most pressing scholarly exigencies of our time. For example, the scholars who were included in the centerfold of the publisher's catalog described at the beginning of this chapter undertook their work to produce knowledge about diverse groups as a contribution to the field but likely applied power upon those groups at the same time they carried out their work. This is one form of surveillance that is facing increased challenge by marginalized groups and that when not challenged leads to representation, which is discussed next.

REPRESENTATION: CONTROLLING THE OTHER

The relationship of knowledge to power encompasses not only the production of knowledge as discussed in the previous section, but also the exercise of that power to represent others, particularly marginalized groups (e.g., their identities, realities, and social relations to other groups). In today's context

> Power does not focus on physical coercion, nor is it directly concerned with one group's sovereignty over others, although domination is always a background issue. Power, in this sense, is productive of social identity rather than instances of repression, violence or coercion. (Popkewitz, 1991, p. 31)

Power, then, has everything to do with controlling the representation of groups in the margin by the center. Fiske (1993) states "the culture of power is a culture of representation. It relies on the ability to reproduce representations of the world and more importantly if less explicitly, of themselves in the world" (p. 147). This is so powerful because representation renders the world knowable and controllable. Education researchers rely on the culture of power to represent urban communities and the marginalized groups that predominate there through spatial and social isolation. These scholars render urban communities knowable and controllable while simultaneously protecting their own identities from examination and representation. Academic researchers are particularly relevant here because the most powerful knowledge is disciplinary, that is, it is produced by a discipline and its discursive practices. "It is important to recognize and examine this discursive machinery if we are to critically interrogate the systematic order through which the Western world managed to construct and discipline the other" (Dei et al., 2007, p. 44). As Fiske (1993, p. 150) suggested, the Other is always a product of representation and, as such, whatever form it may be given, always applies the discursive and material power of representing social order upon that part of the world it has made into its other.

Educational research often now produces knowledge about various racial, cultural and linguistic groups as well as knowledge about urban contexts (as evidenced by the centerfold described at the beginning of the chapter). At one level, research on the margins is essential because in a nation where the Intellectual Enterprise serves as the primary, if not exclusive, regime of truth, research becomes the source of knowing diverse voices, experiences, and realities. For example, the array of sessions at many education research conferences on marginalized groups clearly indicates that the spotlight (read surveillance) is on them. I often overhear graduate students examining the American Educational Research Association's program as they marvel over the sheer number of sessions focused on marginalized groups and urban contexts. Rather than romanticize this process, it is necessary to problematize it when the architects of knowing the "Other" reign from the dominant group as they reproduce and marginalize. Such marginalization occurs through White hegemonic control over the representation of the cultures, histories, consciousness, and realities of racial, ethnic, cultural, and linguistic groups (as suggested by Fiske). This representation is often inaccurate, incomplete, whitened and thus oppressive. But it circulates with authority and certainty while ignoring that knowledge is mediated by the White culture, history and institutions that produce and distribute that knowledge. "Research has often depicted marginalized racial, social-class, and gender groups in stereotypical ways that contributed to their victimization and the denial of democracy and justice. Mainstream researchers also frequently reinforced institutionalized race, class and gender stratification" (Banks, 2006, p. xi). Therefore, research can help to "know" the Other based on generalizations, misinformation, and White perspectives to make them knowable to the world.

Representation occurs when White researchers, through their observations, monitoring, and surveillance, subsequently create, recreate, and make up the stories of those they have placed under their watchful eyes. As a result of their investigative work researchers now can describe, for their purposes, in broad as well as fine detail the culture, behavior, relationship, needs, and problems of those observed. Thus, through a few observations generally within the context of the school, a narrative is created through the lens of the White scholar who has been given carte blanche to other with research as the armor to do so. I am reminded of a White researcher who asserts that his research on African American urban youth is mutually benefitting to them and to him. He believes by merely conducting research on them in their urban school that he is benefitting them because he is using his research to tell their stories or to represent their voices so others will understand them. I stated that I could see the benefit to him in terms of publications and even his recent promotion and tenure based on this form of scholarship but that I could not readily discern the benefit to the African American youth. He became frustrated and stated that maybe he benefitted more but then asked "What am I supposed to do. I have to study someone (a recurrent mantra and excuse to deny that power is being enacted). I need someone to study so I can produce research" he claimed. He did not recognize the acts of power (surveillance and representation) that he set up and sanctioned. This power acts in such a way as to situate research to implicitly say:

> I want to know your story. And then I will tell it back to you in a new way. Tell it back to you in such a way that it has become mine, my own. Re-writing you ... I am still author, authority. I am still the colonizer, the speak subject, and you are now at the center of my talk. (hooks, 1990, pp. 151–152)

Researchers use their university granted authority and power to represent the lives of others in a way that they are unlikely prepared for and should not be given the right to think they should and can do. Because of their power to look and not be seen and because their dominant group acts as invisible and non-racialized, they nonetheless operate to describe what they cannot possibly know or understand. But because of their positions of power over the Other, they believe that they can. I recently heard a leading education researcher authoritatively proclaim in a national forum that researchers should be sent to study inner city schools and students and their families "like sociologist and anthropologist who then can describe them culturally and socially." He seemed to be privileging his fellow White researchers to toss academic disciplines to the wind and to represent Others in any way you desire. His charge to his fellow colleagues was to study not only whom you want but in any way that you want to. This time I had flashbacks of scientists measuring the skulls of African Americans to prove their racial inferiority to whites. Even people who conduct careful research in which issues of observing and representing people from different racial and cultural groups should face and deliberate over the complex ethical and practical challenges (Fine, 1998) in doing so. But many education researchers operate under the assumption that they are qualified to define and describe those they observe and monitor in much the same way that oppressors define and describe those they oppress as acts of control, and they see the spatial and social isolation created in urban communities as their intact play ground to do so. They, subsequently silence, pathologize and trivialize marginalized groups while presenting themselves as neutral, invisible, unveiled, normal and now as sociologist, anthropologists and psychologists.

The converse is not the case. Duneier (1992) states in his reflections of his and other ethnographic works that "Blacks do not tend to conduct sociological studies of White ethnic groups (as do White scholars of blacks)." He further suggested that if they did the assertions made in these studies "without clear and unambiguous evidence ... would have little chance of getting assigned in college classes ... and there would probably be outcry" (Duneier, 1992, p. 137). But because of power and privilege as operationalized through dominant paradigms of research such studies of Blacks by Whites in various fields, not just sociology, are permitted and encouraged without measurable challenge, much less public outcry. In education, such studies are in fact vogue and produce notoriety, fame, and tenure for many White scholars. Simply peruse any research conference program for evidence of this intellectual enterprise—White scholars studying Blacks and Latinos, for example, often with unclear and ambiguous evidence. Some Black scholars, myself included, have begun to openly challenge and question these research practices and the products they produce disguised as truth. Dunier (1992) goes on to suggest that these studies often "confirm inaccurate stereotypes that happen also to be demeaning" (p. 139). This occurs because the researchers:

> Convey[s] his or her essential goodness in relation to others' ... by simply advertising that his or her books present a less stereotyped view of blacks, or by embracing a liberal political program, [that] has afforded a license to make generalizations about the black population that are not supported by firm evidence.

Representation occurs at another insidious, hidden level within education research. In academic communities, research is the primary source of knowledge since too few White academics have too few common experiences with marginalized groups and communities. So they must rely on each other to do the research that discloses the margins to each other.

The knowledge produced is largely produced by White researchers who, due to their own power positions, have "studied" marginalized minority groups in order to make those groups accessible for study by others around the nation. Their representation of minority and marginalized groups is based on their own lenses, privilege, and power to study and represent them. Thus, the knowledge produced is actually power disguised as knowledge. The researchers use research that enables them to own for a time a group that they will eventually rewrite the history, consciousness, realities, and culture of in their own way using their own power to do so. And because of their privileged, intellectual positions in the academy combined with their power to know Others, these interpretations or representations become *truth*. The scholars' own histories, cultures, realities and consciousness are invisible and not acknowledged nor recognized and, as a result, are protected and normalized. Therefore, rather than producing diverse, multiple voices through their research, they actually produce a monovocal representation that ignores rival often contradictory truths.

The knowledge produced through research then becomes activated socially and circulated through discourse. Fiske (1993) defines discourse as representing the world by producing it and exerting control over it because it produces a knowledge of the real which it then presents and re-presents in constant circulation and use. He describes knowledge and discourse as two sides of the same coin that form a coherent system of production, repression and distribution that are totally interdependent. "These discourses operate to constitute who can know the 'truth,' who can speak of the 'truth' and what can be said about the 'truth' " (Dei et al., 2007, p. 48). Through the political process of discourse, education researchers produce certain knowledge about minority and marginalized groups, repress certain information, and distribute what they choose to circulate as truth or knowledge. Discourse applies and carries power because the power to control ways of knowing is power over what is accepted as reality (Fiske, 1993). What is accepted as reality is the product of discourse. Therefore, through the process of producing, repressing, distributing and using the "official" discourse or master narratives, researchers participate in applying power to distribute "the" reality of other groups and controlling that reality regardless of the other realities held by those groups themselves. They produce the definitions, assumptions, and paradigms that serve their unstated, unrecognized and unintended purpose to control and dominate (Popkewitz, 1991; Sleeter & McLaren, 1995) and regulate and subjugate (Dei et al., 2007, p. 43).

Fiske (1993) identifies three forms that representation of groups takes. First, a miniaturization of reality is taken to represent the whole. Second, a representation is used to promote White interests in the world and to extend power beyond immediate conditions. Third, the representation presents selected features of an absent reality or referent. Research is replete with numerous miniaturizations produced through scholarly works that are used to represent the needs, abilities, and realities of those the groups othered. These "findings" then represent the entire group. With this truth of the group, officially produced through research, the interests of White society get extended. The power to commodify and colonize another group through controlling their representation in the world based in rational research has once again been achieved. This process works because the voices of those represented (already marginalized by U.S. structural relations and further marginalized through research) are silenced and cannot therefore challenge the absent reality. With the armor of the undefeatable tools of research, scholars are left to produce reality, dehumanize others and subordinate others without sufficient evidence or risk of challenge from those they represent. Freire (1970) refers to a similar process as cultural invasion in which the invaders (White researchers) penetrate the cultural content of another group (minority and marginalized groups) and impose their own view of the world upon those they invade and inhibit the creativity of the invaded by curbing their expression. In the processes described here, researchers not only invade, to the extent that they impose their world view upon those they invade, they also use their power in such situations to represent the reality of the group they invade, thus curbing the groups' creativity in representing themselves. The researcher becomes located or situated in another's lived experiences [rather than] critically engaging his own experiences as part of the knowledge search (Dei & Johal, 2005, p. 2). More and more racial minority scholars are beginning to resent and reject the numerous representations of their own racial group by White scholars at research conferences. In various professional contexts, such discontent will likely lead to serious conversations challenging surveillance, monitoring, representation and the power, control and the privilege it carries for White scholars.

A presentation I recently attended illustrates the three forms of representation. A White teacher educator presented her "ground breaking" research in which she and her White university students had built an "equal-status" relationship with an urban African American community organization that housed a school. She had also conducted research on the organization, the students, and their families. Rather than equal status, I heard her describe the first form of representation—she miniaturized the reality of a few African Americans to represent the whole. I challenged her on the idea of an "equal-status" relationship based on the marginalizing function of research described here. I was incredulous that the relationship was of equal status thinking that once again a marginalized, minority group was a subject of study for the benefit of White researchers. As I continued to challenge her on what made the relationship "equal-status" she asserted it was trust and respect and her humbleness toward them for allowing her and her students into their "cultural sanctuary." I interpreted this as a condescending response to the Black community organization and the second form of representation (promoting white interests in the world)—that she granted them her trust, respect and humbleness while making them and their children objects of study for her and her students. I again asked quite aggressively, what did the community organization gain if this was an equal-status relationship. She concluded not very much, that indeed she and her university students gained a great deal and the community organization gained little if anything. As a White scholar she could count on those she represented not to be at the conference to challenge her representation of them and their supposed equal-status relations. She presented their absent reality—the third form of representation. After thinking about my questions to her, she later confessed to me one-on-one that the community organization was in fact, an object for her and her students and as a result only an unequal relationship existed. She went on to say, however, that she could not envision how else she could achieve her aims in helping her White students understand Black children. I stated that type of honesty is needed but is insufficient. She had made this presentation around the country (and written it in many research journals) with great confidence and authority and had not been challenged about it from her largely White audiences. Based on the use of her work and others like hers, researchers control their representation and exercise the representation of minority and marginalized groups in urban communities. Hilliard (1999) describes it this way:

> Dominating populations crush or suppress the history of its victims, destroy the practice of the culture of its victims, prevent the victims from coming to understand themselves as part of a cultural family, teach systematically the ideology of white supremacy, control the socialization process, control the accumulation of wealth, and perform segregation and apartheid.

It is not surprising that much of the representation comes out of a discourse of problems with diversity or with others. Although masked as giving voice to marginalized groups, power is reinscribed over others rather than for others. Some would claim such a stand is innocent or unintended. Hillard (1999) states:

> The ideology of "race" drives much of what happens in the world and in education. It is like a computer software program that "runs in the background invisible and inaudible." However, our silent and invisible "racial"

hardware is not benign. It is linked to issues of power and hegemony and the domination of a given group by another.

What he describes is the process of research as an architect of marginalization—a process that is invisible and based on power and domination. And that is what we have left to do in research. We must analyze how our research practices—surveillance and representation—are producing marginalization through invisible power and domination that result in four manifestations of unearned privilege: power, access, status, credibility and normality (Rocco & West, 1998).

Demarginalizing Research

"Generally education as a research enterprise in university settings is poorly articulated with respect to building sustained programs of research and is certainly not organized around a public interest problem or area of concern" (Tate, 2006, p. 255). Instead of this sustained interest in a public problem or concern, researchers serve as spokespersons for social groups (Popkewitz, 1991, p. 233). To disrupt the marginalizing spokesperson role of "White on Black and Brown" research the research community needs to move "with all deliberate speed" to interrogate both the production of knowledge and the ways in which that knowledge produces the representation of others. This means challenging who maintains the privileged status of producing research, research paradigms, what is produced, and the role of the knowledge produced.

Many scholars have thought through what needs to be considered and done to demarginalize research. I present some of the key ideas her in their own voices. They speak with strength from or with the margins, thus no interpretation of their voices is appropriate.

- We believe that in the critical interrogation of race knowledge, multiple voices should be listened to without interruption—to speak both to and with other voices (Dei et al., 2007, p. xiii).
- Whites should resist White flight that ends up "recreating the same old patterns of hierarchy, exclusion, and power somewhere else. Instead, White scholars should "work with rather than on or without colleagues who bring life experiences that broaden the range of ideas on the table, ways of investigating and evaluating those ideas, and actions we might take as a result" (Sleeter, 2006, p. ix).
- Destabilize the inherited rhetoric that gives authority to the world-making images of the intellectual as agents for others (Popkewitz, 1991, p. 241).

- Continue to identify and employ alternatives to the dominant perspective in educational research, which uses its power to determine who will be centered and who marginalized (Welch & Pollard, 2006, p. 3).
- Continue the quest of researchers of color for constructed knowledge, one that moves outside the frames and systems offered in dominant interpretations to provide and create our own analyses of experiences on the margins.... Furthermore, we argue that knowledge construction such as this can become a prime location for resisting objectification as the Other even as it becomes the catalyst for evolving more authentic and inclusive paradigms (Welch & Pollard, 2006, p. 4).
- Value the wisdom in the margins; value marginalized perspectives (Pollard, 2006, p. 15).
- Deconstruct the structures of oppression and critique efforts from the center to define, conduct, analyze, and control research on communities of color (Pollard, 2006, p. 15).
- Challenge the extent of intellectual aggression to which racially minoritized communities have been subjected ... challenge the recolonization of the intellectual space of those racially minoritized (Dei & Johal, 2005, p. 19).
- Ask significant political, theoretical, epistemological, and methodological questions about whose interests continue to be served by social science research (Dei & Johal, 2005, p. 19).
- Pursue transformative research—research that challenges mainstream and institutionalized findings, interpretations, and paradigms (Banks, 2006).
- Ask these questions:

  o Who defined the research problem?
  o For whom is this study worthy and relevant; who says so?
  o What knowledge will the community gain from this study?
  o What knowledge will the researcher gain from this study?
  o What are some likely positive outcomes from this study?
  o What are some possible negative outcomes?
  o How can the negative outcomes be eliminated?
  o To whom is the researcher accountable?
  o What processes are in place to support the research, the researched and the researcher (Smith, 2001).

Clearly to listen to these voices would mark a major struggle and shift in educational research from marginalizing to challenging inequalities through critical questions and challenging who has power to define Others. In his 2008 AERA Presidential Address, Bill Tate states, "It is our civic responsibility as scholars to question the uneven geography of opportunity" (Tate, 2008). That is essentially the challenge presented in this chapter because of the intersectionality of urban social and special isolation and segregation and educational research. If future scholarship does not aggressively engage in the struggle to challenge inequities and the role of dominant research and researchers in producing knowledge of others and using that knowledge to represent others, then the geography of opportunity will continue to be ignored. Instead, educational researchers will be known for exploiting the geography of inopportunity for their advantage. Shifts in power rarely come with ease or without a struggle, but research can play a constructive role in creating more democratic and just communities just as it has played a role in creating undemocratic and unjust communities.

REFERENCES

Banks, J. A. (2006). Series foreword. In G. Ladson-Billings & W. F. Tate (Eds.), (Eds.), *Education research in the public interest: Social justice, action and policy.* New York: Teachers College Press.

Dei, G. J. S., Karumanchery, L. L., & Karumanchery-Luik, N. (2007). *Playing the race card: Exposing white power and privilege.* New York: Peter Lang.

Dei, G. J. S., & Johal, G. S. (2005). *Critical issues in anti-racist research methodologies.* New York: Peter Lang.

Duneier, M. (1992). *Slims table.* Chicago: The University of Chicago Press.

Fine, M. (1998). Working the hyphens: Reinventing self and other in qualitative research. In N. Denzin & Y. Lincoln (Eds.), *The landscape of qualitative research.* Thousands Oaks, CA: SAGE.

Fiske, J. (1993). *Power plays power works.* New York: Verso.

Freire, P. (1970). *Pedagogy of the oppressed.* New York: Seabury Press.

Giroux, H. (1991). Postmodernism as border pedagogy. In H. Giroux (Ed.), *Postmodernism, feminism and cultural politics.* Albany: State University of New York Press.

Gose, B. (2007, September 28). Diversity in academe. *The Chronicle of Higher Education, 54*(5), B3

Haymes, S. N. (1995). White culture and the politics of racial difference: Implications for multiculturalism. In C. Sleeter & P. McLaren (Eds.), *Multicultural education, critical pedagogy, and the politics of difference* (pp, 105–127). Albany: State University of New York Press.

Hilliard, A. (1999). *Race, identity, hegemony and education: What do we need to know and why?* Race, Research and Education. Presentation conducted in Chicago.

hooks, b. (1994). *Teaching to Transgress: Education as the practice of freedom*. New York: Routledge.

hooks, b. (1990). *Yearning: Race, gender, and cultural politics*. Boston: South End Press.

Pollard, D. S. (2006). Women of color and research: A historical and contemporary context. In D. S. Pollard & O. M. Welch (Eds.), *From center to margins: The importance of self-definition in research* (pp. 7–9). Albany: State University of New York Press.

Popkewitz, T. S. (1991). *A political sociology of educational reform: Power/Knowledge in teaching, teacher education, and research*. New York: Teachers College Press.

Rains, F. V. (2006). Making intellectual space: Self-determination and indigenous research. In D. S. Pollard & O. M. Welch (Eds.), *From center to margins: The importance of self-definition in research* (pp. 21–48). Albany: State University of New York Press.

Rocco, T. S., & West, G. W. (1998). Deconstructing privilege: An examination of privilege in adult education. *Adult Education Quarterly 48*(3), 171–184.

Sleeter, C. (2006). Foreword. In D. S. Pollard & O. M. Welch (Eds.), *From center to margins: The importance of self-definition in research* (pp. vii–x). Albany: State University of New York Press.

Sleeter, C., & McLaren, P. (1995). *Multicultural education, critical pedagogy, and the politics of difference*. Albany: State University of New York Press.

Smith, L. T., (2001). *Decolonizing methodologies: research and indigenous peoples*. London: University of Otago Press.

Tate, W. F. (2006). In the public interest. In G. Ladson-Billings & W. F. Tate (Eds.), *Education research in the public interest: Social justice, action and policy*. New York: Teachers College Press.

Tate, W. F. (2008, March). *Geography of opportunity: Poverty, place and educational outcomes*. Presidential Address presented at the meeting of the annual meeting of American Educational Research Association Meeting. New York: Hilton New York.

Welch, O. M., & Pollard, D. S. (2006). Introduction. In D. S. Pollard & O. M. Welch (Eds.), *From center to margins: The importance of self-definition in research* (pp. 1–6). Albany: State University of New York Press.

Young, I. M. (1990). *Justice and the politics of difference*. Princeton, NJ: Princeton University Press.

CHAPTER 4

TRANSFORMATIVE SCHOLARSHIP

Problematizing the Role of the Insider Within Educational Research in Urban Settings

Jody N. Polleck

INTRODUCTION

Four years ago, I began my research on book clubs with urban girls of color in a small urban high school. During my first year of data collection, a colleague asked how I enjoyed conducting research, after being a counselor and teacher for 14 years. "I love it," I told her and enthusiastically began sharing a series of conversations the girls and I were having during these experiences. Once data collection was finished, however, she asked me again how the research was going and my response was much less vibrant. While I loved facilitating the book clubs, hung on every word during transcriptions, and ferociously coded the data, the writing itself was laborious and painful. What could I possibly have to say about these girls whose life experiences overlap with mine in some ways (i.e., being female

Research in Urban Educational Settings: Lessons Learned and Implications for Future Practice, pp. 59–81
Copyright © 2011 by Information Age Publishing
All rights of reproduction in any form reserved.

and growing up in poverty) but in others are so very different from mine (i.e., experiencing life as females of color)? On reflection, I realize that the problem with articulating my work was that I was (and am continually) conflicted by my multiple stances as both insider and outsider—as researcher and teacher, as White woman working with students of color, as woman raised in poverty working with other girls of poverty. My interactions with these girls were complex in that in some ways our identities overlapped but in others they were vastly different. I felt extremely connected to the girls in that we shared similar reactions to texts, similar experiences with our families and friends, and similar struggles related to social class. However, we also differed based on our race, our age, and educational level. It was these internal and external contradictions that in fact silenced me and I struggled with both the analysis and the writing. While I connected with the girls and we shared stories, I knew that at the same time, we were very different and that I needed to constantly be aware of my position of power—particularly as it related to my ethnicity, my age, and my role as researcher and facilitator.

In many ways I felt paralyzed and silenced in that I was worried that I would misinterpret our experiences. In fact, my writing stopped for several months, until one day while having lunch with the girls, I asked them how they felt about being part of the study. Fay, an African American ninth grader, smiled and ardently replied, "Being part of your study made me feel like I was famous!" Sofia, a Latina ninth grader, agreed, "It was like what we had to say was important."

It was at this point that my role became clearer—in that I could not separate the complexities of my identities and insider/outsider stances. Nor could I separate my roles as researcher, advocate, and teacher. In fact, I had to embrace all of these subjectivities and constantly look toward the ultimate goal of my research: to create knowledge that empowers marginalized communities and embraces democratic values (Banks, 1998). The purpose of this chapter is to reveal my own journey as I worked to understand my insider-outsider stance, as a White female researcher working with participants of color, and to simultaneously work to become what Banks (1998) calls a "transformative scholar."

BANKS AND TRANSFORMATIVE SCHOLARSHIP

For centuries, much of the time educational and social science research has harmed low-income students and students of color by portraying them within deficit models (Banks, 1998). Banks thus calls for an alternative research paradigm—a body of literature that instead creates knowledge that empowers marginalized populations while embracing democratic values. This kind of research requires several essential characteristics in order to be transformative. First, while working toward objectivity, researchers cannot ignore that the "heart" of our work—our analysis and interpretations—are affected by our identities and value systems. This does not mean that we cannot work toward nor achieve objectivity, but it does mean that we should be constantly reflective about our data collection systems, our ongoing analysis, and our writing—as our gender, class, age, political affiliation, religion, and occupation are interconnected with how we interpret all of our experiences.

Banks (1998) describes the variety of researchers who exist within the field of educational research and social sciences through a typology of cross-cultural researchers. In revealing his framework, he offers four typologies of researchers that can be placed into two categories: one being the indigenous outsider who exchanges her values and belief systems for mainstream cultures. The external-outsider, on the other hand, is socialized in a community different from the one she is studying and does little to appreciate or respect these viewpoints; in fact this researcher views the studied community's behaviors as pathological or deviant. The other two typologies Banks (1998) describes are much more about empowerment and transformation. Whereas the indigenous-insider endorses the values, perspectives and knowledge of her own culture, the external-insider, while not from the culture in which she is studying, rejects the mainstream cultural assumptions and works to understand and internalize the value systems of marginalized communities.

What I would like to problematize about Banks' (1998) framework is that if we are to become transformative scholars when we are studying communities different from (or the same as) ourselves, we will cross between indigenous-insider and external-insider. Our identities are much too complex to fit within either one. For example, while I am a White woman, and thus have a different ethnicity from my research participants who are African-American and Latina, I do share class and gender with the girls. While all of us are members of the school community, we do differ in education and age. In understanding that identity is dynamic and multifaceted, I wonder if these typologies can remain static and struggle to place myself into one single category. For me, the typology is not as important to define for me individually—but what is more essential is being explicit and conscious of the activities and reflections I participated in so that I could sustain my insider stance. In this chapter, I will be transparent about the process of creating my insider stance within the school and the book clubs, as there are some important lessons to learn as we both enter and engage with communities who are different than we are. As I reveal these processes, I will simultaneously be explicit about the ways I worked to become a transformative scholar (Banks, 1998) where I as a

White researcher continually resisted mainstream cultural assumptions and worked to empower marginalized communities.

ENTERING THE URBAN SETTING AND ESTABLISHING MY ROLE AS AN INSIDER

The purpose of my research was to understand how—if at al—the forum of book clubs could be used as a place of empowerment for urban girls of color. After working directly with this population for many years as an advocate, counselor and teacher, I wanted to extend my impact through scholarship, documenting the voices and experiences of these girls and my own interactions with them. To accomplish these goals, I first had to find an urban school where I felt the staff had a commitment to transforming their students' lives holistically. This is a delicate issue as research on urban school contexts have demonstrated that urban cities experience higher rates of school failure (National Center for Education Statistics, 1996), poverty (U.S. Census Bureau, 2000), and crime (Bureau of Justice Statistics, 2000). Furthermore, academically, urban students are reported to trail far behind their suburban counterparts (Darling-Hammond, 1998; Ladson-Billings, 1994), when studying dropout rates, standardized test scores, advanced placement exams, and college eligibility indexes (Fine, 1991; Morrell, 2004). However, it is important to note that while the educational outcomes of students in urban schools are replete with negative frameworks, researchers and the general public cannot divorce these poor outcomes from these students inequitable access to high educational experiences. In addition to being concerned about the inequitable education that many students in urban settings experience, these poor educational outcomes for students concern me for two reasons. First, I immediately saw urban schools as an area that needed to be explored more so that as a transformative scholar I could work to understand these problems and then participate in overcoming them through supplemental support systems such as book clubs. Simultaneously, I wanted to produce bodies of knowledge that extended beyond simply reporting student outcomes without looking at them within the context of the systems and structures that converged to produce them. More important, I wanted to demonstrate how educational researchers can create transformative spaces by conducting research that more accurately and fully illustrate the lived experiences of often marginalized students whose experiences either are rarely portrayed in the professional literature or distorted when studied.

Many of the poor educational outcomes of students in urban settings addressed above have been attributed to the notion that urban schools are not reflective of, nor responsive to, the students in which they serve. Traditionally, classrooms have devalued urban students' cultural background and experiences, thus placing them at an educational disadvantage (Kretovics & Nussel, 1994). Researchers have faulted these classrooms because of traditional curricula, pedagogical practices, and culturally irrelevant texts (Morrell, 2004). Furthermore, the organizational structures within urban schools face extreme adversity with such limitations as large class sizes, less experienced teachers, ill-equipped classrooms, and poor professional development (Kretovics & Nussel, 1994). The reality is that poor children of color are not being served by insufficiently funded schools nor are they being prepared through culturally-responsive pedagogies. It thus becomes imperative that if we are to become transformative scholars, we not only concentrate our research efforts into urban schools but also start to examine how we conduct our work within these settings as researchers and practitioners to ensure that our work not only extends existing literature but that it directly impacts marginalized communities.

Because of the barriers listed above, I struggled in finding a school where transformative scholarship was embraced. After visiting several locations, I found that administrators were generally distrustful of me as an outsider, and until I offered direct support, many would not continue our conversations. Some schools wanted me to tutor students, while others expressed an interest in professional development. This need was certainly justifiable when seeing the scarcity of resources, the deteriorating facilities, and the lack of experienced teachers. While certainly many researchers would argue that this work is not their responsibility, I would counter that argument because of the dire circumstances that exist within urban schools and the need for educational researchers to bring resources to these environments. In being transformative, we must establish a reciprocal relationship where teachers and administrators see us immersed in their schools and communities, putting our best efforts to offer immediate impact on student achievement and marginalized populations.

After visiting several schools, I decided to work with a new, small high school in the Northeast. Consisting of 300 students, the school had been open for only 3 years and had no senior class at the time of data collection. The school population was primarily Latino (55%) and African American (35%) with 68% of the students qualifying for free lunch. The summer before school started, the principal and I met to discuss my work with book clubs. We agreed that I would spend three days a week as a literacy coach, in order to immerse myself within the community of teachers and students. My responsibilities were to provide professional development and support to the staff and work with struggling and reluctant readers and writers. I served in this capacity for 1 year before starting my research, as I needed to create an insider stance and build trust between teachers and students before starting the book clubs. Although concerned initially about conducting research at the place in which I worked, I believe my insider stance helped me in many ways. One, the students were familiar with me and thus not as hesitant to participate. Second, the teachers understood that I was not just at the school for research but was there to also impact student achievement. This was not a "research and run" study, which is especially important in urban settings. Teachers and students need to believe that our research is not just simply self-motivated, but that researchers, while clearly benefitting from their research activities, have a true commitment to making change not only in the school but nationwide.

UNDERSTANDING RECRUITMENT EFFORTS AS AN INSIDER/ OUTSIDER WITHIN URBAN SETTINGS

After 1 year working as a literacy coach, I began my recruitment efforts in September of the following school year. So that teachers were informed of my research, I sent e-mails to all English teachers, explaining my study and asking for permission to talk to their students about book clubs. Once permission was granted, I visited each classroom, describing the purpose of my research and distributing flyers and surveys. The majority of visits went smoothly, yet despite my best efforts to maintain my insider stance, I did run into one conflict that is important to reveal, as other researchers may confront similar situations when entering urban schools. One of my visits was to a ninth grade class. I gave an explanation of book clubs and my research and passed out flyers which provided information about the study. A tall, African American girl sitting in the back shouted at me as I placed the flyer on her desk, "Why are you giving me this? I'm not going to sign it!"

Slightly thrown by her reaction, I replied, "You certainly don't have to sign it. You can throw it away if you want. It's just to give you additional information if you need it."

Immediately, I wished I could have retracted those words—because as soon as the young woman heard "throw it away," she shoved her chair back, walked across the room, and crumpled up the flyer, tossing it into the garbage can. I smiled at the girl, trying my best to remain unrattled in front of the other students. In my quest to become an insider, I had to demonstrate to my potential participants that I was not going to give up easily. Aware of my difference in ethnicity, age, and race, I did not want to abandon my work with them—a quality that Banks (1998) espouses as important so that transformative research within marginalized communities continues, regardless of the researcher's identity.

Taking a deep breath, I continued to pass out surveys to the students. While students filled these out, I walked over to the young woman and saw the novel *Push* on her desk. Having read this book, I asked her to tell me about it and we shared our reading experiences. It is important for researchers working with students to make a connection with them so that trust is built. While this girl did not fill out my survey, nor join the book club, I believe she did see I was not going to give up on her nor be intimidated by her response. Equally important, the other students saw this as well. As transformative researchers, we must persistently attempt to open doors with all students—even if in some cases the doors are slammed shut. We must continue to try to understand and be sympathetic to the negative responses that we sometimes get from prospective research participants based upon our outsider status and how many communities of color have been treated by researchers in the past. Consequently, we should never take anything or anyone for granted.

THE PARTICIPANTS AND THE RESEARCHER: WHERE INDIGENOUS AND EXTERNAL INTERSECT

By the end of the recruitment stage, two book clubs emerged. The Younger Girls grew to five in number—all in the 9th grade and 14-years-old except for Betsy who was in the 10th grade and 16-years-old. Of these five girls, three are African American and two Latina. This group felt worlds younger than The Older Girls that eventually grew to 7 in number—all in the 11th grade. Of these girls, five are Latina and two are African American.

In seeking a connection with these young women, I reflected on how I could serve as both an external and indigenous insider. Again, problematizing Banks' (1998) framework, in some ways the girls and I had several commonalities: our love of literature, our social class, our gender. However, we differed in several ways too: age, educational level, occupation, and most important, race. Despite these differences, I did not want to be swayed from conducting research with participants who were substantially different from me, especially since the voices of urban girls of color are absent from the professional literature (Way, 1995). Furthermore, traditionally, current theories on adolescent development are void of the experiences of girls of color and those few researchers who do study girls of color caution others to safeguard against inappropriately applying White, suburban theories to this population (Way, 1995). For example, Pastor McCormick, and Fine (1996) argue that urban girls of color are unique in that they may not pursue the autonomy theorized by Erikson because of the challenges of racism, sexism, and classism. Additionally, the information about girls of color that is presented in the professional or mainstream media is often in the form of a deficit model, especially when discussing the disproportionate rate of adolescents of color who are represented in sexuality and childbearing statistics (Murry, 1996). Urban girls of color also have been represented as having higher rates of behavioral disturbances and social withdrawal (Zahner, Jacobs, Freeman, & Trainor, 1993), lower levels of affective strength and poorer school functioning (Dierker, Solomon, Johnson, Smith, & Farrel, 2004), and higher rates of internalizing disorders (Leadbeater, Kupermine, Blatt, & Hertzog, 1999). While the professional literature is replete with this information, how the institutional and economic conditions of racism, classism, and sexism work against them are rarely discussed. Similarly, life experiences of girls of color are rarely mentioned without discussing them within the context of being merely a comparison group for White girls. To counteract this research, I wanted to build my own insider stance with these girls so that I could begin to address their more normative issues such as their relationships with peers and their families and how literature could be used to explore these topics. During the book club, while the girls shared common experiences with texts and each other, they also shared very unique experiences—conveying differences in cultural backgrounds and academic and familial histories. As transformative researchers, while we cannot ignore existing literature on marginalized students that may be grounded in deficit perspectives, we also cannot ignore the *daily* lives of these young girls or the need to present a more holistic representation of their experiences. We must eradicate deficit frameworks and begin to explore what these girls' lives *truly* are without eroticizing or homogenizing them; this can best be accomplished through revealing their individual stories and listening to what they have to say—a positivist approach that can assist our urban educators as they work to be more culturally responsive to the needs of this population.

In this way, I had to be extremely careful in my experiences with the girls and my work to become an insider within their community. This meant being both reflective of my own race and position of power, working to truly understand who these girls were, and how the book clubs could impact and empower them. In the following sections, I will highlight the diverse backgrounds of the girls while simultaneously attempt to be transparent of my own background in that my biography greatly influences my values and the knowledge I have constructed (Banks, 1998). As will be apparent later, my experiences with the girls both were intersecting and conflicting, in that we share gender and class and of course our love for books, but differ greatly across educational access and background, age, and ethnicity and how we experienced our multiple identities.

THE YOUNGER GIRLS

The Younger Girls Group begins with Tia and Joy who are the first young women to express an interest in book clubs. Joy is 14-years-old and speaks softly and quickly with a slight Spanish accent, which she tells me she is always trying to mask. Joy's mother is from Columbia and her father is from Peru. She is the quietest girl in the group, but tells me she enjoys listening to the other girls. She claims she is a daydreamer and describes herself as a good student. If there is a polar opposite to Joy, it is 14-year-old Tia, who is the talker of the girls—the one never at a loss for words. Tia is African American and describes herself as boy-crazy and never shy. Like Joy and Tia, Fay is also a ninth grader. She is Caribbean American and the smallest in the group, standing below five feet. Fay comes from a painful background. Her mother, a Trinidadian teacher, died when Fay was four. Just after the funeral, Fay met her father for the first time. Fay describes herself as fun and says she tries to help people whenever she can. She also tells me that she is a good student who loves to draw and read. The last ninth grader in this group is Sofia, who joins later in the year after being asked by Tia. Fourteen-year-old Sofia tells me she loves "reading like crazy" and that she writes to escape. Her mother is from Ecuador and her father is Cuban. The last member is Betsy, the only tenth grader in the group. She is a 16-year-old African American girl who tells me she is a bit of a loner, describing herself as quiet, shy, and "not very outgoing." Like Fay, Betsy also lost her mother at an early age and she now lives alone with her father.

THE OLDER GIRLS

Like The Younger Girls, The Older Girls Group also starts with two members at first, Gina and Julie, both voracious readers. Out of all the girls, however, 16-year-old Gina is the talker—the one I have to sometimes interrupt so that other girls have a chance to speak. Gina is Dominican and lives with her mother. She tells me that her biggest hobby is reading and her aspirations are to become a lawyer. Julie, also 16, tells me that her personality "varies" depending on the day and her hobbies include writing, reading, and hanging out with her friends. Like Gina, Julie's parents are divorced. Her mother is African American and her father is Puerto Rican and Dominican. Joining after the second meeting, the next girl is Keisha who talks as much as Gina—offering a plethora of comments throughout our discussions. Keisha is a 16-year-old African American who exudes a sense of confidence that is refreshing. Keisha's parents are divorced and she lives her mother. She tells me her favorite hobby is drawing and that she has aspirations of becoming a fashion designer. Eileen also starts book club at the second meeting with Keisha. She is quieter than these three though. At 17, Eileen keeps a busy schedule and is involved in many activities. She works as a sex educator at a community-based organization and is a dancer and singer. While Eileen says she is "not the best of students," she does plan to pursue psychiatry or forensics. Eileen's parents are Puerto Rican and were never married. Pat is similar to Eileen in that she is soft-spoken. She joins the book club later in the year after hearing about our meetings from Gina. Pat is 16-years-old and rarely, if ever, speaks. She tells me she enjoys reading and playing basketball. Pat's parents are Mexican and still married. Pat's best friend is Yoana who she convinces to join the book club. Yoana is the 16-year-old comedian of the group; everything makes her laugh and she is always giggling. When describing her personality, Yoana says she is nice but does not care what people think of her. She lives with her mother and stepfather who are from Ecuador. Yoana's father, also from Ecuador, died 4 years ago. Yoana says she is not doing well in school; when I ask her what her favorite class is, she says, "I just like the book club. That's basically it." The last to join is Carla who is also convinced to come to our meetings by Gina. Carla is 17-years-old and tells me she likes to listen to music, watch television, and read. Carla moved to the United States with her father when she was eight, but her mother still lives in the Dominican Republic.

THE BOOK CLUB LADY:
REFLECTING ON MY OWN IDENTITY AS IT RELATES TO THE GIRLS

After her first week in the book club, ninth grader Sofia coins me as the "Book Club Lady." Not fancy, not eloquent, but certainly my title. Like the girls, my background is unique and is what drew me to working with adolescents. As a transformative scholar and in trying to maintain my insider stance (Banks, 1998), it is imperative that I am reflective of my own history as personal, academic, and professional factors affect my relationships with the girls, my facilitation of the discussions, and my analysis of the data.

For most of my childhood, I lived in lower socioeconomic circumstances, residing in a series of small trailers or apartments in rural and urban settings. Raised by a single restless mother, we moved around frequently. My mother always worked two or three jobs at a time, from x-ray technologist, to waitress, and dog groomer. On the weekends, I spent hours reading books and helping my mother in her barrage of odd jobs. While I share working-class experiences with my participants and therefore act as an indigenous insider, I am White and therefore have not experienced this additional layer of identity and marginalization with the girls—marking my simultaneous role as external-insider. Again, in problematizing the work of Banks (1998), choosing one particular typology is challenging in that our identities are often multifaceted as are those of many of our research participants.

CONDUCTING BOOK CLUBS: AN INSIDER'S JOURNEY INTO THE DIMENSIONS OF SUSTAINABILITY

In addition to being transparent about my own identity, it is equally important to be explicit about the dimensions and characteristics of the book clubs that made my insider stance possible. In terms of external factors, I had to create a physical space that assisted in our building of trust. I struggled with and overcame such barriers as lack of funding, space, and time. Just finding a simple location in overcrowded urban schools is quite a feat. However, it was imperative when doing participatory research—where windows are open because the air conditioners don't work, and where the noise level is overbearing from cars, construction, and people—that we find spaces that are safe, quiet, and comfortable. The physical environment alone helped in blocking out the "outside noise" so that we could focus on one another.

In addition to difficulties of accessing space is the negotiation of common meeting times. Because of their socioeconomic status, many of the girls work jobs and take care of siblings after school. As an indigenous-insider, I understood these barriers and was flexible with the girls about when we met and where. Often, meetings were changed, delayed, or canceled due to these issues, thus why the older girls met during lunch. Once the times were established, however, absences were rare—if ever—and we could work toward building a relationship with one another.

Another challenge was funding for books. I applied for several grants at my university and within the school system for additional monies for new texts. The girls often complained that most of the books at school were not interesting or relevant to their lives. After a lot of reading, I found several culturally-responsive texts—outside of the mainstream curricula—that the girls selected, including *Push, Upstate, Party Girl*, and *Jason and Kyra*. This shift in reading materials was again part of my responsibility as an external-insider who works against traditional curricula and paradigms so that the texts themselves were empowering in that they reflected the voices and perspectives of the girls.

In addition to physical characteristics and resources, I also had to build my insider stance through social conditions in order to build trust and to increase the sustainability of the groups. When conducting transformative research, several key aspects are necessary for successful interactions, especially when the researcher may not be indigenous to the groups in which they are studying. The first dimension was about empowerment—an essential characteristic of transformative scholarship (Banks, 1998). This translated to having the girls establish the group norms at the beginning of the year so they had a common understanding of how to engage with one another. I had little input in these decisions so that I could create a more democratic space where the girls were empowered. Another important quality was the girls selected (and rejected) the texts. Both of these pieces--establishing group norms and selecting texts—allowed the girls to have ownership of the book club and the study itself.

Furthermore, as a facilitator and researcher, and as White woman, I was aware that my role inherently encompassed a hierarchical position and therefore I had to be continually aware of this power imbalance. While I set an agenda for our first meeting, for the rest of our meetings, the girls set the agenda and the pace of the book clubs. Another power shift included student accountability to each other (and not to me), in regards to reading the texts and sharing their stories. Thus, the fluidity of the conversations was directed by the girls so that they could establish trust with one another and with me.

As to the facilitation of the meetings, I constantly reflected upon my own multiple roles as an insider so as to maintain a safe and nurturing environment. In this way, I took on several identities—that of researcher, teacher, facilitator, reader, and friend. This role was dynamic and continually fluctuated between indigenous and external insider, where I participated *with* the girls not just as passive observer. When the girls asked me questions, I responded openly and honestly and always worked to recognize and affirm the girls' linguistic and cultural diversity, so as not to participate in mainstream cultural assumptions (Banks, 1998). This insider stance was enhanced through continual reflection of who I was as a White woman and through listening to and asking questions to learn more about their backgrounds and perspectives.

I also worked to establish a nonauthoritative rapport with the girls—again acting as an external insider where I shed traditional paradigms of power. As an adult, a researcher, and a member of a dominant racial group, a power differential inherently existed and thus contributed to this external-insider position. I had to be constantly aware that my contributions to the discussions could be defined as oppressive or exploitative (Henderson, 1998; Ladner, 1987). I tried as much as possible to counteract mainstream ideologies by primarily listening to the girls and responding in nonjudgmental ways. Despite our differences, I also empathized with the girls in genuine ways by remaining silent and not intruding on their stories—only commenting when my opinion was requested (Crozier, 2003).

This process however was not always easy in that sometimes my viewpoints differed from the girls. It is important to reveal these discontinuities as a transformative scholar requires that we are transparent about our involvement with our participants. The following two examples will help elucidate these conflicts and simultaneously demonstrate how complex our roles can be as both indigenous and external insiders.

As stated before, my role as external insider was reinforced in that I did not share the same ethnicity with the girls. The girls within the group were also different—being both African American and Latina. Because I did not want to impose my own viewpoints or agendas on the girls, they directed the conversations of the groups. I noticed immediately that the issue of race rarely arose from the girls' conversations and I wonder now if this was because I am White. Perhaps the girls were afraid to address issues of racism with each other because of my presence? Or perhaps because the texts they chose did not specifically deal with race issues, the girls also did not address these issues. When the qualifier "White" did arise in conversations, the girls always looked immediately to me and apologized. For example, in the Younger Girls group, 10th grader Betsy explained that her grandmother "hates White people." Immediately after saying this, Betsy apologized to me, but then turned her head to the girls and continued her explanation: "My grandmother is so nice to the White people in her building, and I tell her to shut up in my head because I know she doesn't even like them. She doesn't even realize her own racism."

Betsy then apologized again and I realized that in one way I had been invited into their community, despite my difference in ethnicity. At the same time, because of my presence and Whiteness, the girls felt the need to apologize for their perspectives related to race and may have even altered to some extent their responses in an effort to be respectful and protective of me. Perhaps feeling discomfort, Joy added to Betsy's comment, stating,

> We have problems with ourselves. I don't know what the problem is. Puerto Ricans can't stand Dominicans. Blah. Blah. Blah. No, we're better. No, we're better. Then they start fighting. It's all crazy. We don't even help ourselves so you can say whatever you want cause I know it's true—so much racism. I know.

Unfortunately, this was one of the few explicit conversations either book club had specifically on race—and because often I was acting as facilitator only—I did not feel comfortable pushing the conversation. But perhaps it was my uneasiness of not feeling like an authority on the issue—being that I am White and trying to maintain my external-insider status. What is interesting is that I did feel more at ease pushing the girls when I enacted the role as indigenous-insider, especially as we discussed class or gender. For example, during one meeting with the Younger Girls, they discussed how women bring abuse upon themselves based on their physical appearance. As a feminist, woman, and indigenous-insider, I was disconcerted by this and actively pushed the girls to explore their understandings of this phenomenon. The following outlines the conversation that occurred and how I worked to empower the girls as women:

Betsy: "Today some girls put themselves out there and when they do get abused, they complain about it."

Me: "They do what?"

Betsy: "Some girls think they cute—tight jeans, this, that and the third…. It's like don't put yourself out there cause you'll look like a whore or whatever."

Me: "Do you think it's their fault then?"

Joy and Betsy: "Yes!"

Tia: "Nah, no!"

Fay: "Not always."

Betsy: "Some girls just do it to be doing it and try to look cute about it, but when something bad happens to them, they're going to understand why and feel stupid."

Sofia: "But not all the time. I sort of agree—like I could see why she—why you would say that because some girls do put it out there."

Tia: "That's like you are 14-years-old walking around with your boyfriend who's 27, wearing a mini-skirt. What do you think is gonna happen?"

Betsy: "That's what I'm saying!"

Tia: "And then when you have sex with him and you tell your mother and she gets all upset that was your fault. I mean what do you expect?"

Me: "If you were consenting?"

Tia: "Yeah, if it was consensual sex and you were 14-years-old and your boyfriend is 27. First off what the hell you doing with a 27-year-old?"

Me: "What I'm saying is that if I'm wearing a bikini on the street, then I still have the right to say no and a guy should respect that."

Fay: "No you don't! That's nudity."

Betsy: "I understand that you may have the right."

Sofia: "Although we may not like it, you are flaunting it."

Betsy:	"Jody, if I didn't know you, if I saw you on the street, I'd be like what the hell is she doing?"
Tia:	"If you're near a pool or you're going to a pool, that's one thing."
Betsy:	"That's what I'm saying. We're talking about the city here!"
Fay:	"You can't do that. Not here. That is crack-head!"
Me:	"But if I want to wear a bikini, it still does not give the right to a guy to touch me if I don't want to be touched."
Tia:	But like when you—how you're dressed or how you put yourself out there it gives the guys a different opinion on you."
Betsy:	"How you present yourself outside."
Sofia:	"And they take advantage of you."

While certainly the girls and I did not reach a consensus, it was important for me to reveal my viewpoint, particularly within my analyses so that I was explicit about the way in which I received the stories and opinions the girls shared with me. As Crozier (2003) asserts, presenting contrasting viewpoints including our own "enables the adherence to the principles of participation and demonstrates a commitment to rigorous analysis" (p. 91). In this way, my analysis was about revealing the girls' and my viewpoints—even if they differed—to ensure my commitment of being transparent while simultaneously acknowledging our differences. More significantly, however, in exploring my role as transformative scholar and as indigenous-insider, in discussing our likeness as women, I felt more comfortable being vocal about empowering the girls and offering my viewpoints on issues of gender, rather than race.

Equally important in revealing my own efforts in understanding race, class and gender—and how that affected my role as insider—is being comfortable when asked to reveal my own experiences to the girls—sharing literary and personal responses to the texts and to them. In sharing my stories and removing my "mask," I became vulnerable *and* brave—just as the girls were—working to diminish barriers between us and equalize our relationship (Crozier, 2003). Building trust was taking a risk for all of us in that we revealed positive and traumatic experiences. The conversations—and negotiations—we encountered thus became a balancing act of building trust and taking risks, a task that all of us had to endure in order to promote openness and connection among each other (Crozier, 2003).

Feeling comfortable about revealing our stories and establishing trust was a common theme when I spoke with the girls at the end of the study.

When I asked them about trusting me, ironically, the girls all said they had less concern with me than their counterparts. In fact, the girls were surprised that they could trust each other at all. On her survey, Carla wrote, "I learn[ed] that I am okay around other people knowing my business." Sofia wrote that she is now able "to open up about feelings" while Pat wrote that she can now "express [herself] around other people." During an interview, Betsy told me, "Book club helped me in my personal [life] like trusting certain people." During Eileen's interview, she also illuminated feelings of trust, stating,

> When everyone went on here in the discussions, it was going to stay here and it did. I tried it out for the first time. I sometimes would share my personal experiences and then I was like, okay let me try this. Maybe if we go out you know into the halls? [But] I [wouldn't] hear it, so I know I can trust the group.

TRANSFORMATIVE SCHOLARSHIP THROUGH QUALITATIVE METHODS

Being accepted and "adopted" into the group as an indigenous and external-insider was essential as both a researcher and a facilitator. However, my work to become a transformative researcher was not completed; analysis also required the same level of introspection and reflection about who I was and how that affected my interpretations of the data. Aware of the detrimental research that has been conducted with low-income students and students of color (Banks, 1998), I wanted to produce research that would not further marginalize the girls of color in my study. In this way, qualitative research seemed to provide the most appropriate methodological framework for accomplishing this goal. Qualitative research insists that researchers participate in an in-depth and extensive understanding of the context and the participants and their experiences. This meant spending a substantial amount of time in the field—1 year—before attempting to analyze or create knowledge from the data.

In being transformative, it was also imperative that I use critical theory in revealing and understanding the girls' stories, in that they are from historically, disparaged populations based on their gender, class, and race. Critical theory is political in that the research itself both engages and benefits the participants (Morrell, 2004), upholding Banks' (1998) framework for transformative scholarship. Critical theory asks researchers to explore inequities within the system and to explore how classism, sexism and racism profoundly interfere with our participants, our practice, and research (Lather, 1992). As a critical theorist and transformative scholar, I also had to be aware and reflective of my own background, assumptions, and Whiteness. Sue (1993) insists that White researchers define themselves as racial, cultural beings, thus the need to be reflective of cultural values, biases, and stereotypes. Similar to Banks (1998) "external-insider" typology, Sue (1993) insists that White researchers admit they are not immune from inheriting these assumptions and confront them in an open, non-defensive manner. In taking this external-outsider viewpoint, I had to reject many of my own indigenous assumptions so as to embrace the perspectives of the girls. Furthermore, I had to resist traditional, mainstream, researcher where White scholars have often portrayed participants of color through deficit lenses and defined their behaviors as delinquent or pathological (Banks, 1998; Egharevba, 2001; Sue, 1993).

MAINTAINING TRUSTWORTHINESS AND CREDIBILITY: RESEARCH AS A PARTICIPATORY PROCESS

Being a transformative scholar, especially as an external-insider, I had to reject many of the cultural, mainstream assumptions of White researchers in the analysis and writing of my research. This meant not participating in hierarchal, powerful structures and contributing to deficit models. It also meant that I had to include researchers of color *and* my participants within the research process so that I could establish trustworthiness and credibility. This variety of expertise produced research that was much more "dense" and pluralistic and collaborative in process and product (Fine, 2006). Furthermore, it maintains the stance of transformation and democracy (Banks, 1998) in that we involve others in our research process.

The first step toward credibility was participating in peer debriefing so that I could counteract implicit, hidden biases and collaboratively work to construct meaning of my data (Bogdan & Biklin, 2003; Guba & Lincoln, 1989). Specifically, I participated in a writing group which kept me honest in that my colleagues helped me throughout the research process to probe any biases, explore alternative meanings, and clarify my interpretations (Guba & Lincoln, 1989). Furthermore, I received feedback from researchers and teachers of color so I could unravel, confront, and, where appropriate, reject my own mainstream, cultural assumptions. I also sought feedback from urban teachers of color because I needed to ensure my work would be relevant to urban educators. This social act of sharing my writing forced me to take risks so that I could discover a multiplicity of perspectives and learn to negotiate and collaborate in the meaning making process. While I certainly will never be able to elicit or produce the same picture or story as teachers and researchers of color, I can, as a White woman, contribute to the field, as long as I am reflective of my race, privilege, and biases and continually seek out feedback from those who have been silenced and other-ed. As bell hooks (1989) warns, researchers of dominant groups must be careful "to know better than we know ourselves" (p. 22).

The final condition of credibility was member checking where I verified with the girls interpretations and meaning constructions that developed out of our experiences (Guba & Lincoln, 1989). If we do not allow our participants to engage in research, we only reinforce power imbalances (Banks, 1998; Nygreen, 2006). This collaborative, transformative act forces researchers to be accountable to their participants. I enacted this process formally and informally, giving the girls multiple opportunities to reveal any misinterpretations, to give me additional information, and to judge the adequacy of my study. For example, throughout the year, I discussed with the girls the themes I saw emerging from our conversations. As I completed chapters of my work, I also shared them with the girls so that they could review the content and provide me with feedback. Sharing my data with the girls allowed them to have control over my use of their voices (Crozier, 2003). Both of these measures I had hoped would not only empower the girls, but also further establish my trustworthiness and quest for transformative scholarship.

EMPOWERING URBAN STUDENTS
THROUGH TRANSFORMATIVE SCHOLARSHIP

In writing about my research journey within an urban setting, it is essential that I not only share my own knowledge and experiences but those of the girls as well. In this way, I asked them about their perceptions of participating within a research study. All of the girls told me they felt this kind of work was important. Joy explained, "You have to do this to find out what teens like to read and how they read. I mean, we're the students. We're living it."

"It helps teachers to understand us better so they then can teach us better," agreed Fay.

In talking to the girls, they also revealed the qualities that urban researchers must possess in order to connect with students. Sofia recommended that researchers "keep it to our standard," explaining, "Keep it entertaining. Tell us stuff—personal stuff. And make the research fun. You don't have to ask us a bunch of questions. We got to ask our questions too."

"You gotta know how to connect with us. Don't be boring. Act like a kid!" agreed Joy.

"Even if it's corny," joked Fay, looking over at me slyly.

"Yeah, I hate it when teachers treat us like kids," added Sofia.

"We do understand," agreed Fay. "And kids know when you're being fake."

Connecting to our participants and revealing our own experiences and purposes for research is essential. We must be upfront, honest, and transparent with marginalized students so they feel safe, connected, and empowered. This means acknowledging our own privilege, dismantling the power imbalances, and working in conjunction with our participants-- a democratic and transformative process (Banks, 1998). This is evident in my work where the girls participated in meaning constructions, making decisions about themes, and providing feedback on my analysis and writing. In this way, the girls gave me advice on both content and writing style and, in fact, used the data in their own lives as well. For example, several of the girls shared the chapters with their parents so they could reveal the kind of work they were doing and how they were part of the research process. Sofia explained,

> My dad read a lot of the chapters. When he saw I was confessing a lot of stuff, I was scared he would get mad cause we're not allowed to talk about our problems to other people. But he felt comfortable, cause I could open up to someone. And my mom, she was just happy that I was happy.

In addition to sharing the chapters with her parents, Sofia also asked for the transcriptions so she could use our conversations in order to write a young adult book. She explained,

> This is going to be real. We talk about books, our lives, and our families. It was easy for us to open up. It didn't matter that a tape recorder was there and now I have stuff for my own book.

It is imperative that our research is transparent when working with urban students. We must involve them in the research process and they must see the direct connection and impact this will have on their lives (Banks, 1998). Otherwise, our work only becomes theoretical, abstract, and even exploitative. Collaborative, participatory, transformative research is essential so that we stop treating our participants as "subjects" and work toward an empowering, democratic construction of how we do research (Banks, 1998).

FINDING OUR AUDIENCE AND RECONCEPTUALIZING OUR ROLES AS URBAN EDUCATIONAL RESEARCHERS

In sharing my own journey and reflections into working toward transformative scholarship within urban settings, it is essential to think about the implications this has on our work as researchers. It is important for me to close with the implications transformative research has in the reconceptualization of our roles and the expansion of our audiences and responsibilities. Our first step is to create and publish documents that are accessible to larger audiences. For those in the academic setting, it is imperative that we not only write for theoretical, abstract journals that may never reach our policymakers, administrators, teachers, and participants. While a valid audience *can* be other members of the academy—we must recognize that urban schools are in dire need of immediate assistance and therefore the "trickle down" effect of researcher/professor to researcher/professor to eventually teachers—may be too slow considering the conditions that exist within urban settings. There is a sense of urgency here and we cannot continually strive for "tier one" journals when urban youth need more effective support systems now. Furthermore, in determining merit or tenure, practice journals, book chapters, and books should be weighted just as highly as academic journals. We must remember our purpose—that research is not about obtaining tenure, status or promotion but about our contributions to the field (Anderson, 2005) and to the betterment of the lives of some of our most marginalized communities. And continually we must ask ourselves: Is our research making a difference in the lives of urban children and adolescents? Are we having a direct, immediate impact their lives? If the answer is no, then we are not doing our job. Banks (1998) speaks to the precarious role of "transformative scholars" who are often critiqued for their involvement within the communities and politics. While he warns researchers about the risks inherent in this work, he also celebrates the research of people such as Kenneth Clark who viewed his political actions in the community as an essential extension of his own research.

Additionally, we must resist deficit frameworks used to represent and define urban students of color. We need more research that explores what these students *can* do—and how we can transform our curriculum so it is culturally responsive to their needs. Through examining normative issues and academic achievement and through gaining a deeper understanding of contextual factors such as class, race, and gender, we can begin to promote social and emotional development and academic success for urban students of color (Pollard, 1989). So what does this mean, especially for White researchers? It means that we must be reflective about our assumptions and biases and work to undo these stereotypes, acknowledging and dismantling the power imbalances that are inherent in our privileged positions (Krauss, Goldsant, Bula, & Sember, 1997). We cannot continue to evade or ignore White racism and White privilege and how this implicitly affects our research—from our methods to even our smallest sentence constructions (Sleeter, 1993). In this way, I still have much work to do as an external-insider in understanding my own uneasiness in talking about issues of race and White privilege.

As researchers in urban education, we also need to redefine our roles and responsibilities and begin to see ourselves as activists if we truly wish to make substantial changes. That means becoming politically involved and more immersed in the communities, much like Kenneth Clark has done. It is more than drop-in professional development or "research and run," it is about collaboratively taking part in community efforts to holistically improve the lives of marginalized students (Anderson, 2005). Furthermore, we must also work to not be exploitative and leave the field immediately after our research is completed in order to promote our personal or professional gain (Nygreen, 2006).

Our *methods* within urban research should also be reflective of this activist stance. Under the umbrella of transformative scholarship, we can look to participatory research (Anderson, 2005; Fine, 2006) and activist research (Nygreen, 2006), where we begin inviting our participants to take such roles as data collectors, recruiters, interviewers, presenters, or reviewers of our writing (Banks, 1998; Krauss et al., 1997). In this way we are acknowledging and counteracting the power imbalances that arise in every aspect of our research process from participant recruitment to analysis of our data (Fine, 1991). This means examining who we are and where we come from in relation to the context in which we are studying and our research participants. Unfortunately, this kind of work often is not credible nor validated within university settings (Anderson, 2005). Therefore, we must not only work collaboratively with our communities but also within our own "house" of academe as well. Thus, colleges and universities should strive to remove boundaries and separations between the professors and researchers and our educational communities. In working with one another, breaking down hierarchal structures, and becoming actively involved in redefining how we do research so that it is more inclusive and better representative of the issues at-large within urban settings, power can be dispersed and hopefully we can reach and uplift the population of people who need our assistance the most: our children. As Fay and Sofia so eloquently explained, helping urban students feel "famous" and empowered *is* transformation, in helping them to understand that what they have to say is "important" which should be paramount to the work that we do as transformative scholars and educators.

REFERENCES

Anderson, G. L. (2005). Academia and activism: An essay review of Jean Anyon's "Radical Possibilities." *Education Review, 8*(1), 1–13.

Banks, J. A. (1998). The lives and values of researchers: Implications for educating citizens in a multicultural society. *Educational Researcher, 27*(7), 417.

Bogdan, R. C., & Biklen, S. K. (2003). *Qualitative research for education: An introduction to theory and methods* (4th ed.). New York: Pearson Education Group.

Bureau of Justice Statistics. (2000). *Crime and the nation's households 2000: Trends 1994–2000*. Washington, DC: U.S. Department of Justice.

Crozier, G. (2003). Researching black parents: Making sense of the role of research and researcher. *Qualitative Research, 3*(1), 79–94.

Darling-Hammond, L. (1998). New standards, old inequalities: The current challenge for African-American education. *State of Black America Report.* Chicago: National Urban League.

Dierker, L. C., Solomon, T., Johnson, P., Smith, S., & Farrel, A. (2004). Characteristics of urban and nonurban youth enrolled in a statewide system-of-care initiatives serving children and families. *Journal of Emotional and Behavioral Disorders, 12*(4), 236–246.

Egharevba, I. (2001). Researching an "other" minority ethnic community: Reflections of a black female researcher on the intersections of race, gender and other power positions on the research process. *International Journal of Social Research Methodology, 4*(3), 225–241.

Fine, M. (1991). *Framing dropouts.* Albany, NY: SUNY Press.

Fine, M. (2006). Bearing witness: Methods for researching oppression and resistance—a textbook for critical research. *Social Justice Research, 19*(1), 83–108.

Guba, E. G., & Lincoln, Y. S. (1989). *Fourth generation evaluation.* Newbury Park, CA: SAGE.

Henderson, K. A. (1998). Researching diverse populations. *Journal of Leisure Research, 30*(1), 157–170.

hooks, b. (1989). *Talking back: Thinking feminism, thinking black.* Boston: South End.

Krauss, B. J., Goldsant, L., Bula, E., & Sember, R. (1997). The white researcher in the multicultural community: Lessons in HIV prevention education learned in the field. *Journal of Health Education, 28*(6), 67–71.

Kretovics, J., & Nussel, E. J. (Eds.). (1994). *Transforming urban education.* Boston: Allyn & Bacon.

Ladner, J. (1987). Introduction to tomorrow's tomorrow: The Black woman. In S. Harding (Ed.), *Feminism and methodology* (pp. 74–83). Bloomington: Indiana University.

Ladson-Billings, G. (1994). *The dreamkeepers: Successful teachers of African-American children.* San Francisco: Jossey-Bass.

Lather, P. (1992). Critical frames in educational research: Feminist and post-structural perspectives. *Theory into Practice, 31*(2), 87–99.

Leadbeater, B. J., Kupermine, G. P., Blatt, S. J., & Hertzog, C. (1999). A multivariate model of gender differences in adolescents' internalizing and externalizing problems. *Developmental Psychology, 35*(5), 1268–1282.

Morrell, E. (2004). *Becoming critical researchers: Literacy and empowerment for urban youth.* New York: Peter Lang.

Murry, V. M. (1996). Inner-city girls of color: Unmarried, sexually active nonmembers. In B. J. R. Leadbeater & N. Way (Eds.), *Urban girls: Resisting stereotypes, creating identities* (pp. 272–290). New York: New York University Press.

National Center for Education Statistics. (1996). *Urban schools: The challenge of location and poverty.* Washington, DC: U.S. Department of Education.

Nygreen, K. (2006). Reproducing or challenging power in the questions we ask and the methods we use: A framework for activist research in urban education. *The Urban Review, 38*(1), 1–26.

Pastor, J., McCormick, J., & Fine, M. (1996). Makin' homes: An urban girl thing. In B. J. R. Leadbeater & N. Way (Eds.), *Urban girls: Resisting stereotypes, creating identities* (pp. 15–34). New York: New York University Press.

Pollard, D. S. (1989). Against the odds: A profile of academic achievers from the urban underclass. *Journal of Negro Education, 58*(3), 297–308.

Sleeter, C. E. (1993). Advancing a White discourse: A response to Scheurich. *Educational Researcher, 22*(8), 13–15.

Sue, D. W. (1993). Confronting ourselves: The white and racial/ethnic-minority researcher. *The Counseling Psychologist, 21*(2), 244–249.

U.S. Census Bureau. (2000). *Census 2000.* Washington, DC: Author.

Way, N. (1995). "Can't you hear the strength and courage that I have?": Listening to urban adolescent girls speak about their relationships with peers and parents. *The Psychology Women Quarterly, 19*(1), 107–128.

Zahner, G. E. P., Jacobs, J. H., Freeman, D. H., & Trainor, K. F. (1993). Rural-urban child psychopathology in a northeastern U.S. state: 1986–1989. *Journal of the American Academy of Child and Adolescent Psychiatry, 32*(2), 378–387.

PART II

LESSON LEARNED

CHAPTER 5

A VIEW
FROM THE OTHER SIDE

Practitioner Research on
Critical Mathematics Pedagogy in
an Urban High School

Andrew Brantlinger

THE NEED FOR "INSIDE" RESEARCH

Educational researchers are often outsiders to the schools they study, having never attended or worked in them (Carr & Kemmis, 1986). While the outsider perspective can provide important results, such outsider researchers may have a difficult time understanding schooling from the perspective of teachers and students. As outsiders, these researchers may ask questions and focus on reform agendas that have little value or relevance to local actors. Understanding the perspectives of local participants is important, especially if it is hoped that a new method will be imple-

Research in Urban Educational Settings: Lessons Learned and
Implications for Future Practice, pp. 85–102

mented after a study is completed or if teachers elsewhere will find the report of findings compelling enough to use in their classrooms.

Perhaps because of these flaws, top-down approaches to educational research design generally have not translated successfully into practice in schools (Cremin, 1964; Lagemann, 2002; Spillane, 2004; Stigler & Hiebert, 1999). Failed reform efforts are particularly true for schools that serve the poor and, despite rhetoric about equity and access, educational innovations rarely, if ever, address the actual socioeconomic problems that urban communities face (Anyon, 2005; Berliner, 2006; Noguera, 2003). Some mathematics educators claim that reform efforts in school mathematics fail because they do not adequately conceptualize teachers and do not sufficiently involve and inspire them when they request that teachers try out a new curriculum or pedagogy (Ball & Cohen, 1996). Hence, a growing number of educational scholars point to teacher-initiated/practitioner research as a means to address shortcomings with current research and the key to achieving meaningful educational reform (Carr & Kemmis, 1986; Lampert, 2001; McKernan, 1991; Stigler & Hiebert, 1999).

In this chapter I write about my experiences as a practitioner researcher who studied critical pedagogy in my mathematics classroom with the goal of positively contributing to the lives of urban youth and communities. I became aware of critical pedagogy and critical mathematics (CM) while in graduate school after teaching mathematics for 9 years, 5 years of which I spent in non-selective urban high schools. I begin this chapter by providing a rationale for practitioner research and theory that informed my study, noting its value in advancing evidence in classroom practices. I review the lessons I learned as an urban teacher researching my own attempts to incorporate critical pedagogical goals into my mathematics teaching and document the personal and professional transformation that resulted from engaging in self-study. I then discuss the methodological and ethical issues that I faced in my study and conclude by discussing the implications for conducting future practitioner research in urban schools.

MY PRACTITIONER RESEARCH STUDY: CRITICAL PEDAGOGY AND SCHOOL MATHEMATICS

Similar to other mathematics education scholars (Frankenstein, 1991; Gutiérrez, 2002; Gutstein, 2003, 2006), the larger study that this chapter emanates was designed to advance the understanding of critical mathematics (CM), also known as "teaching math for social justice," for culturally diverse youth in secondary urban classrooms. CM is based on the critical pedagogical theory of Paolo Freire (1971; see also Frankenstein, 1983). CM involves developing mathematics problems that touch on issues of power (e.g., resource distribution, racial or social class segregation) likely to affect the lives and education of working class and poor students.

For example, "South Central" was one CM activity that I adapted from a lesson plan developed by Eric Gutstein (Brantlinger, 2005). In this lesson, my high school students used some of the geometry they had been learning to help them understand resource inequities that might have contributed to the 1992 LA "riots"—what are better described as mass demonstrations against racialized police brutality. In the mathematical component of this activity, I had students use maps to calculate or estimate the areas of two regions: a circular region from South Central LA with a radius of 3 miles and the smaller city of Evanston, Illinois. They used their developing understanding of area to find that Evanston was approximately three times smaller than the circular region of South Central. Next, I provided them with the number of movie theaters, community centers, and liquor stores in Evanston—a largely middle-class urban area—in 2004. I asked them to use this data to estimate the number of these three types of places that were in the South Central region in 1992. My students found that, were South Central in 1992 to resemble Evanston in 2004, it would have had approximately 10 movie theaters, 26 community centers, and 27 liquor stores. However, because South Central was poorer than Evanston, some students guessed that there would be double or triple the number of liquor stores and half the number of community centers in South Central than their calculations indicated. When I revealed that, according to a National Public Radio report, there were no movie theaters, no community centers, and over 600 liquor stores in the circular region of South Central in 1992, many expressed disbelief and shock (see Brantlinger, 2005 for more detail).

At the time I conducted and analyzed my study (2003-2007), scholarship on CM had been largely theoretical. CM advocates argued that CM had the potential, especially for marginalized students, to be more empowering in both a political and mathematical sense than the dominant, traditional and standards-based, instructional approaches that prevailed in schools (Gutiérrez, 2002; Gutstein, 2003, 2006). Because few empirical studies of CM existed, whether or not current CM was more empowering and engaging than dominant forms of instruction remained an open question.

Practitioner research. Practitioner research is an umbrella term that stands for a number of closely related ideas. As Anderson, Herr, and Nihlen (1994) note, there are a dozen or so terms for practitioner research in the educational literature, including "teacher research," "teacher inquiry," and "action research." Whatever the name, researchers in this area share a number of assumptions that McKernan (1991) says, "rest on three pillars":

> [F]irst, that naturalistic settings are best studied and researched by those participants experiencing the problem; second, that behavior is highly influenced by the naturalistic surroundings in which it occurs; and third, that qualitative methodologies are perhaps best suited for researching naturalistic settings. (p. 5)

Elaborating further, Anderson et al. (1994) claim:

> [P]ractitioner research is "insider" research done by practitioners (those working in educational settings) using their own site (class, institution, school district, community) as the focus of their study. It is a reflective process, but is different from isolated, spontaneous reflection in that it is deliberately and systematically undertaken, and generally requires that some form of evidence be presented to support assertions. What constitutes "evidence" or, in more traditional terms, "data," is still being debated.
>
> Most practitioner research is oriented to some action or cycle of actions that practitioners take to address a particular situation.... Like all forms of inquiry, practitioner research is value laden. Although most practitioners hope that practitioner research will improve their practice, what constitutes "improvement" is not self-evident. It is particularly problematic in a field such as education, where there is no consensus on basic educational aims. Practitioner research takes place in educational settings that reflect a society characterized by conflicting values and an unequal distribution of resources and power. (pp. 2–3)

While the idea of a teacher as a practitioner or curriculum researcher might seem unusual, it is in-line with the research that John Dewey and his colleagues engaged in at the turn of the twentieth century. Lagemann (2002) argues that if Dewey's vision for educational science had prevailed historically, rather than the technical vision of such positivists as Thorndike, teachers as instructional designers and researchers would not be atypical now. Nevertheless, the positivist vision won out, resulting in the highly psychologized, techno-rational approach that has kept teachers outside of the research and instructional design process. Their marginalization by top-down university scholars has alienated practitioners and perhaps makes them resistant to educational change.

Practitioner-research seems particularly well suited to the study of critical pedagogy and CM. As Atweh (2004) notes, "[a]ction research is consistent with critical understandings of mathematics education and, particular, of critical mathematics" (p. 108). In conducting practitioner research, my goal was to address these issues and to examine what CM might look like in a secondary classroom from the perspective of an experienced urban mathematics educator. Based on my review of the literature, I believe I was the first researcher to document and examine a critical approach to mathematics instruction at the secondary level. The work of the Algebra Project (Moses & Cobb, 2001) in high schools is relevant, but its relationship to current CM is difficult to gauge. The Algebra Project has not yet shared their curricular materials with the research community (Hall, 2002).

The overriding reason that I chose practitioner research as the means to investigate CM was that it provided me with more flexibility to experiment with critical pedagogy than other research designs would have. There were additional reasons for choosing to do practitioner research. First, much of the outsider research done on teachers' instruction is negative and frequently ungenerous to those who agree to participate in the research (e.g., Cohen, 1990; Nicholls & Hazard, 1993; Schoenfeld, 1988). If I were to have conducted research on another teacher, I would have risked projecting myself as an omniscient researcher qualified to critique someone else's attempt to teach CM, when I had never taught it myself. Second, I felt the insider perspective of practitioner research provided an outlook on education that was unavailable through the use of other methodologies. In tracking my own reflections I gained valuable insights into philosophical, ethical, methodological, and practical issues that reformist and critical mathematics teachers face. The approach allowed me to document my internal conversation on such issues as the potential political utility of school mathematics, racial and social class privilege, school segregation and sorting, and problematic pedagogy.

Third, and relatedly, there was a dearth of information about White teachers being self-critical regarding issues of diversity and equity in the mathematics education literature and I wanted to address this gap. The autobiographical writing of teachers in the broader education genre sometimes ended up being a "celebration of self" (e.g., Codell, 1999). One exception in the literature is Vivian Paley (1979), a White teacher who was open about how she struggled with racial and cultural issues that arose in her teaching. Except for the miracle stories that have been made into films about particular superstar teachers' success in the "urban jungle," there was little at the secondary level that involved teachers developing relevant curricula for urban or lower socioeconomic status (SES) students while reflecting critically on the process (see Gutstein, 2006 for an exception).

Fourth, there were broad theoretical and political reasons for self-study. Specifically, it was a means to collapse academic dualities between theory and practice, and between researchers and those they research. As practitioner research, my study challenges ideas about whether expertise lies with scholars in academia or teachers on the frontline in schools. It challenges assumptions about who should produce educational knowledge

(Anderson et al., 1994; Carr & Kemmis, 1986; Lampert, 2001; McKernan, 1991).

The practitioner research approach I took was similar to work in mathematics education by such scholars as Ball (1993), Chazan (2000), Frankenstein (1991), Gutstein (2003, 2006), Lampert (2001), Lubienski (2000), and Romagnano (1994). To varying degrees, these mathematics educators have all examined their own mathematics instruction using qualitative methods such as participant observation, analysis of their own teacher diaries, student work, and videotaped teaching episodes. In spite of this work, practitioner research is "still somewhat unusual in mathematics education" (Magidson, 2002, p. 17). It may not yet be seen as valid, productive, or respectable in some circles (Carr & Kemmis, 1986; Lagemann, 2002). It is even more unusual for mathematics teachers who teach in non-selective urban schools to research their own teaching. To my knowledge, Gutstein (2003, 2006) and I are the only exceptions in the research literature (Brantlinger, 2007).

THE GUEVARA NIGHT SCHOOL PROGRAM

The setting for my study was in a night school program at Guevara High School (a pseudonym). Guevara is a large non-selective urban high school that was put on "academic probation" by the Chicago Public School system due to low test scores and other indications of failure, including the fact that less than half of the entering freshman at Guevara graduated within a 5-year period. The night geometry course I taught at Guevara ran 2 hours a night, 4 days a week, for 9 weeks. The course was equivalent to one semester's worth of instruction; that is, the students earned one semester's worth of geometry credit toward graduation upon completion of the course.

The Guevara night school students were high school juniors and seniors from lower income Hispanic and African American communities. Most students took the geometry course I taught to make up for a past failure in geometry. They needed the course credit in order to graduate. Despite past failure in mathematics, the night school students had a variety of experiences with, and orientations to, school mathematics. Mathematics was an obstacle for many, but certainly not all, of the enrolled students. While many of my students planned to go to college, others were less certain; four of my students had enlisted in the military either during or prior to completing my course. Because of past academic failure, my students tended to be older than typical seniors and juniors.

Guevara used the night school program both as a place to push out "undesirables" and give them a "last chance" opportunity, common practices in neighborhood urban schools (Casella, 2001). Undesirable student-types at Guevara included chronic truants, gang bangers, and pregnant females. Once we had established trusting relationships, many of the night students were candid with me about issues they faced in their lives outside of school. Several students were open about present and past gang involvement and a few discussed their drug dealing and drug use with me before or after class. Four female students had young children and three were pregnant at the time of the course. Several students lived on their own or with friends or siblings, rather than with their parents.

Low-academic expectations and maximum security at the night school. Academically speaking, not much was expected of students in the night school program. In a pre-interview, Jayla summed up her experiences as a night school student as follows: "we don't really have to do anything in night school, but just be here, and *don't* talk, and just keep quiet" (November 7, 2003). The night school students generally seemed surprised that I expected them to work diligently and collaboratively in order to pass my course. Initially, most students seemed more concerned with getting through my course for accreditation than with learning mathematics. Several students made it clear that they would do the minimum amount of work necessary to pass the class at the outset of my course. When, in an interview conducted before my course began, I told Jayla that there were 33 students enrolled in the class, the following exchange occurred:

Jayla: Yeah, but like, by the *middle*, you'll probably have, like, twelve students. Yeah, cause we only have two days of absence. And, three tardies equals one absence. So not that many people....

Me: Is that what happened last semester in [night school] math?

Jayla: *Ye*-ah. Like we didn't have enough chairs to sit in and everything was all packed up. But at the end of it—I mean—we had more than enough chairs to sit in, cause everybody dropped out. (November 7, 2003)

While 5 students stopped coming or were dropped from the course due to poor attendance, of the 33 students who came to class at some point during the first week, 28 passed the course. It is also important to note, that the despite the generally low academic expectations for night school, by the end of the course the majority of my students conveyed through their behavior, written work, and interviews, that they wanted to learn secondary mathematics.

Although I was accustomed to the "maximum security" (Devine, 1996) of neighborhood urban schools, the tight level of security at Guevara High stood out as particularly excessive. The following fieldnote excerpt from one of my initial visits to Guevara illustrates my feelings about this at the time:

> When I arrive at [Guevara] … three Latino [male] officers in light blue, police-like uniforms with metallic badges stand by a massive, dated, and dingy metal detector…. [T]he security checkpoint is the only thing located on the first floor lobby—a huge space, (probably 200 x 100 feet). One entire floor devoted to security…. The guards are all wearing guns on their belts so that they are visible. Though I've taught in similar neighborhood schools, this security seems excessive to me. Like Guevara students are one step away from jail. When it was my turn to go through the metal check, the youngest and largest of the guards questioned me about my visit to the school and who I wanted to see. I explained. He looked at me and asked, "You want to teach night school?" I responded, "yeah." He then asked, checking me out with a grin, "Do you have a vest and a helmet?" I laughed in response. He lowered his voice and put a hand on my shoulder stating, "No. I'm *serious*. Bring a vest and a helmet. This is *night* school. Only the *sta-ars* come out at night." He chuckled some more. I just smiled back at him not knowing what to say. (Fieldnotes, 11/04/03)

Some scholars claim, and I would agree, that some large neighborhood schools that serve low-income urban students of color prioritize security/discipline over learning (Casella, 2001; Devine, 1996; Noguera, 2003). At the same time, these authors note that violence, the threat of violence, and the disciplinary systems ostensibly in place to deter them, are part and parcel of low-income urban schools—and many other schools for that matter. They further claim that school violence in many lower SES urban schools stems from economic divestment and racial segregation in urban areas. Violence was a frequent topic of student discussions before night class and during break. It was also real; two of my female students were involved in separate fights at school during the 9-week course. The police caught one of my male students when he reportedly was about to shoot at rival gang members. When, early on in the course, I pressured one student to do the class work, he threatened to fight me. It soon became clear that he was drunk. He apologized the next day and promised to come to class sober from thereon. He kept this promise and also began coming early to chat with me before class.

Initially, the focus of my study was on my CM curriculum development and student participation in CM activities. I had not fore grounded an examination of my beliefs in my initial study design, although I understood that these did inform my research design and teaching. However, I had not expected my beliefs about CM to change as much as they did over the course of the study. At the outset of my study, I was convinced that critical pedagogy was the road to student empowerment and equity in mathematics education and was intent on showing the superiority of CM over other forms of school mathematics, particularly for historically marginalized urban students of color (Gutiérrez, 2002; Gutstein, 2003, 2006). As the study progressed, I increasingly questioned both my role as practitioner-researcher along race, social class divides and the validity of the critical theory that informed my study. In particular, I questioned: (1) how *my racialized, privileged* role as practitioner-researcher may have contributed to make an impact on students' responses and our interactions, which led me to reconsider; (2) CM's assumptions that urban students of color were unique in needing a markedly *distinct version of school mathematics* in order to be empowered. To be clear, the practitioner-research perspective was essential in this questioning. Had I conducted research on CM in another teachers classroom, I would not have had access first-hand to insights about CM and might have avoided asking critical questions for fear of being overly critical of another teacher.

MY RACIALIZED, PRIVILEGED PRACTITIONER-RESEARCHER ROLE

Some may argue that trying new pedagogical methods with low-income youth of color is tantamount to testing experimental medications on relatively powerless, unwitting people. My awareness of this ethical issue meant that I was determined to abandon my critical pedagogical aims if I observed that they were doing more harm than good. In fact, there were several occasions when I chose not to implement planned CM activities for precisely this reason (see Brantlinger, 2007). On the other hand, my rationale for choosing students who had experienced past failure in mathematics was that these students might benefit from a critical curriculum that allowed them to use mathematics toward potentially emancipatory ends. Critical educational theory supported my rationale. Of course, ethical decisions are inherently complex, shaped by racial positioning, power and privilege. Decisions about doing the right thing are rarely easy.

The positions of (White male) teacher and researcher are privileged institutional positions based on broader, unequal social class, race, and gender relations in society. My practitioner-research approach was not to try to rid myself of my biases, but rather to become more fully aware of my own position as a middle-class, White, male, mathematics teacher and researcher. Many entries in my curriculum diary elicited problematic local issues and describes my attempts to work through them. For example, in one diary entry I wrote about my implementation of a CM activity called the Mercator Map project (Gutstein, 2003)—an activity where students use their understanding of area to investigate European bias in a popular map projection that makes the areas of Europe and North America look bigger than they are relative to Africa and Central America:

> I felt that I forced my "it's racist" interpretation on [my students tonight when they were finishing up the Mercator Map Project]. The first few groups to complete the assignment claimed they had completed the math components, but I saw that they hadn't addressed the question of whether they thought the map was Eurocentric/racist or not. These "early finishers" apparently hadn't read the prompts in the assignment closely enough. Or, maybe they had and did not want to deal with it [race/racism] or writing down a written response. Several of those who did read it ... shrugged their shoulders and said that the map distortion wasn't done on purpose by Europeans.... I wonder if they think a white male ... can adequately discuss racism with them [all students of color]. Many seem comfortable discussing race and racism with me after class but whole class discussions about race or politics seem formal and forced.... I also wonder if the historic kind of bias in the Mercator Map project is too remote or distant when they experience racialized and classed inequality first-hand. (January 9, 2004)

As this excerpt indicates, I often wondered if my students felt comfortable enough to *formally* discuss such taboo topics as racism and bias with a White teacher or in school. Due, in part to the explicit political nature of CM, I regularly grappled with issues of race, social class, institutional authority, and their effect on my mathematics instruction. I also struggled with related issues such as my privileged and pacifism (that is, whether to challenge students who had chosen to serve in the military to reconsider) and giving advice about college to undocumented students.

Sometimes, I suspected students told me what they thought I wanted to hear rather than what they really thought during CM activities. (This poses problems for critical pedagogy because, in theory, it focuses on authentic student experience, discourse, and ideas.) For example, in one CM lesson I had students examine data on the distribution of recess to urban elementary schools by their racial composition. The data showed that Chicago schools with a smaller proportion of White students were less likely to have recess than those with larger proportions of White students. In what I initially thought was an attempt either to tell me what he thought I wanted to hear or to have fun at my expense, one African American male student maintained that African American students "can't have recess" because they "cause too much damn trouble." However, later in the activity, he stood by this earlier statement claiming, "they banned recess at our school cause they was cussing up the classroom." That is, he seemed sincere. Still other students were openly critical of the racist and segregated school system as I had expected them to be. However, again I suspected that these students were telling me what they thought I wanted hear. While this was a concern for my study, I believe my students generally were honest about their beliefs during CM activities. In fact, a few students even openly challenged the "race and recess" activity—and my broader CM agenda—asserting that it was "racist" to make race a formal part of the school mathematics curriculum as I had.

DISTINCTIVE CURRICULUM FOR A DISTINCTIVE POPULATION

The most powerful ethical issues that I dealt with in my practitioner-research stemmed from creating a distinctive mathematics curriculum for a distinctive population of students. Again, this issue was particularly salient for me because, in contrast to my students, I was socially privileged and had some institutional power. Through teaching and researching CM, it became increasingly clear to me that, in creating an ostensibly utilitarian and politically responsive curriculum for historically marginalized students, CM shares much in common with the problematic and socially polarizing practices and assumptions that undergird school sorting in general and vocational mathematics in particular (Brantlinger, 2007).

As mentioned above, once I entered the analytical phase of my study, I decided to include an analysis of the CM curricular materials I developed to teach with. I drew on Dowling's (1998) sociological framework for the analysis of school mathematics texts in the curriculum analysis. Dowling's approach allowed me to compare one of the CM curricular texts with two similar secondary mathematics texts, namely, a unit section from a standards-based reform textbook and a chapter from an "honors" traditional mathematics text. All three texts were approximately 40 pages long and all three focused on area-related mathematical content.

An important result was that the traditional text was in an academic, or "esoteric," register and provided access to principled content whereas the utilitarian, real world focus and discourses in the CM and standards-based texts actually displaced the development of principled, self-referential mathematics content. The traditional honors text was clearly designed to provide privileged students with disciplinary tools and understandings necessary for advanced mathematics while the CM and standards-based texts were slanted so as to prepare non-privileged students for real world uses of mathematics and, in so doing, diminished access to advanced mathematics. To be clear, by emphasizing critical-utilitarian goals and quantitative data analysis of the newspaper variety, the CM text went beyond the standards-based text in limiting adequate preparation for post-secondary mathematics. Although I make these serious assertions about CM, I also note that results were influenced by the fact that I had to create my own CM texts because none were commercially available and only limited ideas for secondary instruction were included in the CM literature.

Importantly, the curriculum's lack of rigor was not lost on the students. For example, José (a pseudonym) wrote me a note regarding a CM lesson that included the following statement: "I don't think you should teach these because we're wasting time studying things that it doesn't belong in this class. Instead of doing these you should teach us math equations that we have never studied" (January 21, 2004).

Student critiques of CM as seeming not mathematical enough to them stuck with me as I entered the analytical phase of my study. Because of student resistance to CM, and my own growing skepticism of its use in secondary mathematics, I included an examination of my beliefs as expressed in the teacher diary that I kept during the study (for information on this technique see Lampert, 2001; McKernan, 1991). An analysis of the CM curricular materials I developed as part of the investigation also allowed me to gauge how the incorporation of social justice-related themes transformed the secondary curriculum. As discussed further in the next section, I found that the inclusion of critical "real world" activities in my CM materials displaced college preparatory mathematics content, validating José's critique of CM (Brantlinger, 2007). Hence, over the course of my study, I had evolved from an unquestioning advocate of CM to a critical skeptic of it. Because I continued to consider myself a critical mathematics educator, finding flaws with current theorization of CM weighed on me personally. Before vetting my study conclusions to a professional audience, I spent considerable emotional energy worrying that my study would alienate CM advocates and other progressive scholars, people I held in high esteem and several of whom were friends and mentors.

In sum, the three texts in my curriculum analysis, which were aimed at distinctive student audiences, bore the imprint of social stratification. Impoverished students study mathematics for political or vocational purposes (potential use-values) while wealthy students learn mathematics for academic and credentialing purposes (actual exchange-value). Through influencing different audiences distinctively with respect to mathematics the three texts contribute to the reproduction of an unequal social order and appear to have a negative impact on non-advantaged students' academic outcomes.

My analyses suggest that secondary mathematics teachers are relatively powerless in making the curriculum more politically relevant. Secondary teachers who stray from the prerequisites for calculus put their students at risk of not being prepared for college mathematics. This is contrary to what CM advocates imply; they give short shrift to the notion that their political goals may displace academic goals during instruction. While a comprehensive CM curriculum that is both politically relevant and covers the required mathematics curriculum has yet to be developed, advocates assume that CM is or will be superior to dominant versions of school mathematics for urban youth of color (Gutiérrez, 2002; Gutstein, 2003, 2006). CM and other progressive educators gloss over the fact that school mathematics is regulated by the largely non-utilitarian, esoteric activities and discourses of academic mathematicians. With the possible exception of statistics, academic mathematics was not created for direct application to political matters.

Currently, distinctive textbooks, instructional materials, and teaching practices are designed for specific subsets of students according to their ability group, track, and geographically separated schooling arrangements (Anyon, 1981; Dowling, 1998; Oakes, 2005). As was the case historically, current distinctive curriculum designs may be based more on stereotypes and faulty assumptions than actual variations between the needs and learning styles of students (Dowling, 1998; Oakes, 2005; Rist, 1970). In judging whether modifications are valid and constructive, the social and physical distance between educational decision-makers and poor students present a problem (Blanchett, 2006; E. Brantlinger, 2003; Noguera, 2003). Traditionally, decisions about varying instruction have not been based on accurate information about learners or reasonable evidence about the efficacy of certain practices.

Critical and multicultural scholars are right to assert that academic mathematics can lack meaning and real world relevance (Boaler, 1997), in particular for students from subordinated communities (Chazan, 1996, 2000; Gutiérrez, 2002; Gutstein, 2003). Indeed, in their journal entries and interviews, my students were quick to point out how irrelevant secondary mathematics—and the general school curriculum for that matter—was to their everyday concerns. However, the literature on critical mathematics and multicultural education implies that, in contrast to their less advantaged counterparts, middle-class White students find school mathematics to be relevant to their lives outside of school. While middle-class students' perceptions of school mathematics were not the focus of my study, nevertheless I am skeptical of such an assertion. Having been such a student myself, and having tutored several middle-class White students, I doubt that most middle-class students find secondary and college mathematics relevant to their everyday lives. Middle-class students take rigorous, abstract mathematics courses primarily because they expect them to pay off in their adult lives in terms of academic credentials and economic access (Collins, 1979). Because school mathematics is socially and institutionally valued, it allows some students—largely middle-class students—to distinguish themselves from others. If it is true that lower income students are less interested in school mathematics than higher income students, it is likely due to their being less certain about attending college and, hence, benefitting from mathematics skills and credentials. Via tracking, school segregation, lack of availability of college preparatory curricula, lack of highly qualified teachers, and differential test scores, a large number of lower income students also have received the ubiquitous message that they are not cut out for advanced mathematics. Given the cultural capital of advanced mathematics, it is necessary to question any curricular approach that denies access to it, including critical and multicultural approaches.

Although I see benefits to critical pedagogy, I am wary of critical and other utilitarian versions of school mathematics that explicitly or implicitly eschew the exchange-value of disciplinary-focused school mathematics (see Gutstein, 2006). As noted earlier, I found in my curriculum analyses the sociopolitical content of CM displaced academic mathematics content. Thus, it is essential that critical educators better understand the powerful gatekeeper role that school mathematics serves before we reconceptualize school mathematics as a critical literacy for some students. Unless universities change their mathematics requirements, CM and other relevance-inspired reforms will likely not pay off in terms of credentials and institutionally-valued skills for students who receive them (Collins, 1979). While curriculum differentiation is widespread, research has not demonstrated that it is valid. In fact, curriculum differentiation is largely inequitable in practice (Anyon, 1981; Dowling, 1998; Oakes, 2005). While I am not advocating a back-to-basics approach, because of the profound impact of quality distinctions in schooling, certainly the benefits and fairness of "different things for different folks" must be validated. It is also imperative that curriculum and instructional modifications are done with the informed consent of students and their families. The empowered vigilance of middle-class families ensures that the best practices take place in their schools. This same vigilance should be imposed on practitioners and researchers by personnel at urban schools that serve the poor. Assumptions and implementation that reduce the academic level of instruction should undergo particular scrutiny.

CONCLUSION

Educational reform that is neatly packaged, coherent, and powerful in theory often end up being messy, complex, and even contradictory in practice. Reform programs are often tested in "ideal" (i.e., privileged, honors) school settings and researchers hope results will generalize to less privileged settings (Apple, 1992; Cremin, 1964; Lee, 2007). By providing situated, "street-level" perspectives on educational phenomena, in particular in non-privileged settings, practitioner research can augment and improve university-based theory and educational reform agendas (Lipsky, 1980). This is not to suggest that practitioner-research should displace university-based educational research or that practitioner-researchers cannot benefit from top-down educational reforms. In fact, it seems that most practitioner-research in mathematics education was inspired by university-based theories and large-scale reform efforts (e.g., Ball, 1993; Chazan, 2000; Lampert, 2001; Romagnano, 1994). In the practitioner research described here, I drew on methodological approaches, analytical frameworks, and theoretical constructs developed by a diverse range of university-based scholars. My study was informed by and responsive to larger discourses about urban education and reforms in mathematics education.

The practitioner research described here speaks directly to educators and researchers interested in CM but, more generally, to those interested in the reform of urban mathematics education. Whether one agrees with my study results or not, my hope is that they give pause to reform efforts in mathematics education that center themselves on curriculum differentiation for marginalized students or implicitly result in such differentiation.

Practitioner-research, such as that described here, places teacher beliefs front and center and makes researcher bias more visible than it is in much education research. In terms of researcher bias, my study drives homes the point that reforms that make sense to comparably privileged education reformers may not make sense to students. Some of what I learned, including students, racialized and class-conscious view of the mathematics curriculum and curriculum differentiation are important for other researchers and reformers to consider. Again, my students questioned whether CM was linked to lower expectations of them as remedial students in a non-selective setting (i.e., night school)—questions that were laced with social class and racial overtones. With this in mind, two questions for researchers and CM advocates and many other reformers to consider are: Why do reforms in mathematics education target marginalized student populations with differentiated, "real world" relevant, curricula? Would educational reformers advocate similar curricular reforms for their children? Does student disengagement in non-selective settings result from a lack of curricular relevance, as suggested by a wide a range of education reformers, from a lack of perceived social mobility afforded by non-selective tracks, or such things as low teacher expectations?

In closing, I suggest that were more educational scholars to engage in research that takes the perspective of both teachers and students into account, our understandings of urban mathematics education and suggestions for improving it would be better than they currently are (e.g., see Chazan, 2000; Martin, 2000). I would also suggest that current reformers, including CM advocates and practitioner-researchers, have much to learn from historical curriculum reform efforts. In particular, about progressive reforms that sought to displace traditional instruction during the first half of the twentieth century, the historian Lawrence Cremin noted, "[a] protest is not a program" (Cremin, 1964, p. 348). In other words, recommendations based in critique may not smoothly translate into methods that can be trusted to be effective in schools. While I consider myself to be a critical scholar, I contend that, similar to progressive and conservative reformers, critical educators propose idealized educational reforms that are unable to withstand the contradictions of schools for the poor in capitalist U.S. society. That is, while critical scholars present powerful and valid critiques of U.S. schooling and mathematics education, these do not necessarily or readily translate into educational solutions as is implied or asserted.

REFERENCES

Anderson, G. L., Herr, K., & Nihlen, A. S. (1994). *Studying your own school: An educator's guide to qualitative practitioner research.* Thousand Oaks, CA: Corwin Press.

Anyon, J. (1981). Social class and school knowledge. *Curriculum Inquiry, 11,* 3–42.

Anyon, J. (2005). What "counts" as educational policy? Notes toward a new paradigm. *Harvard Educational Review, 75*(1), 65–88.

Apple, M. (1992). Do the Standards go far enough? Power, policy, and practice in mathematics education. *Journal for Research in Mathematics Education, 23,* 412–431.

Atweh, B. (2004). Understanding for changing and changing for understanding: Praxis between practice and theory through action research in mathematics education. In R. Zevenbergen & P. Valero (Eds.), *Researching the social dimensions of mathematics education: Theoretical, methodological and practical issues.* Dordrecht: Kluwer Academic Press.

Ball, D. (1993). Halves, pieces, and twoths: Constructing representational contexts in teaching fractions. In T. Carpenter, E. Fennema, & T. Romberg (Eds.), *Rational numbers: An integration of research* (pp. 157–196). Hillsdale, NJ: Erlbaum.

Ball, D., & Cohen, D. K. (1996). Reform by the book: What is—or might be—the role of curriculum materials in teacher learning and instructional reform? *Educational Researcher, 25*(9), 6–8.

Berliner, D. (2006). Our impoverished view of educational research. *Teachers College Record, 108*(6), 949–995.

Blanchett, W. J. (2006). Disproportionate representation of African American students in special education: Acknowledging the role of white privilege and racism. *Educational Researcher, 35*(6), 24–28.

Boaler, J. (1997). *Experiencing school mathematics: Teaching styles, sex, and setting.* Buckingham, England: Open University Press.

Brantlinger, A. (2007). *Geometries of inequality: Teaching and researching critical mathematics in a low-income urban high school*. Unpublished doctoral dissertation, Northwestern University.

Brantlinger, A. (2005). The geometry of inequality. *Rethinking Schools, 19*(3), 53–55.

Brantlinger, E. (2003). *Dividing classes: How the middle class negotiates and rationalizes school advantage*. New York: Falmer Press.

Carr, W., & Kemmis, S. (1986). *Becoming critical: Education, knowledge and action research*. Lewes, England: Falmer.

Casella, R. (2001). *"Being down": Challenging violence in urban schools*. New York: Teachers College Press.

Chazan, D. (1996). Algebra for all students? *Journal of Mathematical Behavior, 15*(3), 455–477.

Chazan, D. (2000). *Beyond formulas in mathematics and teaching: Dynamics of the high school algebra classroom*. New York: Teachers College Press.

Codell, E. R. (1999). *Educating Esmé: Diary of a teacher's first year*. Chapel Hill, NC: Algonquin Books of Chapel Hill.

Cohen, D. K. (1990). A revolution in one classroom: The case of Mrs. Oublier. *Educational Evaluation and Policy Analysis, 12*(3), 327–345.

Collins, R. (1979). *The credential society*. New York: Academic Press.

Cremin, L. (1964). *The transformation of the school*. New York: Vintage Books.

Devine, J. (1996). *Maximum security: the culture of violence in inner-city schools*. Chicago: Chicago University Press.

Dowling, P. (1998). *The sociology of mathematics education: Mathematical myths/pedagogic texts*. London: Falmer Press.

Freire, P. (1971). *Pedagogy of the oppressed* (M. B. Ramos, Trans.) New York: Seabury Press.

Frankenstein, M. (1983). Critical mathematics education: An application of Paulo Freire's epistemology. *Boston University Journal of Education, 165*(4), 315–339.

Frankenstein, M. (1991). Incorporating race, gender, and class issues into a critical mathematical literacy curriculum. *Journal of Negro Education, 59*, 336–359.

Gutiérrez, R. (2002). Enabling the practice of mathematics teachers in context: Towards a new equity research agenda. *Mathematical Thinking and Learning, 4*(2 & 3), 145–187.

Gutstein, E., (2003). Teaching and learning mathematic for social justice in an urban, Latino school. *Journal for Research in Mathematics Education, 34*(1), 37–73.

Gutstein, E. (2006). *Reading and writing the world with mathematics: Toward a pedagogy for social justice*. New York: Routledge.

Hall, R. (2002). Review of radical equations. *Educational Researcher, 31*, 34–40.

Lagemann, E. C. (2002). *An elusive science: The troubling history of education research*. Chicago: University of Chicago Press.

Lampert, M. (2001). *Teaching problems and the problems of teaching*. New Haven, CT: Yale University Press.

Lee, C. D. (2007). *The role of culture in academic literacies: Conducting our blooming in the midst of the whirlwind*. New York: Teachers College Press.

Lipsky, M. (1980). *Street level bureaucracy*. New York: Russell Sage.

Lubienski, S. T. (2000). Problem solving as a means towards mathematics for all: An exploratory look through a class lens. *Journal for Research in Mathematics Education, 31*, 454–482.

Magidson, S. (2002). *Teaching, research, and instructional design: Bridging communities in mathematics education*. Unpublished doctoral dissertation, University of California at Berkeley.

Martin, D. B. (2000). *Mathematics success and failure among African-American youth*. Mahwah, NJ: Lawrence Erlbaum Associates.

McKernan, J. (1991). *Curriculum action research*. New York: St. Martin's Press.

Moses, R. P., & Cobb, C. E. Jr. (2001). *Radical equations: Math literacy and civil rights*. Boston: Beacon Press.

Nicholls, J. G., & Hazard, S. P. (1993). *Education as adventure: Lessons from the second grade*. New York: Teachers College Press.

Noguera, P. A. (2003). *City schools and the American dream: Reclaiming the promise of public education*. New York: Teachers College Press.

Oakes, J. (2005). *Keeping track: How schools structure inequality* (2nd ed.). New Haven, CT: Yale University Press.

Paley, V., (1979). *White teacher*. Cambridge, MA: Harvard University Press.

Rist, R. C. (1970). Student social class and teacher expectations: The self-fulfilling prophecy in ghetto education. *Harvard Educational Review, 40*, 411451.

Romagnano, L. (1994). *Wrestling with change: The dilemmas of teaching real mathematics*. Portsmouth, NH: Heinemann.

Schoenfeld, A. (1988). When good teaching leads to bad results: The disasters of "well-taught" mathematics courses. *Educational Psychologist, 23*(3), 145–166.

Spillane, J. P. (2004). *Standards deviation: How schools misunderstand educational policy*. Cambridge, MA: Harvard University Press.

Stigler, J., & Hiebert, J. (1999). *The teaching gap: Best ideas from the world=s teachers for improving education in the classroom*. New York: Free Press.

CHAPTER 6

CREATING EFFECTIVE LEARNING OPPORTUNITIES FOR DIVERSE STUDENTS AND FAMILIES

Implications for Conducting Urban Education Research

Kimberley Woo

INTRODUCTION

The increasing diversity of today's classrooms can no longer be overlooked. Students of color currently constitute 40% of the population in the United States (Matuszny, Banda, & Coleman, 2007). The 2001 National Center for Education Statistics (NCES) reports 68% of the student population in 100 of the nation's largest school districts is non-White. By 2050, it is anticipated that 50% of all students attending public schools in the United States will come from diverse—for example, ability,

Research in Urban Educational Settings: Lessons Learned and
Implications for Future Practice, pp. 103–121
Copyright © 2011 by Information Age Publishing

gender, geographic origin, language and communication style, race/ethnicity, sexual preference, social economic status—family backgrounds (Gollnick & Chinn, 2006).

Current public school teachers' demographics do not mirror those of their students'. The previously cited NCES (2001) report reveals that 87% of teachers are White. Brandon (2003) cites Ladson-Billings' (2001) work when describing today's teaching work force: "88% are white and 81% are between 45-60 or more years old." Darling-Hammond and Sclan (as cited by Brandon, 2003) add that "only 3% of new teachers speak a second language."

Given this "typical" teacher profile, it is not surprising that current schooling emphasizes White, middle-class values and overlooks or downplays the strengths of *diverse students*, their families, and their communities. For example, Haberman (2003) asserts that minority students are continuing to be "miseducated." He believes district personnel are allocating resources in ways that maintain bureaucracies instead of improving education, and that the larger society has created institutional and cultural systems that support the successes of middle-class Whites who enjoy education-related privileges; they are more likely to pursue higher education, achieve career goals, and enjoy improved life opportunities. More specifically with regards to the population in this study, Bazron, Osher, and Fleishman (2005) reference Valenzuela's (1999) research on "subtractive schooling" when discussing how Latino students' needs are not being met. Valenzuela argues that many *schools* ignore *students'* knowledge of Spanish, or even treat it as a deficit because it is expensive to provide additional resources to English Language Learners. At the same time, many educators believe that school success depends on students' ability to assimilate into White, middle-class culture so they design curricula that support assimilation and de-emphasize other ways of knowing. Unfortunately, when Latino students' knowledge of their native language is devalued, they may hesitate to ask for help with school work and thereby unintentionally restrict their access to the curriculum. At the same time, when schools ignore or perceive students' knowledge of Spanish as a deficit, Latino students and their parents may feel less motivated to participate in class and school activities (Brown & Souto-Manning, 2008).

Valenzuela's (1999) critique is even more powerful when considered within the context of urban education. Cooper and Liou (2007) discuss likely outcomes for at-risk youth attending urban schools in high poverty settings:

> Studies suggest that by eighth grade almost 40% of African American and Latina/o youth in this country are in situations that cause them to be "at

risk" of school failure ... the National Center for Educational Statistics in November 2001 estimates that each year for the past decade over half a million high school students left school before graduation. (p. 43)

Given these dismal statistics, offering opportunities that engage students and meet their needs early in students' educational experience becomes even more crucial to ensuring they can succeed in school. Historically, classroom teachers, school administrators, and policymakers have assumed primary responsibility for decisions related to school success because of the prevailing assumptions that educators know what is best for children and that most minority parents do not possess the training or experience required for meaningful participation (Garcia & Donato, 1991). Unfortunately, the bulk of their efforts have focused on what can be accomplished in classrooms at school sites and often overlooks the potential impact parents and home life can have in promoting students' successes.

This chapter considers how one second grade teacher tailored her classroom curriculum to meet her students' interests and needs, while also actively involving their parents in the learning process. The teacher's twofold approach included teaching strategy-related games as part of the daily math curriculum, and then inviting parents to participate in a "Family Math Night." It is worth noting that while the teacher's curiosity to study her pedagogical practices motivated her to embark on this study, the literature reveals "early academic performance of children from high-risk or disadvantaged backgrounds is predictive of academic performance in early elementary school" (McClelland, Acock, & Morrison, 2006, p. 488). At the same time, Burnett and Wichman (1997) and Carey (1998) maintain that parent involvement is an equally significant factor to consider when ensuring second grade students' success in math; the range of students' abilities in this subject is most noticeable from kindergarten through second grade. It is hoped that the findings will inspire researchers in their work with diverse student populations to invite reflection on the importance of developing a rapport among all educational stakeholders (e.g., students, teachers, parents), of having fun, and of using data to impact educational policies.

Key Ideas

A brief discussion is offered to clarify key ideas—specifically, to explain stakeholders responsibilities and the ongoing disconnection which exist between home and school.

Parents responsibilities. Parents[1] are the gatekeepers of their children's experiences. They are charged with a range of responsibilities, from determining what world view will shape their children's perspective, to ensuring their safety, to deciding what to serve for dinner each night. For many, the magnitude and gravity of the child-rearing role are not fully realized until they become parents themselves, or work in professions that require parenting skills.

Unfortunately, parents of underserved children have too often not felt welcomed and/or disengaged themselves from their children's education because of work schedule conflicts, language limitations, and/or unfamiliarity with the school culture (Anderson & Minke, 2007; Kainz & Aikens, 2007; Waanders, Mendez, & Downer, 2007). While parents of underserved students may participate at lower levels during school hours, the literature has documents that many of these same parents are demonstrating equal or higher rates of involvement with school activities within the home setting (Sampson, 2007).

Teachers' responsibilities. Within the field of education, *in loco parentis* is a Latin term referring to "the legal responsibility of a person or an organization [that takes] on some of the functions and responsibilities of a parent" (Wikipedia.org). Many educators interpret in loco parentis to mean they are the "parents" of their students during the school day. From cultivating students' critical thinking skills, to nurturing their ability to work in groups toward a common goal, to teaching students how to read and play soccer, today's teachers educate the whole child in the hope of preparing him/her to participate in an increasingly diverse, multifaceted, global community.

(Dis)connection between home and school. Ideally, the worlds of home and school work together to ensure that children receive a meaningful, rich, equitable education while in reality, this is often not the case. Fundamental differences exist across districts, and indeed among schools within the same district. Many factors have been identified as causes of educational inequity. Some of the most compelling studies consider the role students' parents' racial/ethnic make-up, socioeconomic status, and/or educational attainment play in their children's educational success. Lee and Bowen's (2006) comprehensive review of educational research finds that when African American and Hispanic/Latino elementary school students come from homes with "low levels of parental educational attainment ... [these students] are [more likely to be] associated with lower academic achievement" (pp. 193–194). On the other hand, these authors remind researchers that "parent involvement [is] positively related to children's educational performance [and] increasing parental involvement [is] a possible strategy for reducing the achievement gap" (p. 194).

In the face of these findings and the achievement gap they point to in our schools, this chapter focuses upon promising practices that might contribute to the improvement of educational experiences for all children. Working to effect change takes time, patience, resources, and the combined energies of students, parents, teachers, community members, and researchers. The collaboration of all stakeholders in the educational process enables all to learn, including those who often are underserved by today's schools.

AN EXAMPLE OF A PROMISING PRACTICE: STRATEGY GAMES IN A SECOND GRADE CLASSROOM

What follows is a discussion of a teacher-initiated, innovative practice,[2] one that merits particular consideration because it was geared to meet students interests and needs, while also serving as a springboard for increasing parental involvement, and adding to their knowledge base about their children's school.

Research Impetus

Inspirations sometimes have unlikely sources. In this case, a teacher discovered her research interest while watching her friends playing Dominoes. As she looked on, she wondered why adults spend their leisure time playing "children's games." After observing the group for a time, she realized that its members enjoyed the mental engagement and light banter that were part of the game-playing dynamic. Later, the teacher thought of her own children's enthusiasm and laughter as they played board games at their home. The teacher then began thinking about how "game-playing" might benefit her second grade students; she wondered about the possible relationship between game-playing and students' learning. The teacher's "wonderings" evolved into the following research questions:

1. In what ways can strategy-related games[3] be combined with math instruction to enhance math learning?
2. In what ways can strategy-related games cultivate students' social interaction with classmates?
3. In what ways can strategy-related games enhance family interaction? Which games do students and their families enjoy playing?

Description of Participants and Site

The class the teacher taught and studied comprised 17 second grade students, eight (50%) of whom are Second Language Learners. Eight of the students were girls and nine were boys. The primary elementary school that these students attend is located in northern San Diego County. The school site is designated as a Title I school and educates 535 kindergarten through third grade students. Approximately half of the total student population is designated as Second Language Learners.

Before starting on her research, the teacher discussed her ideas with colleagues and school administrators. Their overwhelmingly positive responses added to the teacher's excitement. Everyone expressed support for teaching innovations that would increase students' levels of math engagement, particularly those whose needs were not being met through current curricular approaches.

Research Design

The teacher introduced nine strategy-related games[4] over the course of a school year. Every month, a new game was presented to the class. Students were taught how to play the game and reminded of the need for good sportsmanship. If questions arose during the introduction of the game or while the second graders practiced playing in small groups, the teacher always referred questions back to the class, thereby encouraging critical thinking and collaboration on the part of the students.

Once the second graders demonstrated familiarity with one game, the teacher included it as one choice—the math games option—when the class rotated among math centers. Prior to the start of each rotation, students were reminded of "game-playing behavior": play fairly, play by the rules, be responsible, and do not be "silly." Each rotation lasted between 15–20 minutes, thus allowing the completion of at least one game.

Data Collection

Data were collected in a variety of ways. For example, informal daily observations were jotted in field notebooks. Informal conversations with students about their favorite and least favorite games provided another source of data that were recorded in field notebooks. Report card grades and standardized test scores provided yet another source of data and enabled comparisons of students' performance with reference to other second graders in the school, in the district, and in the state of California.

Research Findings

Though many important findings resulted from this study, three seemed particularly pertinent to the focus of this chapter. The first concerns math-related skills that the second graders sharpened as a result of their exposure to the strategy-related games. The second finding reveals students' increased attention spans and levels of concentration which resulted from playing the games. The third discusses the impact strategy-related games had on increasing family participation and parental involvement in their children's education.

Skills development. One of the most intriguing findings that emerged from incorporating game-playing into the math curriculum was that the second graders honed their problem-solving, reasoning, and strategy-related skills. Many district-approved, textbook and worksheet-based curricula make the same claims; in this case, second graders' interview responses testified to their development in all three areas, and to the fun they had in the process as well. For example, when asked why they preferred some games to others, many of the students remarked that their favorite games were challenging and allowed them to keep improving their "plans." When asked what they meant by the word plan, students described the methods by which they increased their prospects of success—for example, working as teams, sharing ideas with friends, trying "new moves" [strategies]. The teacher believed these comments indicated enhancement of her second graders' problem-solving skills; their responses reflected increasingly sophisticated reasoning and greater willingness to take risks, which improved their chances of winning.

The teacher was then able to help students transfer the game-related skills to other areas of her curriculum. For example, as students collaborated in small groups, the teacher encouraged them to work in a team, to share ideas, and to think about a variety of strategies when solving word problems during math. The teacher felt that the students' abilities to apply knowledge and skills from one context to another were clear indications of their growth as critical thinkers.

When the teacher looked at end-of-the-year math assessments, she noticed that all students demonstrated academic progress; all students increased their report card score by at least one or two percentage points. The teacher was not surprised with this finding for the games provided her students with opportunities to assess information, draw conclusions, work in small groups, and apply critical thinking skills. The teacher was right not to attribute this improvement solely to the incorporation of strategy-related games; however, of the various pedagogical activities—direct math instruction, independent math practice, math homework, and strategy-related games—that combined to raise her students' report card grades, she considered the last most instrumental.

Attention span and levels of concentration. Each month, a new strategy-related game was introduced to the class. In all, nine games were integrated into the math curriculum. Before going further, it is worth noting that students' maturation over the course of the school year may have influenced outcomes. That said, the findings suggest that the playing of the games had a major role in increasing the students' attention spans and levels of concentration.

It seemed students were intrigued by the novelty of learning a game in a classroom setting; they exhibited excitement and heightened attention when a new game was introduced. Students also demonstrated higher levels of concentration while playing games independently, for this allowed them to devise and rehearse game-playing strategies, and then later, try them when playing with classmates. When games were geared to students' ability levels, they held their attention, but if games were above students' abilities, they quickly lost interest.

'Students showed the highest level of concentration when playing familiar competitive partner games such as Othello. Among the boys, the element of competition seemed to intensify their concentration and willingness to collaborate. On a few occasions, when one of the players lost, as the group was setting up for the next game, he would discuss his strategy(s), then along with his peers, they brainstormed ways he could strengthen future game-playing efforts.

'Extending attention spans and levels of concentration strengthens students' capacities to filter information; they become more skilled at retaining necessary information and disregarding unnecessary information. This became evident in this classroom as students learned new game rules and procedures. Those who demonstrated greater adeptness at playing a "new" game seemed to possess greater attention spans and levels of concentration than those who took longer to learn the same game; the latter were easily distracted by "static" events (e.g., playground sounds, peers' comments).

Students who experienced increased attention spans and abilities to concentrate also seemed to demonstrate improved abilities when learning new math concepts. For example, when the teacher began to explain double-digit addition, the class demonstrated readiness and excitement to master this more complicated mathematical application; though the duration of whole group math lessons were approximately the same length as those offered earlier in the year, the teacher noted that students seemed more deeply engaged, on average 3–5 minutes longer, per math lesson since she had introduced strategy-related games as one of the math rotation options.

Family participation. Another interesting result of the implementation of strategy-related games was that the second graders became so excited about the games that they wanted to take games home to play them with their families. In response to her students' enthusiasm, the teacher created a game borrowing system that required that the games be returned in good condition, and that the student and/or the parents complete a game questionnaire before another game was checked out.

At the end of the year, the teacher reviewed the responses[5] and concluded that the families generally enjoyed their time spent playing games. The teacher noticed that many parents felt the games facilitated their taking time out of their busy lives to focus attention on their children. One father offered, "I learned to give time to my kids." Other parents remarked that they appreciated the time together, as it provided opportunities to talk about topics valued by the family.

It is worth noting that while most families indicated they would be willing to purchase their favorite games, there were two families who indicated they would not purchase games. Careful observation of the students and informal discussion led the teacher to conclude that these families could not afford to buy the games. This recalls Lee and Bowen's (2006) findings, which suggest that at least for some families' children, low income delimits access to resources and correlates with low academic achievement. This assertion has particular implications for this study because of the school's Title I designation and because approximately half of the student population was designated as Second Language Learners. Accordingly, the teacher developed math instruction strategies that addressed her students' diverse needs. This teacher's promising practices—the playing of strategy-related games and loaning out of games to play at home—increased students' access to curricular resources, and represented practical strategies to bolster the academic achievement of all.

EXTENDING THE SUCCESS: INCREASING PARENT EDUCATION OPPORTUNITIES

Given the success this teacher experienced in her classroom, she decided to try extending her practice beyond her students and their families to the rest of the school. During a planning meeting for a Family Math Night—one of three Family Nights hosted each year by the school—the teacher suggested that the evening in question focus on strategy-related board games. She cited Caldwell (1998) in proposing that "the idea of a school 'Family Board Game Night' [w]as a way to inform parents of the mathematical benefits of playing board games with their children" (Herrell, 2006, p. 15).

In response to the teacher's proposal, the school's administration initially expressed doubt about the logistics of teaching board games to approximately 150 family members. However, the teachers who volunteered to participate in the event felt that teaching board games was no different from giving classroom instruction. The only accommodation teachers anticipated for this evening was the need for bilingual (Spanish-speaking) "teachers," but as it turned out, students' who were familiar with the games proved both able and willing to teach how to play them.

The teacher analyzed written feedback from Family Math Night and reported that the teaching of games went smoothly, the players learned quickly, and the game-playing was fun for the families involved. The teacher also noted that English-speaking families were generally more familiar with the games played than were the Spanish-speaking families:

> Many English speaking parents shared that they had played these games when they were young and appreciated the opportunity to play the games with their children [while] many Spanish speaking parents were learning to play games for the first time. (Herrell, 2006, p. 47)

The teacher concluded that, regardless of language ability and/or previous experience with the games, virtually everyone—students, families, teachers, and administrators—who participated in Family Math Night felt the evening was enjoyable and educational. Students' comments revealed that they liked being asked to teach others how to play the games; by participating as game instructors, they felt they had contributed to the success of the evening.

Subsequently, many parents reported that they were impressed that their child could now play the games with siblings, often without adult supervision, and that their child was demonstrating leadership skills in the family setting. In addition, many of the teacher's colleagues have begun to implement games or game-related activities in their classrooms; one kindergarten teacher has begun using dominoes to help her students practice their counting skills. This colleague's informal feedback confirmed findings from the teacher's research; she loved having her class work with dominoes because they enjoyed using manipulatives, while at the same time, they also practiced their social skills.

On the whole, the teacher believed that the integration of strategy-related games into her curriculum proved successful. She reflected:

The results of this game project have exceeded my expectations … my students learned skills that I know will be integral to their academic success as well as their futures. At the same time, students discovered that learning is an enjoyable process consisting of both wins and loses along the way. If I am correct in these assumptions, then I believe I have done my job as their teacher. (Herrell, 2006, p. 42)

The teacher here attests to the benefits her second graders enjoyed as a result of her promising practice. What's more, that promising practice had a positive effect on parents. Playing strategy-related games at home with their children and attending Family Math Night increased their educational opportunities in many ways. The following discussion highlights three of those opportunities.

Parents and children (re)learn to play games. As noted earlier in the chapter, all families enjoyed playing strategy-related games, and many Spanish-speaking parents, along with their children, were learning to play these games for the first time. The process of (re)learning something can be very enriching. Among other things, time spent playing strategy-related games involves socializing, engaging in friendly competition, and promoting fairness. It seems reasonable to conclude that for many, playing games is a way to even the playing field; it provides all participants with the chance to experience success. In this case, the "expert" role is not determined by chronological age, but rather by one's level of familiarity with a particular game; parents and children have equal opportunities to develop and demonstrate game-playing expertise.

Mastering the intricacies of game-playing affords all participants considerable satisfaction. At the same time, and perhaps more important, parents (re)learning games bespeaks a commitment to lifelong learning. In this case, they practice what so many preach: Education does not end with graduation, but rather is an endeavor worth pursuing throughout one's life, for the act of (re)learning adds meaning and brings fulfillment to one's existence.

Parents become more knowledgeable about the classroom and school. Lee and Bowen (2006) speak to the important role parents educational involvement has on student success: "Parent educational involvement is associated with child achievement and should continue to be an important focus of school staff" (p. 214). While these researchers believe all children benefit with increased parental involvement, they emphasize the need to pay particular attention to "identifying and reducing barriers among African American, Latino/Hispanic, low-income, and less educated parents"; they believe this parent population benefits most from being "engaged *at school* in their children's education" (p. 214). Just so, attending Family Math Night and playing strategy-related games at home enhanced parents' understanding of their children's math curriculum and school experiences. Participating in school learning activities increased parents' awareness of not only their children's accomplishments, but also areas of needed improvement.

Parents and children have fun. In this era of increased accountability, the focus of school is often on meeting standards. Student-centered, exploratory, project-based approaches to learning are discounted for fear they do not prepare students to perform well on standardized tests. Consequently, student enjoyment of the school experience is typically disregarded. Yet Barack (2006) argues:

> school kids are checking out because they are bored ... 47 percent of students say they left school because ... it wasn't interesting.... Nearly a third of high school students don't graduate on time; among blacks, Hispanics and Native Americans, it's almost half. (p. 4)

Some may consider Barack's findings discouraging, but within the context of this chapter, the teacher's work offers all the more incentive to develop pedagogical practices that engage and stimulate learners. While the aforementioned positive effects of incorporating strategy-related games into one's curriculum are of great importance, perhaps the most important aspect of this promising practice was the level of student engagement it engendered. Again, students always exhibited excitement and heightened attention when a new game was introduced. Students also manifested high levels of concentration while playing games independently when the game was appropriate for their strategy level, with students showing the highest level of concentration when they played familiar competitive partner games such as Checkers. All this indicates that student attention span increases with their enthusiasm for the activity at hand, but even more so when competition is a part of that activity.

At the same time, the teacher believed she could increase the likelihood of her students' math successes if their parents were active partners in the learning process. The teacher provided a creative, educational venue for all, children and parents alike, to engage in second grade math-related activities. Family Math Night was one effective way this teacher increased parents' familiarity with the curriculum and her expectations. In short, the teacher was able to put the fun back into learning, not just for the students, but for their parents as well.

CONCLUSION

Educators can learn much from this teacher's classroom; the positive outcomes of her promising practices can guide our work with diverse student populations in urban settings. Banks and Banks (2006) remind us that today's classrooms are more diverse than ever before, and that it is our responsibility to strive toward increased awareness about the multifaceted interconnections among various cultural, racial, ethnic, and language groups. In particular, we may want to reframe our efforts to be more sensitive to students' developmental and educational needs, and to include their families' cultural backgrounds (Allison & Rehm, 2007). With regards to the findings from this study, teachers and researchers should carefully consider the following: establishing a rapport with participants, having fun, and using data in the creation and implementation of policies that improve education for all students.

Establishing a Rapport

Effective teachers and researchers know that forming relationships with participants is an important part of their work. Carpio (2001) reminds us that, when entering new or unfamiliar settings, establishing a rapport requires knowledge about "unique culture and social contingencies ... in various contexts ... [and that] cultural and psychosocial factors are presumed to play a major role in the ... practices of all people" (as cited by Berg et al., 2004).

The teacher in this study established a wonderful rapport with students during the first month of school. Part of the process involved observing students' learning preferences, levels of frustration, and range of abilities; this information led her to conclude that the best way to incorporate strategy-related games into the math curriculum was to introduce only one game a month. This allowed students enough time to master the rules and develop strategies of that game before learning another game.

The teacher also took time to get to know students' parents. Implementing the game borrowing policy established a connection between home and school, which set the stage for the success of Family Math Night. Because she had established a working relationship with students' parents, they felt a level of comfort with the school culture prior to attending the event.

Again, Lee and Bowen's (2006) research reminds us that "parent involvement [is] positively related to children's educational performance [and] increasing parental involvement [is] a possible strategy for reducing the achievement gap" (p. 194). This may be in part because when students see that their parents are actively involved in their schooling, they feel increased self-worth and motivated to excel. Then, too, when parents are presented with opportunities to become involved and experience first-hand aspects of their children's education, they are then better positioned to contribute to their children's success in school.

Similarly, researchers would do well to keep the teacher's effective approach in mind when establishing relationships with their own participants. Prior to actually entering a site, researchers should spend some time observing the individuals, context, and culture of the setting. In addition, researchers should also make sure their research design supports open communication between researchers and participants. Borbasi, Jackson, and Wilkes (2005) describe research as a personal experience involving "intimacy, self-disclosure, and reciprocity ... with research participants; [and requiring consideration of] power and politics and the moral implications of fieldwork" (p. 493). In particular, a researcher should ensure that participants are clear about his/her study's objectives, as this will help them to feel comfortable while participating in the study. In her work with youngsters, Yuen (2004) recommends "creating a relaxed atmosphere" when conducting focus groups with children. She believes this allows researchers "to gain insight into the children's perspective, to provide structure and focus the[ir] discussion" and that a comfortable approach elicits more meaningful responses from children (p. 468). This indicates it is critical for researchers to establish trust between themselves and their participants in order to attain access to the kind of information that results in insightful findings.

Having Fun

The teacher's decision to incorporate commercially produced strategy-related games was an example of how students can have fun while also learning important content, strategies, and social skills. Game-playing introduced the idea of "chance" and increased students' tolerance for ambiguity; though winning games involved strategizing, students also learned that random rolls of dice could not be controlled. Toward the end of the year, the teacher observed that winning and losing assumed lesser importance than turn-taking, collaborating, and spending time with friends. She concluded that part of the success of her innovative practice rested with students increased enjoyment of learning via the strategy games.

Researchers can integrate this important lesson about "having fun" when conducting research. Research is no longer only an impersonal, quantitative endeavor. The format and tone of today's research are no longer bound by the conventions of "traditional" research paradigms—for example, "objective" reporting of significant findings via charts, graphs, and through the use of the third person perspective. In comparison, much of today's research discusses study limitations by considering how a researcher's background may have influenced the study's design and outcomes, and includes personal reflections about the research process, often expressed in the first person. More researchers are also gearing their writing to address larger audiences. Today's researchers are intending their work to be read by colleagues, classroom practitioners, policymakers, and individuals interested in educational issues. In general, it seems today's postmodern researchers are finally inviting themselves and their participants to have fun when engaging in the research process, and their audience to enjoy reading about that research process in the resulting text.

Using Data to Influence Policies

Policymakers employ statistics to inform their decision making. For example, school districts will reference standardized test scores when determining grade level placements for students within schools and those transferring from other schools, states, or even countries. District-wide data are also used when identifying schools' needs and distributing resources. More generally, national legislation such as No Child Left Behind (NCLB) dictates that students' standardized test scores are reviewed to assess policy effectiveness. Hickok and Ladner (2007) write, "Under NCLB, states are required to test students annually and demonstrate continual progress toward a Federal goal of all students reaching 'proficiency' on state-level exams by 2014" (p. 1).

Clearly, publication of data can also be an effective way to win support for curricula initiatives. Just so, the teacher gave much thought to sharing her data regarding game playing. She began by summarizing findings in a single page, which she shared with students and parents in a brief meeting held after school. The students seemed pleased that their teacher reported significant improvements in math and socialization skills, as a result of their playing of strategy-related games. Students' comments also revealed excitement about having participated in their teacher's project; they hoped to have chances to do "more fun stuff like this again."

Parents' comments during the meeting and as summarized from questionnaires completed during Family Math Night were also very supportive; they focused on two key ideas. Their message was twofold. First, parents expressed their gratitude for the teacher's engaging and content-rich curriculum, and the chance to participate in Family Math Night. Second, parents articulated their appreciation of the teacher's open communication; she always answered their questions and used Spanish translators when needed.

The teacher's successes have initiated thinking about how to build upon her work. The compelling data catalyzed her request to organize another Family Math Night focusing on card games. She plans to incorporate findings from the first Family Math Night into the proposal's rationale requesting that the district purchase sufficient decks of cards, reproductions of card game instructions and extension activities in both English and Spanish, and tote bags so that each family can leave with materials to continue playing card games at home. In addition, as the district embarks on a review of textbooks for the second grade, it is the teacher's hope that her data will prompt others to assess possible texts, at least in part, on their potential to engage student interest.

Researchers can learn much from the way the teacher chose to share her data. Researchers should realize that the students and parents' positive responses to the data resulted because the teacher made the data accessible and only highlighted key ideas. The summary addressed students' and parents limited English language abilities, while still providing salient information. The teacher also created a comfortable forum in which students and parents were invited to respond to her work. Like this teacher, researchers should consider their participants when preparing to share findings. Specifically, data can be presented in ways that support key findings and yet still remain comprehensible to the audience at large.

At the same time, the teacher's strategic use of information may catalyze researchers' thinking about how they can use data to effect policy decisions. Similar to the teacher, researchers might represent key ideas in plain English, and thereby increase the likelihood of legislators and others understanding the reasons underlying their requests, proposals, and/or initiatives. Change is most likely when decision makers have ascertained its rationale. Regarding educational issues in particular, researchers would do well to embed some practice-based data within their arguments, as this can provide a bridge between abstract theory and everyday application.

If we return to this chapter's beginning and acknowledge the tension that exists between the increasing diversity of today's student population and the stability of teachers' profiles, researchers can then see the need to be thoughtful when conducting educational research and making policy recommendations. Ultimately, the goal of both research and recommendations should be to offer students content-rich curricula that engages their interests and promotes their success. Insofar as this is achieved, the educational system will have fulfilled its mission of ensuring all students have equal opportunity to become educated citizens of the world.

NOTES

1. For purposes of this text, the term parents includes all adult caregivers who are part of the children's family groups and are directly involved with the rearing of these children.
2. I would like to express my gratitude to the teacher for inviting me to serve as her masters thesis chairperson and then for allowing me to write about her class.
3. Strategy-related games is a term used to describe "a physical or mental competition conducted according to rules in which the participants play in direct opposition to each other with each side striving to win and to keep the other side from doing so" (Gove, 1961 as cited by Herrell, 2006, p. 5).
4. Nine games were used in this study: Connect Four, Mancala, Kings in the Corner, Uno, Mexican Train Dominoes, Trouble, Kaboodle, Checkers, and Othello. Five criteria were used to select these games: age appropriateness, number of players, variety of skills, the amount of time needed to play a round, and the cost of the game.
5. The data were based on responses from 334 games played by 17 families.

REFERENCES

Allison, B. N., & Rehm, M. L. (November 2007). Effective teaching strategies for middle school learners in multicultural, multilingual classrooms. *Middle School Journal, 39*(2), 12–18.

Anderson, K. J., & Minke, K. M. (2007, May–June). Parent involvement in education: Toward an understanding about parents' decision making. *Journal of Educational Research, 100*(5), 311–323.

Banks, J. A., & Banks, C. A. M. (2006). *Multicultural education: Issues and perspectives*. Indianapolis, IN: Jossey-Bass.

Barack, L. (2006, April). Dropouts: School's boring. Real-world learning could slash dropout rates. *School Library Journal, 52*(4). Retrieved April 7, 2006, from Academic Search Elite: http://www/schoollibraryjournal.com/slj/printissue/currentissue/864455-427/dropouts_schoolamp8217_boring.html.csp

Bazron, B., Osher, D., & Fleischman, S. (2005, September). Creating culturally responsive schools. *Educational Leadership, 63*(1), 83–84.

Berg, B. L., Sanudo, F., Hovell, M., Sipan, C., Kelley, N., & Blumberg, E. (2004, Winter). The use of indigenous interviewers in a study of Latino men who have sex with men: A research note. *Sexuality & Culture, 8*(1), 87–103.

Borbasi, S., Jackson, D., & Wilkes, L. (2005, September). Fieldwork in nursing research: Positionality, practicalities and predicaments. *Journal of Advanced Nursing, 5*(51) 493–501.

Brandon, W. W. (2003, January/February). Toward a white teachers' guide to playing fair: exploring the cultural politics of multicultural teaching, *International Journal of Qualitative Studies in Education, 16*(1), 31–50.

Brown, S., & Souto-Manning, M. (2008). Culture is the way they live here: Young Latinas and parents navigate linguistic and cultural borderlands in U.S. school. *Journal of Latinos and Education, 7*(1), 25–42.

Burnett, S. J., & Wichman, A. M. (1997, May). *Mathematics and literature: An approach to success.* ERIC Report 414–567.

Caldwell, M. L. (1998). Parents, board games, and mathematical learning. *Teaching Children Mathematics,* (4), 365–367.

Carpio, F. F. (2001). Social, cultural, and epidemiological considerations in HIV disease management in U.S. Latino populations. *Topics in HIV Medicine, 9*(2), 34–36. Retrieved August 10, 2003, from http://hivinsite.ucsf.edu/InSite.jsp?doc=md-04-01-11

Carey, L. M. (1998, February). Parents as math partners: A successful urban story. *Teaching Children Mathematics, 4*(6), 314–319.

Cooper, R., & Liou, D. D. (2007, October/November). The structure and culture of information pathways: Rethinking opportunity to learn in urban high schools during the ninth grade transition. *High School Journal, 91*(1), 43–56.

Garcia, H. S., & Donato, R. (1991, Summer). Language minority parent involvement within middle class schooling boundaries. *Community Education Journal, 18*(4), 22–23.

Gollnick, D., & Chinn, P. (2006). *Multicultural education in a pluralistic society.* Upper Saddle River, NJ: Pearson Education.

Gove, P. B. (1961). *Webster's Third New International Dictionary.* Springfield, MA: G. & C. Merriam.

Haberman, M. (2003, January). Who benefits from failing urban schools? An essay. *Theory into Practice, 46*(3), 179–186.

Herrell, W. C. (2006). *Strategy games in a second grade classroom.* Unpublished master's thesis. California State University San Marcos.

Hickok, E., & Ladner, M. (2007, June). Reauthorization of NCLB: Federal management or citizen ownership of K–12 education? *The Heritage Foundation* (2750), 1–9. *In loco parentis.* Retrieved July 14, 2006, from, Wikipedia.org.

Kainz, K., & Aikens, L. L. (2007, October). Governing the family through education: A genealogy on the home/school relation. *Equity and Excellence in Education, 40*(4), 301–310.

Ladson-Billings, G. (2001). Crossing over to Canaan: The journey of new teachers in diverse classrooms. San Francisco: Jossey-Bass.

Lee, J. S., & Bowen, N. K. (2006, Summer). Parent involvement, cultural capital, and the achievement gap among elementary school children. *American Educational Research Journal, 43*(2), 193–218.

Matuszny, R. M., Banda, D. R., & Coleman, T. J. (2007, March/April). A progressive plan for building collaborative relationships with parents from *diverse* backgrounds. *Teaching Exceptional Children, 39*(4), 24–31.

McClelland, M. M., Acock, A. C., & Morrison, F. J. (2006). The impact of kindergarten learning-related skills on academic trajectories at the end of elementary school. *Early Childhood Research Quarterly, 21*(4), 471–490.

National Center for Educational Statistics. (2001). *Characteristics of the 100 largest public elementary and secondary school districts in the United States: 1999–2000.*

Sampson, W. A. (2007). *Race, class, and family intervention: Engaging parents and families for academic success*. Blue Ridge Summit, PA: Rowan & Littlefield.

Valenzuela, A. (1999). *Subtractive schooling: U.S.-Mexican youth and the politics of caring*. Albany, NY: State University of New York Press.

Waanders, C, Mendez, J. L., & Downer, J. T. (2007, December). Parent characteristics, economic stress, and neighborhood context as predictors of parent involvement in preschool children's education. *Journal of School Psychology, 45*(6), 619–636.

Yuen, F. C. (2004). It was fun ... I liked drawing my thoughts: Using drawings as a part of the focus group process with children. *Journal of Leisure Research, 36*(4), 461–482.

CHAPTER 7

"MAKIN' A WAY OUT OF NO WAY"

Forging a Path in Urban Special Education Research

**Monika Williams Shealey,
Liana Gonzalez, and Delsue Frankson**

THE INTERSECTION OF RACE, CULTURE, AND DISABILITY

In spite of the presence of convincing data on the overrepresentation issue and the extant literature challenging special education processes that lead to identification and placement, this problem continues to persist. Its persistence will continue until we reanalyze old premises and reconstruct new premises underlying the field of special education. (Patton, 1998, p. 26)

It is well documented that students living in poverty and those from ethnically diverse backgrounds receive the least qualified teachers and consequently are subject to inequitable educational experiences which result in being placed at greater risk for referral and placement in special education

Change (Transformation) in Government Organizations, pp. 123–142
Copyright © 2011 by Information Age Publishing
All rights of reproduction in any form reserved.

(Artiles, Harry, Reschly, & Chinn, 2002; Artiles & Trent, 1994; Darling-Hammond, 2001). Since the inception of special education, ethnically diverse students have been overrepresented in certain programs in special education and underrepresented in programs for the gifted and talented (Artiles & Trent, 1994; Blanchett, 2006; Dunn, 1968; Ford & Harmon, 2001). Additionally, the special education programs which have predominately served students from ethnically diverse backgrounds, specifically African Americans, represent the most segregated and restricted settings in schools (Harry, 1994; Losen & Orfield, 2002). Further, historically post-school outcomes for students with disabilities, particularly those served in moderate to severe programs, is dismal and in light of the current standards-based reform movement this trend is likely to continue (Blanchett, Mumford, & Beachum, 2005). This is the backdrop from which two National Academy of Sciences panels examined the problem of disproportionate representation (National Research Council [NRC], 2002). As a result of findings from these reports in addition to the work of scholars committed to issues of social justice and equity, there is a growing movement in the field of education advocating for a revamping of special education to include an examination of the dichotomy of disability and diversity which includes specifically addressing the referral and placement process, curriculum and instruction, and the role of family and community engagement.

It is clear that contextual variables such as race, culture, and class are powerful contributing factors in low student performance (Heubert, 2002; McIntyre, 2006; NRC, 2002). Traditionally student achievement has been measured through student performance on standardized assessments. This limited vantage point fails to take into account the influence of family, community and environment variables in the development of instructional practices and policies which directly impact students in urban settings (Anyon, 1997; Nygreen, 2006). This course of exploration has been strikingly absent from the dominant research discourse in special education and has presented unique opportunities and challenges in preparing teachers for diversity in a responsive manner that links rather than dilutes issues such as race, culture, and class (Pugach, 2001; Seild & Pugach, 1998). The inequitable educational experiences of urban students with disabilities are directly related to legislation and reform initiatives which may be perceived as well intentioned yet have failed to address the impact of systemic racism, poverty, and ineffective teaching on student outcomes.

There is agreement in the field of education that student outcomes and teacher quality are essential elements for effective urban school renewal. Yet the stringent methods advocated in No Child Left Behind (NCLB) legislation, which should theoretically address these areas, fail to take into account the extent to which contextual variables such as race, culture, language and poverty impact access to educational opportunities (Shealey, 2006). Therefore, it is essential that urban special education research reflect upon the delimitations of traditional research in effectively examining issues impacting ethnically diverse students and those living in poverty. Reframing issues such as disproportionate representation and the achievement gap require urban education researchers to ask more challenging questions. This shift will ultimately make direct changes in educational policy and address broader societal issues rather than focusing on the symptoms of persistent urban concerns, will move the field toward a framework rooted in activism (Nygreen, 2006).

Research production in special education situated around concepts such as voice and agency represent a departure from what many consider traditional mainstream research. Alternate epistemologies and methodologies have long held a home in social sciences and in the broader educational research community. Although, there are a number of significant studies in special education and disability studies which have advanced new understandings through a reliance on qualitative research methodologies, as well as work that has implicated special education in the continued inequities experienced by traditionally marginalized groups, there remains the privileging of one research methodology over others (Brantlinger. Jimenez, Klingner, Pugach, & Richardson, 2005; McCray & Garcia, 2002). The marginalization of alternate epistemologies in special education reflects a pervasive problem that extends to the ways in which research advocating for "insider" knowledge on issues associated with race, culture, and class on the sustenance of the pipeline of ethnically diverse students and those in poverty into special education programs is valued by the field. This chapter will present an argument for a cohesive and comprehensive urban special education research agenda, which acknowledges the inflexibility of traditional mainstream special education research and offers alternate epistemologies and methodologies in examining the intersection of race, culture and disability. To these ends, we also aim to further research in engaging and mobilizing urban families and communities in advocating for access to resources and supports, and culturally responsive instructional practices in general and special education settings.

COMPLEXITIES OF CONDUCTING RESEARCH IN URBAN SETTINGS

When we dream, we often do not dream original dreams; we merely seek relief from pain. As a result, the dream does not encompass a meaningful plan or strategy which is connected to mobilization. (Hilliard, 1998, p. 177)

Among the many complexities of conducting research in urban settings is the notion that generally research falls short of resulting in action due to its failure to clearly identify and thus expose where the problem lies. Too often urban settings are viewed as places to conduct research from a deficit-based perspective, meaning places where children are typically associated with learning deficits, schools are viewed as crime-ridden institutions, teachers as inept, and parents as generally not invested in their children's education. According to Gordon (2003) the urban context consists of a "number of polarities, such as extreme differences in people, life space, conditions of life, and the concentration of power and resources" (p. 203). These extremes are evident in the curriculum, programs, and instructional practices instituted in urban schools and are central to the many problems currently facing urban education research.

Contradicting these suggested deficits and operating from the principles of Participatory Action Research, the Logan Square Neighborhood Association (LSNA), as part of *The Indicators Project on Education Organizing*, provides residents in urban communities with a forum in which to become advocates and decision makers in their neighborhood schools. As one of five case studies conducted by *The Indicators Project* designed to depict the impact of community organizing on school reform, the LSNA goes beyond theorizing and actually establishes a system of accountability based on performance indicators. The specific indicators chosen typify a collaborative approach to decision making with tenets such as leadership development, community power, and public accountability. The theory of change model employed by the LSNA, establishes the neighborhood school as a resource center that operates based on the needs of the community and follows principles set forth by its very own members. The reciprocity that occurs between the school's culture and the neighborhood's successfully addresses concerns that are of vital importance (Blanc, Brown, Torre, & Brown, 2002).

Bob Moses' Algebra Project is another example of effective, grassroots mobilization designed to promote and highlight the aptitude of minority students in urban areas and the expertise of the teachers that work with them. From a political angle, this type of conscious action toward change from the masses reflects the type of powerful results that can be obtained when marginalized groups are given the opportunity to become autonomous and mobilize toward emancipation (Moses, 2007).

These real-life examples of effective, empowering alternatives to traditional research and methodologies lead to questioning why research on other successful urban-based initiatives is so limited when compared to the extensive database promoting a deficits-based approach. The complexity of conducting research in urban settings does not originate from the socioeconomic constructs traditionally associated with such settings, but rather from researchers' limited perspective on educational problems and the contextual variables which contribute to these problems.

Researchers in urban settings must make a conscious and mobilized effort to decrease the number of studies that exclusively expose the results of the sociopolitical hegemony affecting urban youth and institutions without offering viable action-based solutions to underachievement due to doctrinal disenfranchisement, school attrition, over and disproportionate representation in special education programs. Urban researchers must denounce the policies, social institutions, and political agendas that precipitate these factors (Nygreen, 2006).

In order to honor the proposed call toward a practical, active, and solutions-based approach, research in urban settings must effectively point toward the root of the problem; which is not the community, the children, or the schools; but the political constructs affecting them. Accepting this contention implies that education is a political process and any associated change in its practice becomes a political challenge (Apple, 1990; Giroux, 1983; Kretovics & Nussel, 1994; Nygreen, 2006), as such activism must be the key toward mobilization and change.

DOMINANT PARADIGMS IN SPECIAL EDUCATION RESEARCH

By far, the majority of educational research which critically examines issues of race, ethnicity, language, class, and gender has been conducted and published outside the realms of special education. (McCray & Garcia, 2002, p. 604)

Historically, special education research has sought to script problems related to student learning, teacher preparation, and family and community partnerships devoid of the inclusion of the perspectives of individuals from ethnically diverse backgrounds and those with disabilities (McCray & Garcia, 2002; Patton, 1998). This limited understanding of such complex issues has contributed to the lack of effort and resources devoted to concepts such as voice and agency. Skrtic, Sailor, and Gee (1996) noted that the rise of constructivism called into question the legitimacy of practices historically utilized in remedial and special education, and there is a need to promote scholarship which embraces voice, collaboration, and inclusion in structural, institutional, and social-constructivist reform movements. The voices of individuals from ethnically diverse backgrounds and those living in poverty provide the field with the much needed context essential in challenging a long-standing paradigm in special education which promotes deficit-thinking and reductionism. Consequently, mainstream special education research has not resulted in the advancement of an activist agenda which facilitates the mobilization of urban families and communities in advocating for necessary resources and supports.

Discourse on the pervasive and persistent problem of disproportionate representation has primarily addressed placement concerns and student outcomes (Artiles & Trent, 1994; Harry & Anderson, 1994). It is clear that the manner in which ethnically diverse students are identified as "at risk" for special education is problematic and referral and placement processes are central to eliminating this pervasive problem. Yet, future research will need to attend to what Patton (1998) termed as the scriptwriting which represents the knowledge production in special education to explicate variables such as race, culture, and class and the extent to which these contextual variables influence teaching and learning.

Traditional educational research has historically placed value on highly mechanical, contrived studies that arguably oversimplify the human experience into cause and effect variable relationships. This narrow positivist frame of research contributed to the experiences of the African American students documented in Mercer's (1973) work which offered a counter narrative to the medical deficit-based model of special education which relied upon intelligence testing in making placement decisions. This phenomenon, referred to as the "six hour a day retarded child," resulted in African Americans being labeled as mentally retarded at school and fully competent in their homes and in their communities. Consequently, traditional forms of research, which are the underpinning for much of what takes place in special education raise fundamental, philosophical, epistemological, political and pedagogical questions that challenge the proliferation of non-traditional scholarship and freedom of speech in the academy (Denzin, Lincoln, & Giradina, 2006). The presence of research which shares the voices of families from traditionally marginalized groups and their experiences in a system which theoretically promotes parental participation but in practice sustains barriers leading to limited opportunities for meaningful engagement is a challenging line of discourse but one in need of a broader audience.

It is crucial to acknowledge the influence of past and contemporary sociopolitical movements on educational policy and subsequent paradigm shifts. Engaging in this process not only involves being conscious of the impact politics and society have on education, and celebrating important related victories; but also includes raising awareness to the fact minority children have historically been subjected to politically driven educational paradigm shifts that have not generally been beneficial or supported by research (Conchas & Rodriguez, 2008).

The Civil Rights movement of the 1950s was the catalyst and inspiration for the Disability Rights movement. Focus on the nature and quality of educational practices affecting students with disabilities began in the

1960s during the short years of President John F. Kennedy's administration, and resulted from increased involvement by the federal government in educational policy (Osgood, 2005). Growing interest in special education and consequently the ratification of Public Laws 85–905[1] and 85–926,[2] prompted public awareness and advocacy which echoed the inclusive sentiment of *Brown vs. Topeka Board of Education*, the Education for All Handicapped Children Act of 1975 (renamed the Individual's with Disabilities Act or IDEA in 1990), and promoted general access to a free and appropriate education for students with disabilities.

NCLB has contributed to the schooling experiences of students with disabilities and the extent to which they are included in standardized assessments and ensuring their access to the general education curriculum (Thurlow, 2002; Townsend, 2002; Voltz & Fore, 2006). However, it is important to note that the unintended consequences of stringent requirements associated with NCLB has resulted in a persistent problem of school attrition, which disproportionately impacts students with disabilities (Bost, 2006; Cobb, Sample, Alwell, & Johns, 2006).

Despite the many accomplishments that have resulted from the fight for equality in education, significant hurdles remain in meeting the needs of all students, particularly those from ethnically diverse backgrounds and those living in poverty. Resembling the struggles of other oppressed groups in society and potentially having equally detrimental results (Hehir, 2005; Smith, 2001), the plight of children and youths with disabilities is epitomized by the concept of ableism defined by Hehir (2005) as

> the pervasive system of discrimination and exclusion that oppresses people who have mental, emotional, and physical disabilities.... Deeply rooted beliefs about health, productivity, beauty, and the value of human life, perpetuated by the media, combine to create an environment that is often hostile to those whose physical, mental, cognitive and sensory abilities ... fall out of the scope of what is currently defined as socially acceptable. (Rauscher & McClintock, 1996, as cited by Hehir, 2005, p. 15)

Urban schools and communities play a critical role in the process of creating a more inclusive paradigm in education. It is only through quality educational programming, which places students and their families at the center of teaching and learning, that urban students with disabilities will reap the benefits inherent in the promises of special education, rather than experience continued failure in a system which since its inception has contributed to limited opportunities for access to the general education curriculum and the least qualified teachers. A comprehensive urban special education research agenda embraces culturally responsive methodologies by expanding the lens through which persistent problems such as disproportionate representation and the achievement gap are examined and as a result solutions are developed grounded in an understanding of critical contextual variables such as race, culture, and language and the implications of this interlinking on the lives of urban learners with disabilities and their families.

CONDUCTING RESEARCH WITH
URBAN FAMILIES IN SPECIAL EDUCATION

> In reality, however, realization of this vision of collaborative relationships and family-centered continues to remain elusive, particularly for low-income and culturally diverse families. (Kalyanpur, Harry, & Skrtic, 2000, p. 119)

Another important component in a comprehensive urban special education research agenda is the extent to which research is conducted in collaboration with families in examining issues requiring a deeper understanding of the complexities of urban family dynamics and the role of disability in family functioning and family-school collaboration. Historically, there has been an interest in understanding the contributing influences on student performance and the extent to which the interlinking of these variables are manifested in urban schooling (Burton & Jarrett, 2000; Harry, 2002; Harry, Allen, & McLaughlin, 1995). In order to better understand the dynamics of family functioning and the impact of disability on family functioning and processes within the urban context, research must be conducted which reflects diverse epistemologies and methodologies and effectively documents the cultural, political, and social nuances which contribute to the perceived lack of meaningful engagement of many urban families and communities.

Boyd and Correa (2005) conducted a review of literature related to the experiences of African American families with special education and noted that the perceptions of African Americans of special education have been influenced by three interconnected variables: the sociocultural experiences of African Americans in society, biases toward professionals within the educational system, and their level of acculturation. Further, Zionts and colleagues (2003), in their study of African American urban families of children with severe cognitive disabilities, found six major themes which help to explain families' perceptions of cultural sensitivity by school personnel and the extent to which culture is considered when providing resources and supports to students and families from culturally and linguistically diverse (CLD) backgrounds. The major themes include: respect for families by school personnel, perceived negativity directed toward families, need for information and access to resources and supports, quality and training of educators, and improved teacher-student relationships. Although, this study directly targets African American families in urban settings, the sample reflects families that are active in after-school care groups and parent support networks. However, the findings illuminate the need for further exploration of the satisfaction of families with special education in light of federal mandates for parental participation. Correa and McHatton (2005) in a study of Mexican and Puerto Rican single mothers exposed the discrimination experienced as a result of culture, disability and a combination of both. The perceived discrimination resulted in stigmatization and ultimately impacted the extent to which these family members were able to successfully navigate the special education system. The aforementioned data offers insights into how these urban families make sense of schooling and its influence on their child's post-school outcomes. Finally, Harry, Klingner, and Hart (2005) examined the referral and placement processes for African American and Latino students in a large urban school district. Data from this 3-year study included case studies on 12 African American students with varying disabilities. The findings offer counter stories which contradict the prevailing notion of dysfunctionality between Black families and the impact of ill-conceived beliefs of school personnel about Black families.

Kalyanpur et al. (2000) have asserted the need to deconstruct the assumptions embedded in legislation such as the Individuals with Disabilities Education Act (IDEA), which clearly promotes parent participation in the special education process. Yet, what is missing from much of the discourse on parent participation and collaboration is the understanding of the cultural nuances implicit in working with ethnically diverse families. The authors assert that culture influences families understanding of disability and the extent to which they participate in the schooling experiences of their children. Further, the assumption that ethnically diverse families value opportunities for shared decision making and greater participation in their child's education reflects a Eurocentric ideal that may not be shared by ethnically diverse families. This leads one to question the legitimacy of advocating for family and community engagement in special education when the ways in which students and families are introduced to the system are wrought with misdiagnoses, misassumptions, and misunderstandings and processes aimed in developing collaborative partnerships fail to reflect an understanding of the role of culture.

TRANSFORMING URBAN EDUCATION THROUGH CULTURALLY RESPONSIVE TEACHING

Teachers' knowledge about and attitudes toward cultural diversity are powerful determinants of learning opportunities and opportunities for ethnically different students. For some students they facilitate academic achievement; for others they obstruct learning. (Gay, 2002, p. 613)

The current state of special education in urban schools is disturbing in light of increased calls for accountability and shrinking resources and support for schools in challenging settings. Research has documented that in schools where a large concentration of ethnically diverse students exist a majority of these students will be placed in remediation or lower-level tracks and special education classrooms (Losen & Orfield, 2002). The question of efficacy in special education, particularly for students of color, remains an area of concern particularly in urban settings (Dunn, 1968; Gottlieb, Alter, Gottlieb, & Wishner, 1994). More important, an understanding of the social, cultural, and political dynamics of schooling in urban settings coupled with the "natural variation" (p. 381) among students in an unnatural framework of mainstream traditional special education model is critical in redesigning urban schools (Pugach & Seidl, 1995). Additionally, Morse (2001) asserted that there are four reasons which support the need to examine the appropriateness of curriculum for urban students in special education. These variables include: the unique challenges of teaching students from ethnically diverse students and those living in poverty, the curriculum which has traditionally served students in special education is not reflective on the changing demographics of students living in urban settings, mandates by IDEA which address the extent to which students' individual needs are being met in accessing the general education curriculum, and the role of school personnel in curriculum decision making.

The standards-based reform movement which has resulted in increased calls for accountability and high stakes testing has primarily targeted urban schools which are predominately populated by ethnically diverse students and those living in poverty, many of whom are considered at risk for placement in special education (Townsend, 2000). Although the standardization movement has offered significant opportunities such as raising expectations for achievement of urban students with disabilities, encouraging shared ownership in accountability, and visibility of the individual needs of students with disabilities (Voltz & Fore, 2006); the unintended consequences of school reform initiatives such as NCLB are the overreliance on a rigid and narrow curriculum, increased retention rates for ethnically diverse students with disabilities, and special education being perceived by administrators as a quick fix which results in an increase in students referred for special education services (Seidl & Pugach, 1998; Townsend, 2000; Voltz & Fore, 2006). These conditions provide a backdrop for the discussion of the attitudes and beliefs of preservice teachers about working in urban schools with ethnically diverse learners and the impact of these beliefs and attitudes on the current instructional practices utilized by urban teachers.

It is clear that the problem of disproportionate representation must be examined through a sociopolitical lens, which is undergirded with an understanding of disproportionate representation as the perpetuation of the arrangement of power and privilege in America's schools. This arrangement is based on the presumption of power, which grants privileges to some and penalizes others (Day-Vines, 2000). Patton (1998), and other critical theorists support the notion that special education is grounded in structured power relationships designed to serve the interests of the dominant social, political and economic classes. Eradicating the misassumptions, misdiagnoses and miscommunications which lead to ineffective teaching, labeling, and segregated placements for students of color requires one to acknowledge the role of systemic racism, White privilege and a political agenda which continue to blame and punish those in poverty for their circumstance (Blanchett, 2006; Harry et al., 2005). In a country where the student population grows more culturally and ethnically diverse each year (National Center for Educational Statistics, 2000) and conversely a teaching population continues to reflect the dominant culture more so than the cultures of the students they serve (Terrill & Mark, 2000); responding to the needs of all learners and building relationships with students and their families is essential to countering a system which has historically failed to produce equitable outcomes for all students.

Culturally responsive teaching represents a belief in placing students' culture at the center of teaching and learning rather than placing students and their families at the center of educational problems such as low student performance and an increasing high school dropout rate. The roots of culturally responsive teaching lie in constructivism and multicultural education. Gay (2000) defines culturally responsive teaching as "using the cultural knowledge, prior experiences, frames of reference, and performance styles of ethnically diverse students to make learning encounters more relevant to and effective for them" (p. 29). Elements of culturally responsive teaching include: communicating high expectations, using active teaching methods, facilitating learning, fostering positive perspectives of students and families, demonstrating cultural sensitivity, reshaping the curriculum, promoting student-controlled classroom discourse, and encouraging small-group instruction and cooperative learning (Shealey & Callins, 2007). Irvine and Armento (2001) reported that the term "culturally responsive teaching" can be used interchangeably with other terms such as culturally responsible, appropriate, congruent, compatible, relevant and multicultural. These terms all imply teachers are recognizing and valuing the cultural contributions of their students and use this knowledge to inform their practices and employment of instructional strategies.

Critical components guiding the development of culturally responsive teaching are as follows: understanding of culture as a powerful tool which influences teaching and learning, effective teaching research and its compatibility with culturally responsive pedagogy, teacher knowledge and reflection as important considerations, and high standards and expectations for students of color (Irvine & Armento, 2001). In further elaboration of how the evolution of multicultural education has supported the use of culturally responsive teaching, researchers have explored the extent to which culture impacts student learning. Many have noted that for students of color, culture represents their way of life (Ogbu, 1988; Utley & Obiakor, 2001). People interact with the dominant society and as a result become aware of different ways of acting, different expectations and thus may change their way of thinking individually or collectively (Shade, Kelly, & Oberg, 1997). With that in mind, there is a discontinuity between the cultural values, norms and beliefs of students of color and the culture of schools. This discontinuity or incongruence has led many to believe cultural differences are major contributors to the school failure of students of color (Irvine, 1990).

The compatibility of effective teaching research and culturally responsive teaching is another critical element guiding the development and implementation of culturally responsive teaching in America's public schools and colleges. Cruickshank (1990) proposed that effective teachers are identified by: their character traits, what they know, what they teach, how they teach, what they expect from their students, how their students react to them, and how they manage the classroom. Furthermore, Ladson-Billings (1994) made the distinction between excellent teaching and excellent teachers in her depiction of culturally relevant teachers and reports that culturally relevant teachers acknowledge and value culture as means to empower students and help them achieve excellence. Additionally, Gay (2000) posited that teaching is contextual and situational and thus effective teaching must take into account ecological factors and they are included in instruction. Teacher reflection and knowledge are critical considerations in culturally responsive teaching. Culturally responsive teachers use their knowledge of effective teaching to inform and guide their practice (Irvine & Armento, 2001). Ladson-Billings (2001) asserted many teachers due to increased demands fail to participate in reflective practice and this is often viewed as a luxury. Nonetheless, reflective teaching should be emphasized as teacher development is an ongoing process of experiencing practical teaching and learning situations and developing ones own insights into teaching through the interaction between personal reflection and theoretical notions offered by the expert (Korthagen & Kessels, 1999).

The final critical component of culturally responsive teaching includes holding high standards and expectations for students of color. The elements of culturally responsive teaching are also compatible with the standards and performance indicators proposed by organizations such as the Council for Exceptional Children (CEC), the National Board for Professional Teaching Standards (NBPTS) and the Interstate New Teacher Assessment and Support Consortium (INTASC), which all explicitly acknowledge the importance of teachers working effectively with diverse learners as well as Effective Schools research. Many researchers have acknowledged the relationship between teachers' expectations and student performance (Gill & Reynolds, 1999; Good & Brophy, 1994; Terrill & Mark, 2000). According to Good (2001) "teacher expectations may affect perception by causing some teachers to see what they expect and less likely to notice the unexpected" (p. 2). Researchers have further noted the role of teacher expectations in the disproportionate representation of learners from culturally and linguistically diverse backgrounds in special education programs and the ability of students to reach their maximum potential (Daniels, 2001; Obiakor & Algozzine, 1993). Yet, Nieto (2000) believes the term "teacher expectations" should be downplayed due to the overwhelming responsibility of holding teachers solely accountable for student achievement. Nieto further asserted that the focus on teacher expectations distances schools and society for taking on responsibility in student underachievement. Gay (2002) proposes that prior to implementing culturally responsive teaching, it is critical to address obstacles related to negative teachers' attitudes and expectations of students of color as well as the lack of understanding the dichotomy of diversity and disability. Here there needs a transition sentence to the next thought.

Currently, the empirical evidence available on the effectiveness of special education for ethnically diverse learners remains inconclusive (Artiles & Trent, 1994). What is known about the issue of disproportionate representation in special education is that students enter schools with what Bourdieu and Passeron (1977) refer to as cultural capital or funds of knowledge, a term coined by Moll and Greenberg (1990). Yet, this type of knowledge is not recognized or built upon by educators and thus may lead to ineffective teaching and inappropriate labeling and placement in special education programs (Meyer & Patton, 2001). The inclusion of culturally responsive teaching in teacher preparation programs for general and special educators may provide far-reaching implications in addressing a number of issues related to diversity and disability (Utley & Obiakor, 2001).

As suggested earlier, perhaps the greatest challenge to an urban special education research agenda is acknowledging the ways in which traditional and deficit-based research have framed the experiences of poor and ethnically diverse students in special education and rescripting persistent problems such as disproportionate representation. Additionally, it is critical to address the proliferation of Master Scripting, which refers to the official school curriculum and the subsequent instructional practices which accompany the curriculum; both of which reflect the knowledge valued by the dominant culture (Blanchett, 2006; Swartz, 1992, 2003).

The work of Boykin and Cunningham (2001) highlights the extent to which the use of cultural knowledge directly impacts student engagement and consequently performance. In a study of the effects of the use of cultural factors in lesson presentation and content of task materials on performance, African American elementary-aged students demonstrated that in the area of reading they performed better in situations that utilized high movement expression. High movement expression is characterized as the use of music and movement in the presentation of reading text. Although as previously noted, urban settings are characteristically unique and diverse in that there are schools which promote student engagement and higher-level thinking skills while others rely upon a curriculum which emphasizes rote learning and mastery of basic tasks. Traditionally, special education classrooms in urban settings are underresourced and understaffed which contribute to the proliferation of ineffective teaching practices and limited opportunities to cultivate the talents of urban students with disabilities.

A study investigating methods to increase the participation of ethnically diverse students in programs for the gifted and talented across the nation revealed the importance of selecting curriculum and instructional design. Seven programs for the gifted and talented were selected for in-depth study. In these programs a continuum of services was evident and incorporated into instructional methods which included: "individualized instruction, use of advanced content, training in research skills, development of creative and critical thinking skills, differentiation, questioning strategies, project/interest based activities, hands-on experiences, problem solving, and enrichment opportunities" (Briggs, Reis, & Sullivan, 2008, p. 138). Additionally, curriculum decisions were made taking into consideration the unique needs of ethnically diverse students which included helping students making connections between curriculum, program components, and students' language and culture. Findings from this investigation of promising programs aimed at attracting gifted and talented students from ethnically diverse backgrounds suggest that successful programs recognize the significance of disproportionate representation, increased awareness of the role of culture in student performance, and established support staff and educators who were prepared to make substantive changes.

CONCLUSIONS

A potential paradigm shift in special education research includes understanding and evaluating the results of past and current research which has framed an understanding of students from ethnically diverse backgrounds and students in poverty within a narrow and mainstream lens which fails to reconceptualize the needs of all learners and meet those needs in a comprehensive manner. While undoubtedly great contributions to the field of education have been made possible through research, it is still imperative to elicit action and change in research and program development. The current and future emphasis of studies should shift from the evaluation of institutions, programs, and pedagogy and focus on examining the sociopolitical constructs from which these operate.

Education is not linear, but rather a reciprocal process or relationship where the students and teachers make sense of their environment from within the framework of their own sociocultural capital. With this in mind, the relationship between education, power, and politics must be scrutinized by researchers committed to social justice and equity. The foundation for meaningful and collaborative interactions and the development of reciprocal relationships with urban communities rests in the ability of urban special education researchers to challenge dominant paradigms in special education research and contribute to a growing community of scholars transforming the educational experiences of students with disabilities in urban settings.

NOTES

1. PL 85-905 authorized loan services for captioned films for the deaf.
2. PL 85-976 provided Federal support for training teachers to for children with Mental Retardation.

REFERENCES

Artiles, A. J., Harry, B., Reschly, D. J., & Chinn, P. C. (2002). Over-identification of students of color in special education: A critical overview. *Multicultural Perspectives, 4*(1), 3–10.

Artiles, A. J., & Trent, S.C. (1994). Overrepresentation of minority students in special education: A continuing debate. *The Journal of Special Education, 27*(4), 410–437.

Anyon, J. (1997). *Ghetto schooling*. New York: Teachers College Press.

Apple, M. (1990). *Ideology and curriculum*. New York: Routledge.

Blanc, S., Brown, J., Torre, A. N., & Brown, C. (2002). *Case study LSNA: The Logan Square Neighborhood Association: The Indicators Project on Education Organizing*. Retrieved October 7, 2007 from: (Park, Miller, Mary, Budd & Jackson) http://pdf.researchforaction.org/rfapdf/publication/pdf_file/16/Blanc_S_Strong_Neighborhoods_Strong_Schools_LSNA.pdf

Blanchett, W. J. (2006). Disproportionate representation of African American students in special education: Acknowledging the role of White privilege and racism. *Educational Researcher, 35*(6), 24–28.

Blanchett, W. J., Mumford, V., & Beachum, F. (2005). Urban school failure and disproportionality in a post-Brown era. *Remedial and Special Education, 26*, 70–81.

Bost, L. W. (2006, July). *Effective interventions in dropout prevention for students with disabilities: Putting the evidence into practice*. Paper presented at the Critical Issues in Urban Education Harvard Summer Institute, Boston, MA.

Bourdieu, P., & Passeron, J. (1977). *Reproduction in education, society, and culture*. London: SAGE.

Boyd, B. A., & Correa, V. I. (2005). Developing a framework for reducing the cultural clash between African American parents and the special education system. *Multicultural Perspectives, 7*(2), 3–11.

Boykin, A. W., & Cunningham, R. T. (2001). The effects of movement expressiveness in story content and learning context on the analogical reasoning performance of African American children. *The Journal of Negro Education, 79*(1/2), 72–83.

Brantlinger, E., Jimenez, R., Klingner, J., Pugach, M., & Richardson, V. (2005). Qualitative studies in special education. *Exceptional Children, 71*(2), 195–207.

Briggs, C. J., Reis, S. M., & Sullivan, E. E. (2008). A national view of promising programs and practices for culturally, linguistically, and ethnically diverse gifted and talented students. *Gifted Child Quarterly, 52*(2), 131–145.

Burton, L. M., & Jarrett, R. L. (2000). In the mix, yet on the margins: The place of families in urban neighborhood and child development research. *Journal of Marriage and the Family, 62*, 1114–1135.

Cobb, B., Sample, P. L., Alwell, M., & Johns, N. R. (2006). Cognitive-behavioral interventions, dropout, and youth with disabilities. *Remedial and Special Education, 27*(5), 259–275.

Conchas, G. Q., & Rodriguez, L. F. (2008). *Small schools and urban youth: Using the power of school culture to engage students*. Thousand Oakes, CA: Corwing Press.

Correa, V., & McHatton, P. (2005). Stigma and discrimination: Perspectives from Mexican and Puerto Rican mothers of children with special needs. *Topics in Early Childhood Special Education, 25*(3), 131–142.

Cross City Campaign for Urban Schools Reform. (2002). *Logan Square Neighborhood Association*. Retrieved 7 October 2007 from: the Research for Action website http://www.lsna.net/content/2/documents/LSNAindicatorsstudy.pdf

Cruickshank, D. (1990). *Research that informs teachers and teacher educators*. Bloomington, IN: Phi Delta Kappa Educational Foundation.

Darling-Hammond, L. (2001). Inequality and access to knowledge. In J. A. Banks, & Banks-McGee (Eds.), *Handbook of research on multicultural education* (pp. 465–483). San Francisco: Jossey-Bass.

Daniels, V. I. (2001). Responding to the learning needs of multicultural learners with gifts and talents. In C. A. Utley & F. E. Obiakor (Eds.), *Special education, multicultural education, and school reform* (pp. 140–154). Springfield, IL: Charles C Thomas.

Day-Vines, N. L. (2000). Ethics, power, and privilege: Salient issues in the development of multicultural competencies for teachers serving African American children with disabilities. *Teacher Education and Special Education, 23*(1), 3–18.

Denzin, N. K., Lincoln, Y. S., & Giardina, M. D. (2006). Disciplining qualitative research. *International Journal of Qualitative Studies in Education, 19*(6), 769–782.

Dunn, L. M. (1968). Special education for the mentally retarded-Is much of it justifiable? *Exceptional Children, 35*, 5–22.

Ford, D. Y., & Harmon, D. A. (2001). Equity and excellence: Providing access to gifted education for culturally diverse students. *Journal of Secondary Gifted Education, 12*, 141–147.

Gay, G. (2000). *Culturally responsive teaching: Theory, research, and practice*. New York: Teachers College Press.

Gay, G. (2002). Culturally responsive teaching in special education for ethnically diverse students: setting the stage. *Qualitative Studies in Education, 15*(6), 613–629.

Gill, S., & Reynolds, A. J. (1999). Educational expectations and school achievement of urban African American children. *Journal of School Psychology, 37*(4), 403–424.

Giroux, H. (1983). *Theory and resistance in education: A pedagogy for the opposition south hadley*. MA: Bergin & Garvey.

Good, T. L. (2001). Expectancy effects in the classroom: A special focus on improving the reading performance of minority students in first-grade classrooms. *Educational Psychologist, 36*(3), 113–127.

Good, T. L., & Brophy, J. E. (1994). *Looking in classrooms*. New York: HarperCollins College.

Gordon, E. W. (2003). Urban education. *Teachers College Press, 105*(2), 189–207.

Gottlieb, J., Alter, M., Gottlieb, B. W., & Wishner, J. (1994). Special education in urban America: It's not justifiable for many. *The Journal of Special Education, 27*(4), 453–465.

Harry, B. (1994). *The disproportionate representation of minority students in special education: Theories and recommendations*. Alexandria, VA: National Association of State Directors of Special Education. (ERIC Document Reproduction Service No. ED374637).

Harry, B. (2002). Trends and issues in serving culturally diverse families of children with disabilities. *Journal of Special Education, 36*(3), 131–138.

Harry, B., & Anderson, M. G. (1994). The disproportionate placement of African American males in special education programs: A critique of the process. *The Journal of Negro Education, 63*, 602–619.

Harry, B., Allen, N., & McLaughlin, M. (1995). Communication versus compliance: African American parents' involvement in special education. *Exceptional Children, 61*(4), 364–378.

Harry, B., Klingner, J., & Hart, J. (2005). African American families under fire. *Remedial and Special Education, 26*(2), 101–112.

Hehir, T. (2005). *New directions in special education: Eliminating ableism in policy and practice.* Cambridge: MA: Harvard Education Press.

Heubert, J. P. (2002). Disability, race, and high stakes testing. In D. J. Losen & G. Orfield (Eds.), *Racial inequality in special education* (pp. 137–166). Cambridge, MA: Harvard Education Press.

Hilliard, A. G. (1998). *SBA: The reawakening of the African mind.* Gainesville, FL: Makare.

Irvine, J. J. (1990). *Black students and school failure: Policies, practices, and prescriptions.* Westport, CT: Greenwood.

Irvine, J. J., & Armento, B.J. (2001). *Culturally responsive teaching: Lesson planning for elementary and middle grades.* New York: McGraw-Hill.

Kalyanpur, M., Harry, B., & Skrtic, T. (2000). Equity and advocacy expectations of culturally diverse families' participation in special education. *International Journal of Disability, Development and Education, 47*(2), 119–136.

Korthagen, F. A. J., & Kessels, J. P. A. M. (1999). Linking theory and practice: Changing the pedagogy of teacher education. *Educational Researcher, 28*(4), 4–17.

Kretovics, J., & Nussel, E. J. (1994). Introduction: School reform and transforming urban education. In *Transforming urban education.* Boston: Allyn and Bacon.

Ladson-Billings, G. (1994). *Dreamkeepers: Successful teachers of African American children.* San Francisco: Jossey-Bass.

Losen, D. J., & Orfield, G. (Eds.). (2002). *Racial inequity in special education.* Cambridge, MA: Harvard Education Press.

McCray, A. D., & Garcia, S. B. (2002). The stories we must tell: Developing a research agenda for multicultural and bilingual special education. *Qualitative Studies in Education, 15*(6), 599–612.

McIntyre, A. (2006). Activist research and student agency in universities and urban communities. *Urban Education, 41*(6), 628–647.

Mercer, J. R. (1973). *Labeling the mentally retarded.* Berkeley: University of California Press.

Meyer, G., & Patton, J. M. (2001). *The nexus of race, disability, and overrepresentation: What do we know? Where do we go?* Denver, CO: National Institute for Urban School Improvement.

Moll, L. C., & Greenberg, J. (1990). Creating zones of possibilities: Combining social contexts for instruction. In L. C. Moll (Ed.), *Vygotsky and education* (pp. 319–348). Cambridge: Cambridge University Press.

Morse, T. E. (2001). Designing appropriate curriculum for special education students in urban schools. *Education and Urban Society, 34*(1), 417.

Moses, B. (2007). *The Algebra Project: Math Literacy is the Key to 21st Century Citizenship.* Retrieved 7 October 2007, from the Algebra Project website: http://thealgebraproject.org

National Center for Educational Statistics. (2000). *Digest of Educational Statistics.* Washington, DC: Government Printing Office.

National Research Council. (2002). *Minority Students in Special and Gifted Education.* Committee on Minority Representation in Special Education. M. Suzanne

Donovan & Christopher T. Cross (Eds.), Division of Behavioral and Social Sciences and Education. Washington, DC: National Academy Press.

Nieto, S. (2000). *Affirming diversity: The sociopolitical context of multicultural education* (3rd ed.). New York: Longman.

Nygreen, K. (2006). Reproducing or challenging power in the questions we ask and the methods we use: A framework for activist research in urban education. *The Urban Review, 38*(1), 1–26.

Obiakor, F. E., & Algozzine, B. (1993). Urban education, the general education initiative, and service delivery to African American students. *Urban Education, 28*(3), 313–328.

Ogbu, J. U. (1988). Diversity and equity in public education: Community forces and minority school adjustment and performance. In R. Haskins & D. Macrae (Eds.), *Policies for America's public schools: Teachers, equity, and indicators*. Norwood, NJ: Ablex.

Osgood, R. L. (2005). *The history of inclusion in the United States*. Washington, DC: Gallaudet University Press.

Patton, J. M. (1998). The disproportionate representation of African Americans in special education. *The Journal of Special Education, 32*(1), 25–31.

Pugach, M. C. (2001). The stories we choose to tell: Fulfilling the promise of qualitative research for special education. *Exceptional Children, 67*(4), 439–453.

Pugach, M. C., & Seidl, B. L. (1995). From exclusion to inclusion in urban schools: A new case for teacher education reform. *Education & Urban Society, 27*(4), 379–396.

Rauscher, L., & McClintock, J. (1996). Ableism and curriculum design. In M. Adams, L. A. Bell, & P. Griffen (Eds.), *Teaching for diversity and social justice* (pp. 198–231). New York: Routledge.

Seild, B. L., & Pugach, M. C., (1998). Associate editors exchange responsible linkages between diversity and disability: A challenge for special education. *Teacher Education and Special Education, 21*(4), 319–333.

Shade, B. J., Kelly, C., & Oberg, M. (1997). *Creating culturally responsive classrooms*. Washington, DC: American Psychological Association.

Shealey, M. W. (2006). The promises and perils of scientifically-based research for urban schools. *Urban Education, 41*(1), 5–19.

Shealey, M. W., & Callins, T. (2007). Creating culturally responsive literacy programs in inclusive classrooms. *Intervention in School and Clinic, 42*(4), 195–197.

Smith, G. (2001, July 20). Backtalk: The brother in the wheelchair. *Essense*, p. 162.

krtic, T. M., Sailor, W., & Gee, K. (1996). Voice, collaboration, and inclusion: Democratic themes in educational and social reform initiatives. *Remedial and Special Education, 17*, 142–157.

Swartz, E. (2003). Teaching White preservice teachers: Pedagogy for change. *Urban Education, 38*(3), 255–278.

Swartz, E. (1992). Emancipatory narratives: Rewriting the master script in the school curriculum. *Journal of Negro Education*, 341–355.

Terrill, M., & Mark, D. (2000). Preservice teachers' expectations for schools with children of color and second language learners. *Journal of Teacher Education, 51*, 149–155.

Thurlow, M. L. (2002). Positive educational results for all students: The promise of standards-based reform. *Remedial and Special Education, 23*, 195–202.

Townsend, B. L. (2002). Testing while Black: Standards-based school reform and African American learners. *Remedial and Special Education, 23*(4), 222–230.

Townsend, B. L. (2000). The disproportionate discipline of African American learners: Reducing school suspensions and expulsions. *Exceptional Children, 66*(3), 381–392.

University of KMT Press. (2007). *Dr. Asa Hilliard: A tribute.* Retrieved October 7, 2007, from http://www.ukmtpress.com/id31.html

Utley, C. A., & Obiakor, F. E. (2001). *Special Education, multicultural education, and school reform: Components for quality education for learners with mild disabilities.* Chicago: Charles C. Thomas.

Voltz, D. L., & Fore, C. (2006). Urban special education in the context of standards-based reform. *Remedial and Special Education, 27*(6), 329–336.

Zionts, L. T., Zionts, P., Harrison, S., & Bellinger, O. (2003). Urban African American families perceptions of cultural sensitivity within the special education system. *Focus on Autism and Other Developmental Disabilities, 18*(1), 41–50.

PART III

NEGOTIATIONS AND COLLABORATIONS

CHAPTER 8

SERVICE AND SCHOLARSHIP

How Opportunities to "Give Back" Foster Culturally Responsive and Respectful Research Projects

Raquel Farmer-Hinton

INTRODUCTION

A deficit discourse about race and intelligence, race and academic achievement, and race and social mobility has plagued academic scholarship for many years (Milner, 2007; Solorzano & Yosso, 2001). This misplaced *blaming of the victim* has fixated the academy and ultimately prevented the academy from providing informed analyses to help resolve inequities in the U.S. (Ladson-Billings, 2006). The greatest challenge is that there is a lack of culturally sensitive research that situates cultural knowledge as the core of the research investigation and analyses (Tillman, 2002). As a result, scholars such as critical race theorists are calling for researchers to become more culturally aware in order to "advance the research literature in ways that validate and give voice to people who have

Research in Urban Educational Settings: Lessons Learned and Implications for Future Practice, pp. 145–162

often been silenced, misinterpreted, misrepresented, and placed on the margins" (Milner, 2007, p. 397). In this chapter, I am suggesting that scholar service is a potential avenue in which scholars gain greater cultural knowledge of school communities of color. Service, as a form of experiential learning, can lead to greater cultural knowledge and understanding of school communities of color, particularly if that service experience is coupled with immersion in the appropriate literatures on race, culture, and structural inequality. In the pages that follow, I will first share why scholar service is one way to provide restitution for the misplaced blaming of the victim and the ensuing lack of informed analyses. Then, through my own service experiences, I will also share how an added benefit of service provision is greater cultural knowledge that can be utilized in research investigations. Last, I will discuss the challenges of this service-scholarship approach through reflections on a case study that I conducted as a result of my service experiences.

SERVICE AND PAYING DOWN THE EDUCATION DEBT

Academic appointments are often based on a combination of research, teaching, and service responsibilities with research and teaching using most of the allocation of time. Ward (2003) discusses the distribution of service activities to include both internal service and external service with scholars engaging more in internal service due to its alignment with their respective campus roles and positions. External service, however, receives less faculty attention and is rewarded less within the academy. Thus, scholars such as Boyer (1990) have tried to legitimize external service by extending the conceptualization of *traditional* scholarship in order to include the "scholarship of application," which refers to the ability of scholars to apply their knowledge bases in order to serve the needs of local communities. Yet, our attention to service is not just important because civic engagement is a positive attribute of individual scholars and the university community, it is also important because the academy owes its time for its role in perpetuating the "education debt."

In 2006, at the annual meeting of the American Educational Research Association, Gloria Ladson-Billings delivered her presidential address, which was entitled "From the Achievement Gap to the Education Debt: Understanding Achievement in U.S. Schools." In that presidential address, Ladson-Billings critiqued our conceptualization of the "achievement gap" as well as the use of the phrase in dictating educational policies and practice. She used the national debt as a metaphor to help the audience of practitioners, scholars, and policymakers to reevaluate what is currently referred to as the achievement gap to a more comprehensive and accurate phrase called the education debt. She suggested that the education debt more accurately captures the reality that current achievement disparities between students of color and low-income students compared to their White and more affluent counterparts are the result of the generational divestment of equal schooling opportunities, equal school funding, social justice, and social responsibility from communities of color and low-income communities. Ladson-Billings charged her audience to address the debt because continual refusal to acknowledge the debt in our practice, research, and policymaking activities will only lead to further misguided attempts to address the achievement disparities faced by communities of color and low income communities.

However, her implications for the academy were more comprehensive than just a critique of current practice, research, and policy analyses. First of all, Ladson-Billings implied that knowing and understanding the education debt means that the academy has to recognize its role in sustaining the education debt. She reviewed various educational studies and literatures which placed the blame for the achievement gap on students, students' home environments, and students' cultures. She also critiqued literatures for misplaced attention on the so-called "gap" because that misdirected focus has only led to "short-term solutions that [were] unlikely to address the long-term underlying problem" (Ladson-Billings, 2006, p. 4). As a result of the misplaced blame and attention by the academy, teachers, administrators, and school communities are faced daily with the "magnitude of the education debt" (p. 9). Since scholars have not provided the kinds of resources and tools that schools have needed, teaching and administrative roles in schools are preoccupied with "debt service," which Ladson-Billings (2006) said are what "teachers and administrators pay each year against what they might rightfully invest in helping students advance academically" (p. 9). Moving forward, if we understand the academy's role in perpetuating the education debt, then surely scholar service is an appropriate way to pay down what the academy owes toward the debt service occurring in school communities.

Second, Ladson-Billings implied that knowing and understanding the education debt should impact our research methodologies. She suggested that attention to the cumulative nature of the education debt is missing from our research investigations. She pushed us to "move beyond the documentation of the inequalities and inadequacies" and to investigate the cumulative effects of what it means to have had a generational divestment from equal schooling opportunities, equal school funding, social justice, and social responsibility (Ladson-Billings, 2006, p. 9). She used the example of school funding. She implied that school funding inequities are not just harmful because in one particular school year students in predominantly poor or minority school districts received disparate funding as compared to their more affluent and predominantly White counterparts. School funding inequities are also harmful because that one school year of disparate funding represents at least 1 year out of 12 in which students' teachers and their schools' instructional resources and infrastructures were not operating on an optimal level. This issue of cumulative effects is reminiscent of Kozol's (1991) *Savage Inequalities* in which he quoted a principal saying, in each successive school year, "there's one more toilet that doesn't flush, one more drinking fountain that doesn't work, one more classroom without texts" (p. 37). Moving forward, if we are to give issues related to the education debt "full and sustained hypothesis testing" (Ladson-Billings, 2006, p. 9), we have to reacquaint ourselves with schools using the lens of the education debt. Since we have virtually ignored the education debt in the academy, we need to learn and fully understand what the debt service faced by teachers and administrators feels like, how it operates, and what it means in terms of student learning. Scholar service is an appropriate way to get involved with schools so that we cannot only pay our share of the debt, but we can also be in a position to experientially learn about debt service so that our research is more informed and applicable toward improving schooling opportunities for low income students and students of color.

In consideration of what the academy owes toward the education debt, service-learning programs provide a unique framework from which to launch scholar service toward *paying down the debt*. Service learning programs have existed in various formats since the late 1800s (Titlebaum, Williamson, Daprano, Baer, & Brahler, 2004). More recently, service learning programs have become a resource for universities interested in greater community outreach (Chibucos & Lerner, 1999; Kellogg Commission on the Future of State and Land Grant Universities, 1999). This current interest in community outreach is born out of an effort of restitution since the academy has drifted from its *traditional aim* of community service (Boyer, 1996). In practice, service learning is generally conceived as a program where students engage in community service activities and are allotted structured time with which to reflect on their role in the service activity. This dual process of learning and volunteering is intended to enrich participants' civic engagement and participants' ability to learn from the volunteer experience (National Service-Learning Clearinghouse, n.d.). Service learning programs are also intended to affect the organization or community for which the service is being provided because students who are engaged in service learning activities should use the knowledge or skills gained in order to inform or foster change within that community or organization (Eyler, Giles, Stenson, & Gray, 2001).

Yet, beyond the rewards gained such as civically engaged students and faculty or greater university outreach (see Boyer, 1996; Fiske, 2001; Ward,

2003), service learning can lead to greater cultural knowledge and understanding (see Eyler et al., 2001) and the reduction of stereotypes (see Astin & Sax, 1998). [In this book, Eustace G. Thompson argues that greater cultural knowledge and understanding is needed because stereotypes can permeate teaching and learning in the academy.] Curran (1999), for example, compared the perceptions of students enrolled in a service-learning course section and those students not enrolled. The students enrolled in a service-learning course section, where they worked within a community of adults with physical and mental disabilities, were more likely to respond favorably to survey items on the empowerment of those adults than the students who were not enrolled in the service-learning course section. However, service-learning does not always lead to reduced stereotypes and greater cultural awareness. In fact, just the opposite can occur. Grady (1998) found that the stereotypes and cultural deficit views of poor and minority families were reinforced among pre-service teachers enrolled in a service-learning course. The author suggested that the race and socioeconomic backgrounds of the service-learning participants fostered notions of privilege and power, leading the participants to stereotype the families they met during their service activity. Thus, it is important, as Butin (2006) argues, that service-learning evolves from "charity-based perspectives to justice-oriented ones" (p. 486). An example includes service-learning aligned with diversity education that focuses on critical multiculturalism, antiracist education, structural and historical inequality, and cultural identity (Adams, Ajirotutu, & Jay, 2007). Adams and colleagues (2007) found that the combination of service-learning and diversity education led to service-learning participants' increased community awareness, their understanding of diverse cultures, and their articulation of how power and privilege operate in the United States.

In applying service learning to scholar service, there are important caveats to consider in the practical application of scholar service. First, scholar service, like service learning, provides two important outcomes—it provides assistance for the community in which the service experience is implemented and it improves the person providing the service. However, Butin (2007) argues that the traditional approach to service-learning will ultimately not achieve either outcome with any depth. He suggests that service learning is not always transformative of either the person or the community in receipt of said service because the approach to the service activity is beset with privileged orientations. These privileged orientations are the result of people's "authorized institutional role" as university members and/or their perception that the completion of the outreach activity is more important than the actual process of engaging with the community (p. 3). This critique is particularly valuable toward the application of scholar service since scholars also operate in the university context, which has traditionally fostered elitism and hierarchical privileges. Therefore, it is essential with scholar service, as it is with service learning, that service providers are immersed in the appropriate literatures on critical multiculturalism, power and privilege, and structural and historical inequality. Immersion in these kinds of literatures improves cultural awareness and knowledge as well as the critical thinking skills to question unequal power arrangements during service activities (Adams et al., 2007; Astin & Sax, 1998; Curran, 1999; Eyler et al., 2001). Further, immersion in these kinds of literatures is what Tillman (2002) and Milner (2007) suggest as prerequisites for scholars who want to engage with school communities of color and who want to be culturally respectful and responsive.

Another important caveat to consider is the marginalization of service and outreach within the university community. While there have been some modest improvements in the academy's perception of the importance of service and outreach (see Chibucos & Lerner, 1999; Kellogg Commission on the Future of State and Land Grant Universities, 1999), there are several challenges to the institutional valuation of service as comparable to research and teaching (Berberet, 1999; Butin, 2006; Ward, 2003). Of primary concern is the devaluing of service when it comes to faculty members' annual merit point allocation and tenure promotion activities. Since service has yet to be perceived as a scholarly activity in the same way that research and teaching are perceived, service activities are not rewarded equally and the lack of a comparable reward system does not encourage faculty service and outreach (Ward, 2003). An additional concern exists because the academy has traditionally used "objectivity" to define "legitimate scholarship" (Butin, 2006, p. 488). Thus, service and community engagement can lead to questions of validity and bias in research endeavors rooted in scholar service. While I am suggesting that scholar service places scholars in a position to experientially learn about debt service so that our research is more informed and applicable toward addressing the debt, scholar service is a non-traditional path in the current academic climate, and it is risky to scholar advancement and promotion as well as the acceptance of their scholarship within academic circles.

In this chapter, I am suggesting that scholars engage in service because the academy owes its time for hindering school communities in which people of color and poor people are educated. In the following pages, I will describe how, for scholars, an added benefit to scholar service is greater cultural knowledge and respect of school communities of color and how that cultural knowledge and respect can be used in research investigations. I will share my experiences as a tutoring program organizer and how those experiences led to a research agenda on an important and timely topic for the education debt community—college preparation. College preparation is an important topic with which to be culturally sensitive due to the long association of college preparation with elites, Whites, and males (Cookson & Persell, 1985; Peshkin, 2001; Powell, 1996). Further, since launching a research program through service experiences is risky, I will also discuss the challenges of this non-traditional, service-scholarship approach.

BECOMING CONNECTED THROUGH SERVICE

According to Ladson-Billings (2006), the achievement disparities between students of color and low-income students, and their White and more affluent counterparts, is the result of the generational divestment of equal schooling opportunities, equal school funding, social justice, and social responsibility. Schools have not been successful in addressing achievement disparities because the academy has focused on the achievement gap and provided short-term remedies for school communities. I am proposing that scholar service serves as restitution for what the academy owes toward the education debt occurring in school communities. I am also proposing that scholar service be an avenue for scholars to learn and fully understand what the debt service faced teachers and administrators feel like, how it operates, and what it means for student learning.

Getting started. I organized a tutoring program for a school because one of the members of the school's Board of Directors told me that school administrators were seeking young role-models of color for their students. I sent a few e-mails to my peers and the tutoring program was born. In preparing for the program, I sought out the school administrators to help schedule and organize the program. I also provided the announcements to be read over the intercom so the students knew about the program in advance. After students signed up, and even weekly throughout the program, I called students to encourage their attendance in the tutoring program. Lastly, I recruited and retained the tutoring staff and matched students to tutors based on a combination of academic and occupational interests.

In order for scholars to get involved with school communities, scholars have to submit themselves to the role of being service providers. This submission is important because of the traditional role of scholars as authority figures as well as the lessons learned from service-learning programs in which university members have weighed the completion of the outreach activity higher than the actual process of engaging with the community (Butin, 2007). In practice, this means that forging a service relationship with schools has to be an effort humbly pursued by the scholar. Schools are busy places and staff members are often very active meeting the instructional and non-instructional needs of students. So, scholars will have to actively reinforce their interest in serving, share their professional background, and provide very practical ways in which they are willing to help. However, scholars should note that the school should dictate their utility, and the service activity should not distract school staff from their daily routines. This is an appropriate approach because scholars often believe that their expertise is more extensive than that of the school leaders and teachers.

Experientially learning. I arrived at the school without any knowledge of the local community. Like most scholars, I was a new transplant to the area. Since I had recently finished my doctoral studies, I was keenly aware of how power and privilege operate in the United States and why social justice should be a priority. Also, since I had spent my formative years in what Kozol (2005) calls America's "apartheid" schools, I was familiar with what inequalities looked like and felt like. Similar to where I grew up, the effects of segregation, deindustrialization, commercial and white flight, and racialized housing policies fostered the divestment of the community surrounding the school (see Farmer-Hinton, 2006).

The students' social, economic, and educational backgrounds represented what Ladson-Billings (2006) says are the effects of a generational divestment from equal schooling opportunities and equal school funding. Students talked about being the first in their families to get an opportunity to attend college. They spoke about growing up in a poor neighborhood and attending an elementary school with poor resources. They talked about the teachers that they perceived as effective (and ineffective) and what those characteristics were. They also spoke about an adult in school (or the lack of adults thereof) who mentored them through difficult educational or social periods in their lives. I understood why students perceived adult social support as valuable.

Making connections. After 2 years, student participation dwindled and the tutoring program came to an end. Did the tutoring program have a *measurable* impact on the school community? No. However, I believe that the presence of and students' access to young adults of color who were able to mentor younger students of color about their social mobility and how to cope with racialized boundaries, was, in some way, beneficial for the students who attended the program. I believe it was important to them because of their continued desire to stay in contact with us by attending church, e-mailing us with questions about their college majors and occupational futures, or inviting us to their high school and college graduations. Besides, as Butin (2007) argues, the service activity itself does not have to engender a huge social movement, it only has to lead to the questioning of power and privilege.

Did the service experience change me? Yes. I changed because I realized that much of what I had read or researched in terms of school reform was missing the mark. In the spirit of my experiences, I researched literature on the local social and educational history of the community and wrote a paper called "The Chicago Context: Understanding the Consequences of Urban Processes on School Capacity" (2002). In that paper, I argued that historical and racialized policies and practices have segregated African Americans into divested communities, and the cumulative nature of living in said communities is often at odds with what today's schools can offer toward social mobility because schools have also been divested. Thus, the educational and social support that is warranted by students and their families is not aligned with schools' capacities.

Did the service experience change my research agenda? Yes. When the tutoring program ended, I was looking for an alternate way to stay involved with the school. So, I asked the administrators if I could conduct a case study of their school. I wanted to know more about how the school would impact the postsecondary plans and experiences of its students. This work became important to me because if this school could develop students who were made educationally and socioeconomically vulnerable from historical community and educational divestment into college bound students—then so can other schools. This work also became important to me because college preparation still has elitist connotations, and the cultural knowledge gained from this school community could inform a research community overly focused on test scores and dropout rates, which is arguably another form of deficit discourse (Milner, 2007).

LEARNING FROM DOING

After the tutoring program concluded, I embarked upon a research investigation of the school community. The cultural knowledge gained from my service experiences helped me to dissect the literature on college preparation, particularly the race-specific, structural impediments to the access of college preparation by low-income students of color. The cultural knowledge of the school community gained from my service experiences also helped me design a 4-year, mixed method case study that could capture the school's college preparatory mission, student-staff relations, and college preparatory activities.

Service, cultural knowledge, and extant literature. In deciding to conduct a case study of the school, I started reviewing the literature on college preparation. Relying on my experiences as a tutor while reading the literature on college preparation, I realized that there appeared to be a gap between what I experienced and what the literature said about college preparatory schools and their students [Eustace G. Thompson discusses a similar disconnect in his chapter]. First of all, in the literature college preparatory is still associated with White and affluent students. In the literature, "college prep" schools are feeder institutions for elite colleges and universities (Armstrong, 1990; Cookson & Persell, 1985; Powell, 1996) and the power elite use these schools to reinforce their families' social and economic status (Cookson & Persell, 1985; Graham, 2000; McDonough, 1997; Peshkin, 2001; Powell, 1996). Since traditional college prep schools serve as the archetype for college prep schools and college preparation, the cultural knowledge gained from my service experiences helped me to see why a case study of a college preparatory school for low-income students of color was needed to address a gap in the literature. The cultural knowledge gained from my service experiences also helped me to see why the methodological tools should gauge whether the archetypal college prep model was transformed in order to meet the educational and social needs of diverse students.

Second, the college choice process is still framed as an individualized or familial process. In the literature, the college planning and choice models are primarily based upon White and affluent students, and those models structure college planning and choice as a three-stage process where students' predisposition to college as well as students' searches for college and their eventual college selections are isolated within the family unit (Hossler, Schmidt, & Vesper, 1999; Schneider & Stevenson, 1999). Yet these models provide limited evidence on the extent to which these college planning and choice stages are applicable to students of color. The cultural knowledge gained from my service experience helped me to understand why the individualized and familial approach to college planning are not as applicable for low-income students of color whose college planning appeared to be more interdependent through reliance on school personnel as well as their families for college planning tools and support (see Billingsley, 1992; Ceja, 2000; Freeman, 1997, 1999; González, Stone, & Jovel, 2003; Levine & Nidiffer, 1996; Noeth & Wimberly, 2002; O'Connor, 2000). The cultural knowledge gained from my service experience also helped me to see that the methodological tools should try and capture the kind of social support associated with college planning in the high school.

Service, cultural knowledge, and methodological approaches. In relying on the cultural knowledge gained from my service experiences, I knew that students' college planning was interdependent, which is key to capturing the role of student social support in their college planning activities. This cultural knowledge gained from my service experiences was important in exploring the school's college preparatory context and its structure for student social support. So in order to incorporate what I knew, I designed a 4-year, mixed-methods case study that could capture the school's college preparatory mission, student-staff relations, and college preparatory activities. I used faculty and staff interviews, senior survey and senior student focus groups and extant data sources. For the purposes of this chapter, I will only use illustrations from selected methods and analyses from the focus groups and staff interviews.

Sample methods and analyses: Focus groups. The student focus groups were conducted with senior students in spring 2002, 2003, 2004, and 2005. The intent of these focus group interviews was to capture how the features of the college preparatory school context impacted these seniors' postsecondary plans. The only criteria for the focus groups were a balanced array of students with grade point averages both higher and lower than 2.5 and at least one group in which all students had a grade point average of 2.5 or higher. The focus group interviews lasted approximately 40–50 minutes each, and each group discussed questions regarding college planning at their school, staff academic and social support, family and peer expectations for educational attainment, and seniors' postsecondary plans. Over the 4 years of the study, 55 seniors participated in the focus groups, and the majority of the focus group participants were African American.

During the focus group interviews, my experiences as a tutor helped me garner a discussion about students being the first in their families to get an opportunity to attend college. We talked about their family's expectations for college as well as their own self-perceptions of being college bound. Many of the students said that their parents did not attend college yet wanted them to attend college so that their economic and occupations' futures were not as constrained as those of their family members. While the students tended to adopt these familial expectations, they were also insecure about their ability to live up to those expectations. Their insecurities appeared during their senior year college application activities, and the social support from school staff played a key role in keeping students on-track to transition to college. While students said their parents were supportive toward their college aspirations, the students relied more on school staff for individualized monitoring and confidence building during the application process.

Sample methods and analyses: Staff interviews. During each spring, faculty members were recruited from the staff roster for face-to-face interviews lasting 1 to 1.5 hours. We discussed the school's mission, student social support, and college preparatory activities. Over the 4 years, I annually interviewed an average of 29 faculty and staff members out of about 43 staff members on the school's roster. Since data were collected over a 4-year period, there are 2–4 data points on most staff members and at least 75% of core academic units and departments are represented in the interview data. The interview data is also highly representative of racial and gender demographics with about half of the interview respondents being African American and about half being female.

The cultural knowledge gained from my experiences as a tutor helped with some of the questions about student social support and the disparate staff views on whether the school should be "hard-core college prep" or offer college preparation tailored to fit their students' academic and social support needs. Staff members discussed how organizational challenges such as staff turnover and building rehabilitation took time away from refining the mission, resulting in disparate staff views on how college prep should be conceptualized. Those staff showing allegiance to the college prep construct considered the meritocracy ideology as a superior belief system and selective colleges as superior to other colleges. Staff who wanted to define college prep so that their students' academic and social needs were prioritized believed that their model inherently challenges the archetype since the school was founded to address the unequal college opportunity structure in the neighborhood. As a result, the extensiveness of students' social support also varied by teachers' and staff members' beliefs in what the school should focus on.

To sum, a culturally responsive and respectful researcher is knowledgeable and aware of the school community and how schools and students have been affected by the larger issues of race, class, power, equity, and social justice. Through service activities, researchers have an opportunity to establish trust and gain cultural knowledge that can inform their research agenda. The service experience not only helped me to experientially learn about debt service, but also helped me to develop a research plan in which I could use the lens of my service experiences to dissect the literature as well as design a project that is culturally sensitive and applicable toward improving schooling opportunities for low-income students and students of color. The findings from this work, particularly that social support is an integral function of college preparation for low-income students of color, add a new dimension to the established literature that focuses on individualism in college preparation versus interdependence in college preparation. If I had strictly relied on the literature, I could have applied a deficit view that low-income students of color did not have the wherewithal to complete the college application process on their own, which would attribute to the gap in college attendance and access.

In this chapter, I am discussing the cultural knowledge gained from serving within a specific urban school community with a history of racialized housing segregation, white flight, deindustrialization (70,000 jobs lost) and concentrated poverty among African Americans. The cultural knowledge gained from my service experiences helped me to see why the social context of the neighborhood was related to the social support service delivery and student utilization of social support services. I want to emphasize that students of color and low-income students attend schools across all regions and locales in this country and, as a result, their schooling experiences vary according to the school communities and neighborhoods in which they live. Eustace G. Thompson (in this volume) cautions against any "homogenized understanding of African American students because those monolithic views stifle the academy's ability to affect change" (p. 183). So, while the larger issues of race, class, power, equity, and social justice affect all school communities, the cultural knowledge gained should reflect the specific social context of the neighborhood (e.g., community demographics, historical events, economics, politics, social movements, residential patterns) and the school (e.g., student and staff demographics, school funding, school size, school reform, resource allocation). Diamond (2006), for example, used the "racialized educational terrain" as an analytical tool to examine the achievement disparities between African Americans, Latinos, and Whites in an affluent suburban school (p. 497). By using the lens of the racialized educational terrain (instead of a cultural deficit theory), Diamond concluded that school tracking practices were aligned with residential segregation such that African American and Latino students were sorted into lower level classes that would eventually keep them from accessing upper level mathematics courses and learning the necessary skills for higher mathematics achievement. While some African American students in this school community may have been wealthier than their counterparts in urban schools, they were still affected by the larger issues of race, class, power, equity, and social justice because the specific way they were stratified within schools was related to that community's history of racial segregation. This knowledge helped Diamond to attribute the achievement disparities to students' limited access to advanced courses and instruction instead of students' academic weaknesses.

SERVICE, MERIT POINTS, AND RESEARCH VALIDITY

In this paper, I have argued for a new conceptualization of service to be a platform of restitution to school communities of color for the misplaced blaming of the victim and the ensuing lack of informed analyses that could have helped school communities of color. I have also argued that service, as a form of experiential learning, can lead to greater cultural knowledge and understanding of school communities of color, particularly if that service experience is coupled with immersion in the appropriate literatures on race, culture, and structural inequality. However, coupling service with scholarship is risky since service is typically marginalized in the academy (Ward, 2003). Coupling service with scholarship is also risky because the academy has traditionally used "objectivity" to define "legitimate scholarship" (Butin, 2006, p. 488). Thus, service-scholars have to be sure to address the validity of the research as well as the validity of their service provision.

In coupling service with scholarship, the researcher has to take concrete steps to address validity. A major concern would be whether the service provision can be attributed to any of the *cause and effect* that are observed. Thus, the researchers have to decide if their service provision and the research study are too intertwined to ensure validity. If so, other approaches may be more appropriate such as participatory action research so that the service experience becomes an integral part of the research study. In my own example, I was not interested in studying the impact of a tutoring program. Also, since the tutoring program was short-lived and only twenty or so students ever participated in the program, I did not structure the research study to have the service experience at its core. In order to address concerns about validity, I took several approaches such as, (1) data triangulation with data internal to the study (i.e., collecting data from students and staff members, collecting data within and across school departments and units, and using a combination of focus groups, surveys, and interviews), (2) data triangulation with data external to the study (i.e., utilizing extant student survey data collected by the school district and a local data clearinghouse), (3) using multiple time points for data collection (i.e., extending the study over 4 years in order to provide a longer time span for insights into the case and the views of the respondents), (4) using staff meetings and follow-up interviews to address interpretive validity, and (5) seeking negative cases to assess researcher bias toward selective observations. In general, scholars use some of the aforementioned techniques to address validity in their research. However, those engaged in service-scholarship should devote more attention to validity issues due to the intimacy offered through service provision that can be a threat to research validity.

Establishing the validity of the service provision is also challenging since external service is still marginalized within the academy (Ward, 2003). During annual performance reviews, scholars' distribution of time is often literally or metaphorically calculated in order to access the proportion of time spent on research. Also, even the kind of research one conducts is prioritized. Within the university context, the history of extractive research in which predominantly poor and minority school communities have become "big business" for both the university (through the indirect costs generated from large grants) and for the scholar (through the generation of grant submissions and publications) encourages many scholars to build their careers without being accountable for helping those schools' communities from which the data were extracted. The stress to "publish or perish" can often deflect our natural roles as service providers. Yet, though external service is not always rewarded, we most hold true to the commitment to and nature of our work in which service has always been a traditional aim (Boyer, 1996). Scholars should hold themselves accountable and immerse themselves within a community of scholars who can hold them accountable for meeting performance outcomes without losing the spirit of our professional responsibility to serve others.

CONCLUSION

Through illustrations from my own experiences, I have shared how the cultural knowledge gained from service experiences can lead to research investigations that are more culturally sensitive. In my own experiences, the cultural knowledge gained from my service experiences helped me to employ a critical lens to a literature that has placed the college preparation of students of color on the margins. From experientially learning from service, I was able to utilize research methodology that centers my research investigations on the college preparation experiences of students of color. Yet, service-scholarship is a nontraditional path in the current academic climate. In the current climate, skewed notions of "validity" are used to foster distance between researchers and the school communities that are the focus of the research. So, the intimacy afforded through service experiences places any subsequent research at risk of critique. Thus, scholars have to employ extensive validity measures for the study.

Overall, the positive attributes of scholar service outweigh the negative attributes because scholar service serves two important ends. It helps to make amends to school communities of color for the academy's misplaced blaming of the victim and, consequentially, the lack of informed research to improve school communities of color. It can also help scholars become more equipped to develop research projects that are culturally responsive and respectful, leading to the identification of an appropriate theoretical framework and the development of culturally responsive and respectful research questions and methods. Most important, scholar service helps to address the education debt because it is an avenue for scholars to enhance their research approach and methodologies "beyond the documentation of the inequalities and inadequacies" that Ladson-Billings (2006) cautions against (p. 9) to research projects that are more informed and thus responsive to the school communities facing the education debt.

REFERENCES

Adams, S., Ajirotutu, C., & Jay, G. (2007). Service learning, multicultural education, and the core curriculum: A model for institutional change. *Diversity Digest, 10*(2), 9–11. Retrieved October 15, 2007, from http://www.diversityweb.org/Digest/vol10no2/vol10no2.pdf

Armstrong, C. F. (1990). On the making of good men: Character-building in the New England boarding schools. In P. W. Kingston & L. S. Lewis (Eds.), *The high status track: Studies of elite schools and stratification* (pp. 3–24). Albany: SUNY Press.

Astin, A. W., & Sax, L. J. (1998). How undergraduates are affected by service participation. *Journal of College Student Development, 39,* 251–263.

Berberet, J. (1999). The professoriate and institutional citizenship: Toward a scholarship of service. *Liberal Education, 85*(4), 33–39.

Billingsley, A. (1992). *Climbing Jacob's ladder: The enduring legacy of African American families.* New York: Simon & Schuster.

Boyer, E. (1996). The scholarship of engagement. *Journal of Public Outreach 1*(1), 11–20.

Boyer, E. (1990). *Scholarship reconsidered: Priorities of the professoriate.* New York: The Carnegie Foundation for the Advancement of Teaching.

Butin, D. (2006). The limits of service-learning in higher education. *The Review of Higher Education, 29*(4), 473–498.

Butin, D. (2007). Justice-Learning: Service-learning as justice-oriented education. *Equity & Excellence in Education, 40*(2), 1–7.

Ceja, M. (2000, November). *Making decisions about college: Understanding the information sources of Chicana students.* Paper presented at the annual meeting of the Association for the Study of Higher Education, Sacramento, CA.

Chibucos, T. R., & Lerner, R. M. (1999). *Serving children and families through community-university partnerships: Success stories.* Norwell, MA: Kluwer Academic.

Cookson, P. W., & Persell, C. H. (1985). *Preparing for power: America's elite boarding schools.* New York: Basic Books.

Curran, J. M. (1999). *College students' attitudes towards mental retardation: A pilot study.* Paper presented at the Biennial Meeting of the Society for Research in Child Development, Albuquerque, NM.

Diamond, J. B. (2006). Still separate and unequal: Examining race, opportunity, and school achievement in "integrated" suburbs. *Journal of Negro Education, 75*(3), 495–505.

Eyler, J., Giles, D., Stenson, C., & Gray, C. (2001). *At a glance: What we know about the effects of service-learning on college students, faculty, institutions and communities, 1993B2000.* Washington, DC: Learn and Serve America National Service Learning Clearinghouse. Retrieved October 15, 2007, from http://servicelearning.org

Farmer-Hinton, R. L. (2002). The Chicago context: Understanding the consequences of urban processes on school capacity. *Journal of Negro Education, 71*(4), 313–330.

Farmer-Hinton, R. L. (2006). Savage inequalities: Children in America's schools. *Educational Studies, 40*(1), 84–91.

Fiske, E. B. (2001). *Learning in deed: The power of service-learning for American schools.* Battle Creek, MI: W. K. Kellogg Foundation.

Freeman, K. (1997). Increasing African Americans participation in higher education: African American high-school students' perspectives. *The Journal of Higher Education, 68*(5), 523–550.

Freeman, K. (1999). The race factor in African Americans' college choice. *Urban Education, 34*(1), 4–25.

González, K. P., Stone, C., & Jovel, J. E. (2003). Examining the role of social capital in access to college for Latinas: Toward a college opportunity framework. *Journal of Hispanic Higher Education, 2*(1), 146–170.

Grady, K. (1998). *Constructing the other through community service learning.* Bloomington: University of Indiana. (ERIC Document Reproduction Service No. ED 431 698) Retrieved October 15, 2007, from http://www.eric.ed.gov/

Graham, L. O. (2000). *Our kind of people: Inside America's Black upper class.* New York: HarperCollins.

Hossler, D., Schmit, J., & Vesper, N. (1999). *Going to college: How social, economic, and educational factors influence the decisions students make.* Baltimore, MD: The Johns Hopkins University Press.

Kellogg Commission on the Future of State and Land Grant Universities. (1999). *Returning to our roots: The engaged institution.* Washington, DC: National Association of State Universities and Land-Grant Colleges.

Kozol, J. (1991). *Savage inequalities: Children in America's schools.* New York: Harper Perennial.

Kozol, J. (2005). *Shame of the nation: The restoration of apartheid schooling in America.* New York: Crown.

Ladson-Billings, G. J. (2006). From the achievement gap to the education debt: Understanding achievement in U.S. schools. *Educational Researcher, 35*(7), 312.

Levine, A., & Nidiffer, J. (1996). *Beating the odds: How the poor get to college.* San Francisco: Jossey-Bass.

McDonough, P. M. (1997). *Choosing colleges: How social class and schools structure opportunity.* Albany: State University of New York Press.

Milner, H. R. (2007). Race, culture, and researcher positionality: Working through dangers seen, unseen, and unforeseen. *Educational Researcher, 36*(7), 388–400.

National Service-Learning Clearinghouse. (n.d.). *What is service learning?* Retrieved October 15, 2007, from http://www.servicelearning.org/what_is_service-learning/service-learning_is/index.php

Noeth, R. J., & Wimberly, G. L. (2002). *Creating seamless educational transitions for urban African American and Hispanic students.* Iowa City, IA: ACT Policy Research Center.

O'Connor, C. (2000). Dreamkeeping in the inner city: Diminishing the divide between aspirations and expectations. In S. Danziger & A. C. Lin (Eds.), *Coping with poverty: The social contexts of neighborhood, work, and family in the African American community.* Ann Arbor: University of Michigan Press.

Peshkin, A. (2001). *Permissible advantage? The moral consequences of elite schooling.* Mahwah, NJ: Lawrence Erlbaum Associates.

Powell, A. G. (1996). *Lessons from privilege: The American prep school tradition*. Cambridge, MA: Harvard University Press.

Schneider, B., & Stevenson, D. (1999). *The ambitious generation: America's teenagers motivated but directionless*. New Haven, CT: Yale University Press.

Solorzano, D. G., & Yosso, T. J. (2001). From racial stereotyping and deficit discourse toward a critical race theory in teacher education. *Multicultural Education, 9*(1), 2–8.

Tillman, L. C. (2002). Culturally sensitive research approaches: An African-American perspective. *Educational Researcher, 31*(9), 3–12.

Titlebaum, P., Williamson, G., Daprano, C., Baer, J. & Brahler, J. (2004). *Annotated history of service learning 1862B2002*. Retrieved October 15, 2007, from http://www.servicelearning.org/filemanager/download/142/SL%20Comp%20Timeline%203-15-04_rev.pdf

Ward, K. (2003). *Faculty service roles and the scholarship of engagement*. ERIC Digest. (ERIC Document Reproduction Service No. ED 480 469) Retrieved October 15, 2007, from http://www.ericdigests.org/2004-3/faculty.htm

CHAPTER 9

INSIDER AND OUTSIDER

Reflexivity and Intersubjectivity in Ethnography

Jamie Lew

REFLEXIVITY AND INTERSUBJECTIVITY IN ETHNOGRAPHY

For the past few decades, conventions of writing or representing ethnography and qualitative research have been heavily criticized. There has been much critical analysis of how fields and observations are actually "constructed" in the writing process, and that the pretense of objectivity has resulted in researchers' objectification of the indigenous voices of "informants." Predicated on the understanding that observations and stories are rarely "captured," but instead, framed by experiences and perspectives of a particular researcher, the interpretivist approach deeply challenges researchers to interrogate and disclose their own subjectivity and positionalities. Researchers argue that such reflexivity challenges the more positivist paradigm, breaking down the power relations in dichotomous oppositions of researcher and researched, outsider and insider, knower and the known. Influenced by a more postmodern inclination,

Research in Urban Educational Settings: Lessons Learned and
Implications for Future Practice, pp. 163–176
Copyright © 2011 by Information Age Publishing

reflexivity therefore draws from epistemological relativism, subjectivity, and positionality, invoking political or even moral commitment of research practice by challenging the power relations inherent in ethnographic fieldwork.

In anthropology, theoretical discussion of reflexivity has been developing for decades. And today, the value of reflexivity has been widely accepted not only by anthropologists but by researchers in various fields conducting fieldwork or qualitative research. In Scholte's (1972) important essay, *Toward a Reflexive and Critical Anthropology* he argues that reflexivity is a paradigm shift from a "scientist" to a "hermeneutic" approach, which involves moving away from an objectivist view toward a more relativistic one. He underscores the constant awareness and assessment of the researcher's own contribution to and interpretation of research Afindings.@ Indeed, for Scholte (1972), this intersubjective process also leads to an emancipatory action. "We have once again come the full hermeneutic circle: The comparative understanding of others contributes to self-awareness; self-understanding, in turn, allows for self-reflection and (partial) self-emancipation; the emancipatory interest, finally, makes the understanding of others possible" (p. 448).

In his seminal essay, *Grief and a Headhunter's Rage*, Rosaldo (2000) describes how intersubjectivity and reflexivity provide him an opportunity to realize his own "positions" and limitations of doing fieldwork with the Ilongots in the Philippines. He points out that all accounts are partial and argues that there is no objectivity, only different views from different positions, both structural and experiential.

In addition to noting the significance of positionality and relativism in ethnography, reflexive discourse in education has also been implicitly and explicitly interrogating status of power and privilege of researchers' positions, in forms of race, class, and gender. Some of these questions note how researchers' own identity impacts the way questions are developed and conceptualized, research data are collected and analyzed, and analysis are interpreted and written (Denzin & Lincoln, 1994; Ladson-Billings, 2000; Usher & Edwards, 1994).

For instance, in Gordon's research on reflexivity of White privilege, she examines the ways in which race was negotiated and interpreted in her school community. She interrogates her own role as a White researcher, and how this privilege allowed her to implement various strategies as a way to avoid questions of race with her school personnel. By outlining series of negotiations and discursive practice employed in the research process to avoid or manage race talk, she interrogates her own White privilege and how she was implicated in reproducing it (Gordon, 2005; Macbeth, 2001; McIntyre, 1997; Sleeter, 1993, 1994; Thompson, 1998, 1999, Warren, 2001). Gordon (2005) states in her conclusion, "Color-blindness, avoidance of race talk, selective attrition race, containment, and Whitewashing, constitute a repertoire of logics that I used in the data collection process. That repertoire bespeaks my complicity with sustaining White privilege and reinforcing inequitable power relations" (p. 298). As such, engaging in critical reflexivity reminds researchers that it may be much easier to analyze racism located elsewhere, turning attention away from ourselves as researchers to racism of others in our research. In doing so, researchers may overlook their preconceived ideas, privileges, and strategies used to reproduce inequality of power status.

Drawing from a tradition of auto ethnography, reflexivity demands personal narrative as a reliable mode of expressing findings from a field—a field that is racialized, gendered, sexualized, embodied (Coffey, 1999). That is, research fields are embodied as active sites of contestation. In doing so, it attempts to challenge dichotomous dualist standpoint of self and other, insider and outsider, researcher and researched. For instance, Briggs (1970) classic writing, *Never in Anger: A Portrait of an Eskimo Family*, is a good example of research based on auto ethnography or intersubjectivity. Through a process of constant reflection of her own feelings and actions, Salzman (2002) notes that Briggs reflective work should have been subtitled "all about Jean" (p 806) as it primarily focuses on the author's own story as a researcher. In her description of living with the Eskimos, she writes:

> I describe the feelings that I myself had in particular situations. My justification for this is that I was an intrinsic part of the research situation. The responses of my hosts to my actions and my feelings, and my own reactions to the situations in which I found myself—my empathy and my experience of contrasts between my feelings and those of my hosts—were all invaluable source of data. (Briggs, 1970, p 6)

Notwithstanding the significance of reflexivity and auto ethnography, some researchers suggest that self-reflexivity should be placed in larger social contexts. That is, larger social forces and changing contexts release different mechanisms that impact process and outcome of reflexivity (Cain, 1990; Pawson & Tilley, 1997; Roberts & Sanders, 2005). Ethnographic process should take into account structural conditions— conditions that may either promote or limit the research process, and how this process impacts reflexivity at different stages of research (Roberts & Sanders, 2005). For instance, Roberts and Sanders (2005) call for a more realist standpoint they coin "pragmatic realism" (p. 296), and argue that "contexts trigger particular mechanisms: resources, structural as well as individual, that provide individuals with the means to conduct research" (p. 296). They highlight specific resources, capacities, and opportunities that may be significant for mechanisms of reflexivity to be activated.

These include structural factors such as access to research funding, research context, and research respondents. Therefore, for Roberts and Sanders (2005), reflexivity is not something that is condoned to fieldwork per se, but one that is negotiated throughout the various phases of the research process:

> What is sometimes absent or unreported from such reflexive accounts is a recognition that dilemma inevitably emerge temporally for the researcher *before* they make contact with the research setting, *during* the process of ethnographic research, and subsequently in the time taken to unravel the theoretical importance of the research *after* the fieldwork has ended. (p. 296)

Using this framework of pragmatic realism (Roberts & Sanders, 2005), I will delineate how my research—before, during, after fieldwork—activated mechanisms of reflexivity and intersubjectivity: (1) Before fieldwork—I will reflect on the process of arriving at my research topic, my own local biographical context, and gaining access to respondents; (2) During fieldwork—I will reflect on how my own shared biography and background with the respondents were both a source of strength and limitation. It also signifies constant negotiation of my own multiple identities and ethical implications for how these shifting identities provide access to our respondents; (3) After fieldwork—I will reflect on analyzing data and writing for academia, drawing relationship between personal experiences with theoretical framework, and challenge of generating valid "findings" in an environment where quantitative and traditional positivist approach to research prevails. I argue that in all of these stages of research; it is only through active reflexive process that one can arrive at a meaningful ethnographic study. Moreover, while subjective experiences are extremely important, it is also important to relate this personal intersubjectivity with larger structural mechanisms that greatly impact how reflexivity may be facilitated or impeded. I suggest that it is important for researchers to draw integral relationship between "self" and larger social context at all stages of the research process. Individual subjective voices, regardless of how insightful and aware, are also operating within the context of changing social and power structures that greatly influence one's reflexive standpoint. Exposing some of these forces in reflexivity may only strengthen the ethnographic process. As Roberts and Sanders (2005) explain, "the advantage of this realist approach to ethnography enables a greater degree of specificity of understanding how mechanisms and contexts help to change our reflexive standpoint throughout the ethnographic enterprise in order to produce different outcomes" (p. 309).

RESEARCH SETTING

Spanning more than three years, I have examined how structural and cultural factors of social class, community networks, and schooling resources affect achievement variability among Asian American students. To do so, my research specifically compared schooling experiences of middle-class Korean American students who are attending a competitive academic magnet high school, with working-class Korean American high school dropouts in a community-based GED program in NYC. Although I analyzed student academic data and demographics, most of my research consisted of fieldwork in schools and interviews with teachers and students themselves (Lew, 2006).

The study is based on fieldwork and in-depth interviews with a total of 72 Korean American youths attending urban high schools in New York City: 42 Korean students attended one of the elite magnet high schools, which I call "Magnet High," or MH; 30 Korean high school dropouts attended a GED preparatory program at a nonprofit organization, which I call "Youth Community Center," or YCC. My informants consisted of both 1.5- and second-generation children—1.5-generation: born in Korea but raised in the U.S. since the age of ten, with at least one Korean parent; second-generation: born and raised in the United States, with at least one Korean parent. The students' ages ranged from 14–20 years old.

School Context

Magnet High School (MH). As a competitive elite high school in New York City, MH prides itself on student academic achievement paralleled by few public high schools. According to the annual school report (NYC Board of Assessment, 2002–2003), approximately 2,700 students were enrolled, and since entrance to the school was based on a competitive standardized exam, students commute to the school from all five of New York City's boroughs. Almost half of the students were Asian, 46.5%, while 37% were White, 9.1% Hispanic, and 7.4% Black. Only about 1% consists of recent immigrants to the U.S.—those who immigrated to the U.S. within the last 3 years.

Approximately 99% of the students graduate and pursue a 4-year college education. An overwhelming 97% graduate with a regents diploma, 2.2% with local diploma, and less than 1% with a GED diploma. Students. average SAT scores were 626 verbal and 671 math scores on each segment of this test range from 200 to 800—compared to the average of 443 verbal and 472 math for New York City schools. Meanwhile, students' academic performance correlates to their socioeconomic backgrounds. From 2001 to 2003, the percentage of MH students eligible for reduced and free lunch was 19.5 (2001), 19.3 (2002), and 25.2 (2003); by comparison, schools citywide averaged 48.4 (2001), 51.3 (2002), and 54.0 (2003).

Youth Community Center (YCC). The Youth Community Center is a nonprofit community-based organization in Queens, New York. Although the organization provides social service programs to diverse racial and ethnic communities, it primarily serves Korean Americans in Queens. Its education and outreach programs provide students and adults with counseling, tutoring, classes on the Test of English as a Foreign Language (TOEFL), English-as-a-second language (ESL) classes, and preparatory classes for the General Educational Development (GED) exam.

All of the Korean students in the GED program had officially dropped out of their respective neighborhood public high schools in New York City, and had been referred to the program by teachers, counselors, parents, community members, and peers. The Korean high school dropouts in the GED program came from various public high schools in New York City, most of which had a record of low student academic performance and high school dropout rates, as well as a disproportionate number of poor minority students and recent immigrants. Since the students came from numerous schools, it is difficult to give detailed information and statistics for all of them. However, as a point of reference, I will cite statistics from one particular urban high school in Queens, New York, since it was the one most commonly attended by the Korean American high school dropouts.

According to the annual school report (NYC Board of Assessment, 2002–2003), the school had approximately 2,400 students, and most of them lived in Queens. Almost half were Hispanic, 45.4%, while 25.6% were Asian, 22.4% Black, and 6.6% White. Approximately 18%—compared with 10% of high school students citywide—were recent U.S. immigrants, those who immigrated to the U.S. within the last 3 years. Among these recent immigrants, 20% were from Korea, 20% from Ecuador, and 40% from China.

Academically, the students struggled: 42.3% had graduated on time, 34.8% were still enrolled, and 22.8% had dropped out. Only 26.5% of the students graduated with a regent's diploma, 73.5% with local diploma, and less than 1 percent with a GED diploma. Students' average SAT scores were 419 verbal and 460 math scores on each segment of this test range from 200 to 800—compared to the average of 443 verbal and 472 mathematics for New York City schools. Meanwhile, a disproportionate number of students were eligible for the reduced and free-lunch program, which reveals their low socioeconomic backgrounds. Between 2001 and 2003, the percentage of eligible students steadily rose from 47.7 (2001), to 60.4 (2002), to 70.3 (2003); the citywide average was 48.4 (2001), 51.3

(2002), and 54.0 (2003). Teacher qualifications were not quite on par with the magnet high school: approximately 90% of the teachers were fully licensed and permanently assigned to the school; the percentage of teachers with a master's degree or higher was 77.2% (2002) and 78.6% (2003).

REFLEXIVITY IN CONTEXT

Before Fieldwork

Scholars have long advocated for using life histories and experiences as the basis of sociological inquiry (Goldsmith, 2003; Kempny & Burszta, 1994; van Maanen, 1988; Wright Mills, 1959). Wright Mills (1959) suggests that researchers must use one's own life history in intellectual work as a way to choose objects of enquiry. This is important for Wright Mills (1959) because research should begin with a set of issues or questions that one cares about most deeply, even if it seems "trivial." Thus personal background and life history often lead to topics and questions that researchers choose, which in turn could lead to better understanding of one's own culture and history. This has implications for the interpretation and influences of the possibilities within ethnography, where learning about "our" culture is also about culture of "others." (Kempny & Burszta, 1994; Robert & Sanders, 2005). Therefore, it is important to take a reflexive stance toward one's reason for choosing a research topic and entering specific field in the first place, even before the research actually takes place (Roberts & Sanders, 2005).

This is certainly the case for choosing my research topic. As a 1.5-generation Korean American growing up in New York City with immigrant parents and communities, I was deeply concerned about the invisibility of Asian American children and families in schools and research. Although I was relatively privileged growing up with middle-class parents who were able to provide important resources for their children, I also faced many challenges in and outside of schools. These challenges and complex negotiations that involved both structural and cultural forces were rarely discussed in schools, work, or research. Moreover, through community activist work in Asian American communities, I understood too well the diversity and variance of social class, ethnicity, language, achievement, and immigrant histories within Asian American communities, as well as salience of class, race, and gender in shaping variegated experiences among Asian American children. Yet these issues were often disguised in cultural discourse of model minority that blamed the victims for their plight and kept minority groups from building an important coalition against inequality, racism, and injustice. No doubt, I arrived at this research topic because of my own personal biography, as well as my work experience and political conviction hoping that my work could make a difference to educators policy makers, and ultimately to students themselves. My rationale for choosing this topic was indeed lofty, idealistic, and personal.

So with the topic in hand, I tracked back to the community I knew well—the Korean American community in New York City. Growing up as a 1.5-generation Korean American, as well as having worked in community-based Asian-American human service organizations in New York City, I spent a good part of my childhood and adult life involved in the community I was studying. Indeed, my personal background was very similar to the high-achieving Korean American students in my study who attended the specialized magnet high school. As a child of post-1965 Korean immigrants, I grew up and attended one of the academic magnet high schools in the study. Similar to many of the middle-class parents in the study, my parents were also college educated and professionals in Korea who immigrated to the United States for educational and economic opportunities for their family. Growing up with immigrant parents who had little knowledge of English language or the U.S. school system, I faced many challenges while in school. Nevertheless, we were privileged to grow up with middle-class college-educated parents whose social and cultural capital enabled them to provide various opportunities for their children. Similar to many of the middle-class students in my study, my parents were able to provide important cultural capital and structural support for us to achieve in school and ultimately bridge the gap between our educational aspiration and achievement.

If not for my personal background, my professional background also deeply connected me to the lives of the working-class Korean American high school dropouts. As a high school teacher in New York City, I have worked with many poor minorities and their families. Similar to many educators, I was outraged by the blatant segregation within our school system and the limited funding and resources for poor minority children. While teaching, I became more involved with community-based organizations and their efforts in implementing programs that directly impact the lives of the students and their families. Throughout the years, I became increasingly involved with human service and political organizations serving disenfranchised Asian American and minority communities in New York City. I helped develop educational programs to support poor immigrant parents and their children in schools, as well as politically mobilizing Asian American women against domestic violence and labor exploitation. Many of the community-based programs were serving these very invisible families and children who were dropping out of high school, facing myriad structural barriers at home, communities, and schools. No doubt, the lives of these children too became an integral part of my life and I was committed to tell our story.

The initial entrée into both of these communities therefore was relatively easy. Indeed, if it was not for my personal experience growing up as a child of an immigrant, I would not have had the understanding of the complex negotiations, challenges, and privileges that the middle-class students experienced. Moreover, without the political and community work with Asian American communities, I would not have been as aware of the class disparities and ongoing struggles within the Asian American communities, such as those faced by working-class and poor high school dropouts and families. A combination of my personal childhood schooling and professional adult experience also illustrate how diverse Asian American communities are. Even within one ethnic group in an urban setting, structural forces of class, race, ethnicity, gender, for instance, play a critical role in shaping multiple sets of experiences. Being a Korean American, speaking the language, and having worked in the Korean community over the years, many of the students and organizations considered me an insider, allowing me to gain trust of my informants relatively quickly.

During Fieldwork

Although my personal experience and background provided me an insider status, negotiating my status was not always smooth sailing. Throughout the research, I often found myself straddling or caught between competing and opposing identities. Although I was an insider, I was also an outsider. I was both an adult and a student. Having immigrated at the age of nine, I was neither a first-generation nor second-generation, but considered a 1.5-generation.

Moreover, even though I may have been considered an insider, the variability and diversity within the Korean community posed negotiation of power status that I was not fully prepared for. This was especially true in my relationship with the working-class high school dropouts. Even though I was a Korean American, my status as a middle-class professional in authority status placed me in an outsider position. For instance, throughout the research, the working-class Korean American high school dropouts spoke of discrimination and ostracism they experienced from other middle-class and educated Korean Americans. In this respect, my status as a relatively successful middle-class Korean American college professor represented the very power structure and oppression that they and their family deeply resented. Their narratives poignantly illustrated how the Korean American community was divided deeply along class lines.

During this phase of research, I was struck by a myriad of moral and ethical questions of "othering" that took place. In ways that I did not anticipate, I quickly realized that what initially appeared as strengths of shared biographies sometimes became limitations of assumptions and preconceived ideas. Many respondents from the middle-class achieving group often assumed that I should simply "understand" their experiences. Other times, they were reluctant to speak out against their Korean parents or immigrant communities because they believed that I represented an authority adult figure who would judge them if they did not fit into a model minority status. Likewise, the working-class Korean dropouts often felt that they had to give me "correct" answers because I simply represented an authority figure from the Korean community who labeled them as "failures." Particularly for the dropout population, they had a long history of mistrust with authority figures and met therefore with strong resistance. Moreover, as the working-class dropouts began to explain their resentment and ostracism from the middle-class Korean communities, it became extremely difficult to negotiate my own status as a member of the privileged middle-class Korean American community. Throughout the interview and fieldwork process, I found myself shifting my identities to negotiate my power status in changing contexts.

I grappled with the purpose of my shifting identities, and how these negotiations were often in the interest of generating openness and gaining access to my respondents. Despite my shared Korean American history and background, it was through revealing narratives about my own biography and history that I was able to build trust and rapport with my respondents. I would share my background and biography, especially when students asked me, but I was also selective in what information I shared and how those experiences were conveyed. For instance, while I openly shared my personal experiences of attending magnet school as a child and graduate school as an adult, I downplayed this part of my background when talking with the working-class dropouts. Instead, to the dropouts, I spoke more about my work in Asian and Korean communities as an activist and the ways in which I "understood" their personal issues of poverty, racism, and limited structural support at home and school. Although I remained as transparent as I could during the research phase, such negotiation and selective process also meant dealing with preconceived notions and assumptions from my respondents, forcing me to (re)negotiate my own multiple and shifting identities in the field. Often when we are involved in research, especially with respondents who may share similar backgrounds and histories, observed meanings have deep resonance (Hervik, 1994). During the research phase, I experienced an ongoing negotiation and relation with the "other" and the ethical implications for my own shifting identities. As essential openness may be for ethnographers, it is just as if not more important to realize the purpose for the openness. As we generate openness with our respondents to develop trust and tolerance, we also engage openness as a way to generate willingness on the part of other to share materials with the researcher. Moreover, in my case, what appeared as shared biographies and experiences between my respondents and me did not always warrant "openness," but rather involved a dialogic negotiation with the other within one's own community.

Such negotiation of self-reflexivity and multiple-self within the Korean American community becomes even more poignant because of the ways in which they are often portrayed as a monolithic group. Particularly in urban contexts, Korean American communities have been touted as a homogeneous group of middle-class urban entrepreneurs who are uniformly achieving social mobility. Researchers often underscore the Korean American success story to their access to urban ethnic enclave and co-ethnic networks. However, as I have shown in my earlier study (Lew, 2006), while the middle-class Koreans are more likely to be entrepreneurs or owners of business, the working-class and poor Koreans are more likely to work for these entrepreneur bosses and cannot afford to own businesses. That is, Korean American communities in urban contexts, despite their homogeneous portrayal of model minority status, are deeply divided along class lines. In fact, few studies point to the variegated experiences within Korean American ethnic enclaves and the ways in which issues of class, race, and ethnicity may play a critical role in shaping multiple experiences. It is no surprise, therefore, experiences of those Koreans who are poor, dropping out, and downwardly mobile are rarely exposed, rendering them invisible to both researchers and educators. Particularly for those poor Korean students living and attending urban schools, issues of poverty, racial segregation, and limited resources become even more salient.

After Fieldwork

After one has spent years in the field, how does he or she make sense of a body of discrete "data" and draw relationship to larger theoretical framework? Moreover, in what ways is this notion of "theoretical reflexivity" (Roberts & Sanders, 2005, p. 308) influenced by academic institutions and values placed on different kinds of knowledge? Last, how does a researcher unravel both intellectual and emotional experiences accumulated over number of years, and grapple with the "messiness" of ethnography, especially when it has to be now grounded in theory and written for a particular audience? These are some of the key questions that came up for me after fieldwork when I had to engage in the process of analysis, transcription, and meaning-making of the massive amount of data collected.

For many researchers, especially graduate students, there is much to be said about the power relations inherent in academia and who makes decisions about what is considered "valid" data. When low-status graduate students choose to conduct research with a population who are also marginalized, it becomes even more challenging to validate such findings and claims in academia. This is why it is imperative that such research is grounded in a strong theoretical framework. That said, such process involves complex power dynamics between a more traditional positivist approach that is still upheld in many fields in social sciences. In this context, where is there room for critical reflexivity and personal biographical account?

In an academic culture that still favors quantitative methods and positivist approach, it is no surprise that I often reverted to research methods that seemed most familiar and safe—a traditional positivist approach applied to a qualitative study. During this phase, I tried to remain as detached, neutral, and separate from the subjects and their lives as much as possible. In doing so, I believed that I was "capturing" moments of their lives and experiences without subjecting them to my own views and opinions that may sway their interviews. I actively resisted making any personal connections with my respondents' comments, despite my genuine understanding of and empathy for their experiences. I believed that these were necessary steps toward conducting a "valid" sociological research that would be fair to both informant groups, and hold up to my academic audience.

However, my attempt to remain "detached" and "neutral" often seemed false and unjust, bordering on exploitive. I wanted to challenge the conventional research method rooted in positivism, and question how dichotomous notions of subject and object, insider and outsider, political and personal, and knower and known could be reimagined and reconstructed.

Foremost, it meant grappling with and challenging my own privileged status as a "researcher" who's detached positivism—remaining separate, neutral, and distant from my subjects—proved not only naïve but bordering on exploitive. As I analyzed my findings for the academic audience, I struggled with questioning conventional dualism and separation between socially coded binary oppositions: personal/political; public/private; knowledge/known; insider/outsider. I was not fully prepared for the inescapable features of research: Conflict of emotions and interest between research and researched, as well as messiness of ethnography and the significance of "partial truths." More important, how this liminality could actually be written for and accepted by the academic audience was an important question. Despite the supportive graduate school environment, there were also institutional restrictions on what was considered "sociological" and "valid findings."

CONCLUSION

Issues of positionality and reflexivity in ethnography have raised the significance of interrogating status of power and privilege of researchers' positions. More specifically, it has also raised critical awareness of how researchers' own identity and position impacts the way research questions are developed and conceptualized, data are collected and analyzed, and how analysis is interpreted and written. In the reflexive discourse however, there has been less attention paid to significance of structural conditions—conditions that may either promote or limit the research process, and how this process impacts reflexivity at different stages of research. As argued in this chapter, it may be important to highlight specific resources, capacities, and opportunities that may be significant for mechanisms of reflexivity to be activated. By critically engaging in the process of intersubjectivity in all the stages of research—before, during, after fieldwork—researchers may assess how different social contexts help release various mechanisms for reflexivity. Some important questions arise at different stages of research and elicit different negotiations depending on the kinds of structural resources and social contexts within which we operate. Some important questions addressed are: how does one arrive at a research topic and gain access to respondents before fieldwork?; how does one negotiate multiple identities during fieldwork and the ethical implications for how these shifting identities are positioned to gain access to our respondents?; how does one write for academia and develop valid findings in an environment where quantitative and traditional positivist approach may still prevail? Through process of critical reflexivity at all stages of research, we can underscore how individual subjective voices may also be operating within the context of changing social and power structures.

REFERENCES

Briggs, J. L. (1970). *Never in anger: Portrait of an Eskimo family.* Cambridge, MA: Harvard University Press.

Cain, M., (1990). Realist philosophy and standpoint epistemologies or feminist criminology as a successor science in L. Gelsthorpe & A. Morris (Eds.), *Feminist perspectives in criminology,* Buckinghanshire, England: Open University Press.

Coffey, A. (1999). *The ethnographic self: Fieldwork and the representation of reality*. London: SAGE.

Denzin, N., & Lincoln, Y. (Eds.). (1994). *Handbook of qualitative research*. Thousand Oaks, CA: SAGE.

Goldsmith, A. (2003). Fear, fumbling and frustration: Reflections on doing criminological fieldwork in Colombia. *Criminal Justice, 3*, 103–125.

Gordon, J. (2005, November). White on white: Researcher reflexivity and the logics of privilege in white schools undertaking reform. *The Urban Review, 37*(4), 279–302.

Hervik, P. (1994). Shared reasoning in the field: Reflexivity beyond the author. In K. Hastrup & P. Hervik (Eds.), *Social experience and anthropological knowledge* (pp. 78–100). London: Routledge.

Kempny, M., & Burszta, W. (1994). On the relevance of common sense for anthroplogical knowledge. In K. Hastrup & P. Hervik (Eds.), *Social experience and anthropological knowledge* (pp. 12–138). London: Routledge.

Ladson-Billings, G. (2000). Racialized discourses and ethnic epistemologies. In N. K. Denzin & Y. S. Lincoln (Eds.), *Handbook of qualitative research* (2nd ed., pp. 257–277)., Thousand Oaks, CA: SAGE.

Lew, J. (2006). *Asian Americans in class: Charting the achievement gap among Korean American youth*. New York: Teachers College Press.

Macbeth, D. (2001). On "reflexivity" in qualitative research: Two readings and a third. *Qualitative Inquiry, 7*(1), 35–68.

McIntyre, A. (1997). *Making meaning of Whiteness: Exploring racial identity with White teachers*. Albany: State University of New York Press.

Pawson, R., & Tilley, N. (1997). *Realistic evaluation*. London: SAGE.

Roberts, J. M., & Sanders, T. (2005). Before, during, and after: realism, reflexivity, and ethnography. *The Sociological Review*, 294–313.

Rosaldo, R. (2000). Grief and a headhunter's rage. In R. J. McGee & R. L. Warms, (Eds.), *Anthropological theory* (2nd ed., pp. 521–535). Mountain View, CA: Mayfield.

Salzman, P. C. (2002). On reflexivity. *American Anthropologist, 104*(3), 805–813.

Scholte, B. (1972). Toward a reflexive and critical anthropology, In D. Hymes (Ed.), *Reinventing anthropology* (pp. 430–457). New York: Pantheon.

Sleeter, C. E. (1993). How white teachers construct race. In C. McCarthy & W. Crichlow (Eds.), *Race, identity, and representation*. New York: Routledge Press.

Sleeter, C. E. (1994). White racism. *Multicultural Education, 1*(4), 5–8.

Thompson, A. (1998). Not the color purple: Black feminist lessons for educational caring. *Harvard Educational Review, 68*(4), 522–554.

Thompson, A. (1999). Colortalk: Whiteness and off white. *Educational Studies, 30*(2), 141–160.

Usher, R., & Edwards, R. (1994). *Postmodernism and education*. London: Routledge.

Van Maanen, J. (1988). *Tales from the Field: On writing ethnography*. London: University of Chicago Press.

Warren, J. T. (2001). Performing whiteness differently: Rethinking the abolitionist project. *Educational Theory, 51*(4), 451–466.

Wright, Mills, C. (1959). *The sociological imagination*. New York: Oxford University Press.

CHAPTER 10

ONE EDUCATOR'S PERSPECTIVE OF THE DISCONNECT BETWEEN THE ACADEMY AND AFRICAN AMERICAN SCHOOL DISTRICTS

Eustace Thompson

INTRODUCTION

Although I embraced the two worlds of the academy and public education over the course of my career, I am presently experiencing a disconnect between my past role as educational leader and my current position as assistant professor in an educational leadership program teaching prospective administrators. In this new role I find I am experiencing a crisis of confidence I attribute to the academy's failure to effectively utilize and honor the wealth of experiential knowledge I bring to educational leadership programs. The sources of my disconnect are functions of a colorblind

Research in Urban Educational Settings: Lessons Learned and
Implications for Future Practice, pp. 177–199
Copyright © 2011 by Information Age Publishing
All rights of reproduction in any form reserved.

perspective embedded in leadership research, epistemological constraints of a White middle-class constructed curriculum, including research that does not differentiate leadership roles in Black schools. In addition, the challenge of delivering a social justice oriented curriculum to classes of predominantly White students with negative perceptions of Black schools or little interest in problems of Black schools is a source of disconnect. The relationship between a school administrator's experience and the agenda of a school leadership program is particularly important because of the expectation that these areas would be complementary. As a former African American male administrator with more than 30 years in an urban predominantly Black district, I am in a unique position to provide a dual critique of urban school leadership and the academy's educational leadership program with a focus on educational leadership program improvement.

PERSONAL IDENTITY AND RACE, SOCIAL STATUS, AND GENDER

The transition from a predominantly Black urban public school system to the academy challenged me to rethink issues of race, social status, and gender. In my practitioner life these issues were integrated and aligned to my administrative work. However, in my work as an academic I find challenges to these areas of my identity that require me to reassess my race, social status and gender in the academy setting. One significant difference moving from a Black school district to the academy was a decrease in the number of professional people of color I interact with on a daily basis. In the academy the students in my classes are predominantly White as are my colleagues in the school of education. We in the academy openly discuss the issues of race related to hiring more people, creating a diverse faculty, and attracting more students of color. However, few academy policies and procedures address or ensure ethnic diversity. What we find in practice are relatively few faculty members of color and those Blacks have adjunct and assistant professor status. In addition to the lack of faculty diversity, there are few individuals of color at administrative levels.

In my district I had thoughtfully constructed my identity as an African American male responsible for instructional design and delivery. The recognition that a Black male was successful in a direct instructional role and not a tangential role of discipline or athletics gave me significant legitimacy with staff and parents. I viewed safety, student management, and the co-curricular issues exclusively as contributors to academic success and not as independent goals. On entering the academy, this perspective and my extensive experience was marginalized to that of urban school specialist at best and at worse a source to confirm the negative ingrained perceptions of Black schools held by my colleagues. I am cognizant that the role of assistant professor is to demonstrate a contribution to body of leadership knowledge; however, disconnect occurred as I realize my research agenda is tangential to what program wants me to do.

The success of my work in Black schools was known to my university and was the basis of my invitation to join the educational leadership faculty. However, a source of annoyance during my tenure as a principal and deputy superintendent in such close proximity to the university was that neither I nor other administrators in my district were asked to mentor administrative interns. The incongruity of my utility to the academy as a Black male faculty member reflecting its diversity as opposed to my former role as a deputy superintendent being excluded from the mentoring of predominantly White students was not lost to me. Upon my entry into the educational leadership program of the academy, I observed that several administrative internship placements are primarily based on convenience. Districts identified for student placements are based on our relationships with superintendents who have completed our doctoral program and who were primarily White administrators in White districts. In addition, internship districts are restricted to areas that adjunct faculty responsible for supervising interns were willing to visit based on proximity to their homes and issues of safety.

This description of how the academy has challenged my professional persona must be discussed in the context of the academy. I am focusing on educational leadership programs. I believe my personal identity relative to race, gender and social status conflict with the interdisciplinary matrix of my educational leadership program. Specifically, the manner in which African American schools are perceived and understood by educational leadership programs has marginalized my contribution to the leadership program and has limited my ability to focus attention on what I believe is essential to the core knowledge of all practicing administrators. It is my belief that leadership theory, strategies, and practices must be applied to varied settings that elucidate the totality of ethnic, social status and gender issues.

PARASITISM: THE BLACK SCHOOL AND THE ACADEMY— SCHOLARSHIP, TEACHING, AND SERVICE

An understanding of the relationship between African American schools and educational leadership programs is essential if we are to determine why these schools are marginalized. I maintain based on my observations that this relationship is parasitic, one in which the academy benefits while the African American school is impaired. More specifically, I view the academy as parasitic in a very specific way. The parasitic relationship is termed biotrophic, meaning the academy relies on the survival of the African American school. This biotrophic relationship is extremely successful for the academy but not necessarily for the African American school.

A number of scholarly articles identify the parasitic effects of the academy's relationship with all schools (Goldring & Sims, 2005). McClintock (2007) asserted educational research is uniformly harmful because it is irrelevant to schools and administrators. He identified the compositions of faculty as poor because of the use of extraneous research as a criteria for hiring faculty. He indicated that the myth that research could improve schools results in lower morale and confidence in all school administrators. Last, he maintained that good schools do not operate effectively in the pedagogical culture created by educational researchers. Other studies with a critical race theoretical perspective (Bell, 2004; Delgado & Stefancic, 2001; Ladson-Billings & Tate, 2006) maintain educational leadership programs have limited African American schools to marginalized roles that serve restricted research agendas such as the focus on gap analysis and the slavish integration/desegregation debates. This research suggests that my experiences, despite my success leading a successful Black school, will be less valued or required because this parasitic relationship places Black schools in subordinate positions to White schools.

To determine the extent of this assertion, I am analyzing this negative relationship through the three aspects of faculty roles in the delivery of the educational leadership program. The academy uses teaching, scholarly research, and service (university and community) criteria for the evaluation of faculty (Boyer, 1990). As an untenured assistant professor I am intently focused on aligning my experiences with these criteria, and am keenly aware of the constraints placed on the application of my experiences within these criteria. I will use the lenses of these academy activities to discuss my perception of the failure of educational leadership programs to address the needs of African American schools and thereby marginalizing my experiences as a former Black administrator in predominantly African American schools. The legitimacy of using my personal experiences related to being Black, male, and an assistant professor is supported by Donmoyer (1995) His study of the knowledge base in educational administration that identified racism, sexism and classism as significant barriers to the effectiveness of educational administrative programs.

RESEARCH AND THE HIDDEN CURRICULUM—SHAPING THE AGENDA OF BLACK FACULTY

Research is integral to the academy and functions as the connective thread through all of these evaluative criteria. I recall during my interview with the dean of the school of education discussing the issue of my research agenda and the need for me to develop a distinctive voice. I identified my interests in the role of school leadership in creating structures of improving the performance of children of color. I thought that this area of interest and experience would effectively correspond to the three areas of scholarship, teaching and service. I was mistaken. I entered with a misunderstanding of the type of research that academia values. What I found was research regarding educational leadership programs is flawed in two critical ways. The first is that it does not serve the interest of African American administrators and secondly supports a hidden curriculum that provides negative portrayals of African American schools, administrators, and teachers.

The rationale for the use of research as a lens is embedded in the purpose of research. If research does not serve and actually excludes African American schools, then it is not "good" research (Hostetler, 2005). Hostetler indicated that good research serves the well-being of people. He identified the issue of generalizability as the tension between qualitative research competing for legitimacy with quantitative research. Although he maintains that inquiry into human well-being can and does lead to generalizations about what good human life entails, he cautions that these generalizations suppress "particular factors and experiences essential to individuals and subpopulation well being" (p. 18). I maintain that leadership research is relatively silent on what happens in African American schools. When conducted it does not contribute to or benefit African American schools. McClintock (2007) states that schools of education injure practitioners, "The myth that fixing the schools somehow depend on the magic of educational researchers deflects attention, material support, and respect from those charged with the real tasks of keeping school, diminishing their morale and confidence" (p. 4).

The "hidden curriculum" in this document refers to the attitudes and values embedded in school experiences and relationships (Silberman, 1970). Middle-class home value systems of most teachers, both White and Black, who enter administrative preparation programs, are aligned to the curriculum of administrative programs. However, this hidden curriculum is populated with labels that influence what I teach and what my students learn. Through my experience I challenge the labels that restrict my thinking and actions regarding leading African American schools. However, my pedagogy is continually restricted by the labeling (use of terms fostered by the language) that defines this discipline (Cooper, 1996). Educational leadership uses its own language for conversing and writing, and it is through this language that a new researcher can initially be acknowledged in the field. The knowledge coming from educational leadership programs is often revered because we are seen as authorities. And as a recognized support profession for school administrators our professional language and presentation of content shape the beliefs of our students (Edelman, 1977). Henry Giroux (1989) and hooks (1995) maintain that the language of researchers links schools to ideologies and practices of domination and control. This argument regarding academic language and research knowledge, according to Cooper (1996) has a more powerful claim than knowledge acquired through experience. My experiential knowledge that I assumed would be most valuable to the academy and the program I found to less valued than the texts and articles read by my colleagues and students.

SCHOLARLY RESEARCH

The scholarly research of educational leadership does not complement my experiences as a Black practitioner and limits my voice as a teacher in the leadership program. The research typically has limited utility for African American administrators, because the literature does not permit students to differentiate between leadership roles related to Black districts in urban vs. suburban settings, the depiction of African American schools is viewed with a colorblind perspective, and Blacks are almost exclusively associated with high needs urban settings.

Research in the form of published works is not particularly friendly to or even neutral with regard to African American schools, districts, faculty, or students. McClintock (2007) suggests that the state of educational research from scholars is useless to school administrators because it is contradictory, unfocused, and irrelevant. He points to the 2007 fourth edition of the *Handbook of Research on Teaching* for this argument. He states, "It assembles work, pointless in a deep existential sense, for the research goes off in every direction, leaving those in 'practice-policy, school administration, teaching, instruction, and parenting' without a clue what to do" (p. 1). If indeed, this is a view of research in the broad field of education, what does this state of research portend for African American school administrators? I want to clearly differentiate educational leadership literature from foundations of education literature because candidates in educational leadership programs are rarely required to take foundations courses and foundations is usually viewed in the academy as a distinct program.

A source of dissatisfaction with educational administration programs is the lack of perceived benefit to districts, schools, teachers, and administrators from published research in the form of articles or dissertations. There should be minimally two factors of benefit to administrators. The first is the ability to point to a specific study and state with pride that a school/district participated and the findings presented the district/school in a positive manner. The second is participation in studies that pose research questions that are sufficiently broad to have applicability to policy or practice for their schools.

In my experience, I could identify few studies in the district where I was deputy superintendent that portrayed my schools in a positive manner. Although, the level of requests for our participation was huge because our schools "looked" more like White schools statistically than other African American schools, the findings consistently focused on negatives. For example, the findings of one study with three districts, all White with the exception of mine, indicated that, although not statistically significant the White districts out performed the African American district on several important scales. This study again highlighted an unfavorable gap between African American districts and White districts and overlooked the positive academic accomplishment of an African American district.

Leadership scholarship does not permit students to differentiate between leadership roles related to Black districts in urban versus suburban districts. The challenges of Black student achievement are a major concern for administrators who exit leadership programs with a homogenized understanding of Black students. A significant body of research suggests that middle-income Black students in suburban school settings experience school differently from Black urban school students (Fordham, 1996; Ogbu, 2003; Zweigenhaft & Domhoff, 2003). These researchers point to the importance of understanding Black students in non-urban contexts. Their findings, although controversial, offer leadership programs critical alternative perspectives for viewing the education of Black students in different settings. Pattillo-McCoy (1999) described middle-class experience in the neighborhood context by investigating how racial segregation, changing economic structures, and disproportionate Black poverty affect the residential experience of Black middle-class youth. Ogbu (2003), based on studies in middle-class integrated school districts maintained African-Americans' own cultural attitude is a serious impediment to their academic success and that is too often neglected. He maintains that structural changes in schools will not address the academic gap between Black and White students. Griffin, Allen, and Kimura-Walsh (2007) found that even when racial minorities and Whites attended the same schools, they could have radically different experiences because of tracking and teacher expectations. Fordham (1996) said she feared that the "acting-White" idea has been distorted into blaming the victim. Her research focuses on how race itself is a social fiction, rooted not just in skin color but also in behaviors and social status. Zweigenhaft and Domhoff's (2003) study sheds light on this debate—it concludes that while the importance of class has increased in the past few decades, race is still the paramount factor in the personal and social identity of Blacks. The implication of these studies underscores the need for administrators to develop understandings of Black students in urban and suburban settings. The implication for administrators is that class distinctions between Blacks affect the quality of their experience in schools regardless of composition and require the use of different administrative strategies and skills.

As I reviewed the educational leadership required readings of the courses in the educational leadership program, I found the role of administrators in ethnic settings is given minimal attention. There is what I consider a "primitive" belief that effective leadership is not bound by setting and minimizes the experiences of any administrator not practicing in a majority district. The indirect affect of the color blind perspective is that administrators fear and distort differences (Park & Judd, 2005). Research typically doesn't serve African American administrators. Scholarly literature does not address the individual or special needs of administrators in multiple Black district settings. In essence educational leadership research is basically "color blind" in orientation. This theory within the social psychology posits that attention to race results in stereotyping that result in prejudice and racism (Mazzocco, 2006). Bonilla-Silva (2003) debunked this theory suggesting that failure to recognize racial disparities and racial structural factors results in color blind racism. The damaging results for educational leadership is that students exit programs blaming people of color for disparities and believing that race-targeted programs are inconsistent with notions of equality. The work of Park and Judd (2005) uses the social cognition perspective to challenge the color blind approach stating that racial categories occur automatically and silencing discussions of race does not reduce prejudice. Hilliard (1995) indicated that educators are taught to view schools as neutral settings that offer quality instruction to all students. This reasoning is fostered by the failure of leadership programs to contextualize the administrator/school relationship to Black instructional environments.

In summary, the scholarly research we use in preparation programs does not permit me to readily utilize my practitioner experiences as a Black academician. The colorblind approach embedded in research does not give value to my unique perspectives as a former school administrator in a predominantly Black district. In addition, absence of programmatic conversations about Black social status in urban and suburban settings potentially curtails my course selections of research literature. The body of research literature is considered by some in the academy as relatively useless for school administrators and does not recognize the Black school experiences as multifaceted.

TEACHING

I considered my expertise in the area of professional development to be strong. As a "teacher" of administrators and teachers in my district, I believed that the teaching strand would be a natural fit as I moved to the academy. Teaching is purported to be equally important to scholarship especially in our program that is directly and solely responsible for providing educational leaders. Unfortunately I find significant restraints to my pedagogy as I attempt to deliver a balanced and representative curriculum. The areas of teaching I find most troubling is the lack of discussion of leadership as related to the context of Black schools, the relative absence of social justice sensibilities in the delivery of educational leadership course content, the limitations and exclusionary practices of internship experiences, and the negative perceptions of white students toward a Black professor regarding challenges to their beliefs.

Teaching About Black Schools in Context

According to Levine (2005) school leadership programs in comprehensive universities are not innovative and in general, by design, fail to address site-specific practice in African American and other subgroup educational settings. The effectiveness of teaching in educational administrative preparation programs in the area of teaching depends on understanding the importance of embedding context into the curricula. I expected that the primacy of context would make the selection of scholarly research applicable to my expertise as an administrator in Black schools. My view is supported by researchers and practitioners who agree that school and district context is critical to the preparation of educational leaders. In a recent comparative study, Orr (2007) surveyed 696 principals from exemplary and conventional preparatory programs. The variables examined included school improvement progress, school climate and direct principals' work. Although the researcher did not specifically study administrators in African American urban schools or African American school settings, her findings related to school context were significant. She found school context of poverty positively moderated the influence of leadership practice improvement and the context of challenging school problems negatively meditated the leadership practice improvement. This study not only reaffirms the importance of context for the preparation of school leaders, but also identifies the two critical variables of poverty and administrative challenges as mediators of administrative effectiveness. Both of these variables are descriptive of some African American school contexts.

Leithwood, Louis, Anderson, and Wahlstrom (2004) narrowed the discussion of context by focusing educational leadership preparation of student learning outcomes. He is critical of literature that merely identifies characteristics of effective university-based preparation programs. He maintained the programs that are long-term and job embodied, and have coherent curriculums and a variety of instructional methods, tend to be more effective but they still do not identify student learning as the "fundamental criterion for success" (p. 87). That being stated, at the crux of the debate is whether learning that takes place in preparation programs should be monolithic in its applicability for administrators in all schools, or whether significantly different skills and dispositions are needed by African American school administrators. Leithwood et al. identified "problem-relevant knowledge" as critical for all administrators. Administrators will be effective when they solve problems in the social and physical context in which the problem is embedded. This view requires administrators to be knowledgeable about the culture of the school and district, and the individuals and groups within the school and community.

In my certificate program, the formal curricula is too limited in course requirements to offer an in-depth environmental understanding of the African American school, and existing courses that provide quality problem-relevant knowledge for administrators are not offered. Administrative prep programs leading to state certificates are typically lock-stepped. Some are cohort organized with prescribed courses. An example of course titles from one northern university includes five sequenced required courses: Leading Learning Organizations, Building Learning Organizations, Framing Problems and Making Decisions, Educational Program Development, and Delivery and Assessment and Engaging External Environments. Within the same department, courses excluded from the certification program but available as electives in other programs included such titles as: Children of Color: The Social Construction of Race in American Schools, Urban Education, and Contemporary Educational Movements. One could argue the relegation of these courses to elective status outside of the course program requirements is reflective of marginalization of the African American school and directly limits the intellectual capital of administrators in African American schools. Other reasons offered for course limits include the need to cram courses and content into financially manageable programs for students, and the belief that core skills and understandings are effective for administrators in all schools regardless of ethnicity or socioeconomic status.

SOCIAL JUSTICE

The work of Ladson-Billings (1995) and Theoharis (2007) moves the discussion of context from Orr's (2007) recognition of the importance of the urban context of poverty and administrative challenges and Leithwood et al.'s (2004) view that contextual problem solving is most critical in failing schools, to the specific skill requirements administrators need in urban schools to be successful. He identified the distinctions between good leaders and social justice leaders. One example references instructional programs: a good leader "supports a variety of programs for diverse learners," however, a social justice leader "strengthens core teaching and curriculum and insures that diverse students have access to that core" (p. 252). A second example addresses the use of data: good leaders "use data to understand the realities of the school" whereas social justice leaders "see all data through a lens of equity" (p. 252).

The construct of social justice was an intrinsic strand of my leadership in Black districts where I served. My major focus in these schools was to establish a vision that parents, teachers, and community members could identify with to maximize the performance of marginalized students. My agenda was to promote high quality instruction by developing strong curriculum structures and identifying school and district barriers to student achievement. Without this social justice agenda I would have been unable to use strategies to transform school cultures and the structures related to curriculum, pedagogical practices, and management. I expected that the social justice agenda espoused by the academy would be a strong support for administrators in African American schools and an orientation that I could relate to and teach in my courses.

The curricula of educational preparation programs minimize ethnic diversity and are barriers to social justice instruction. In a study of seven urban school principals (Theoharis, 2007) recognized as school leaders for social justice, the researcher asked what resistance they encountered in their social justice work. They found the educational administration curricula of the academy were major impediments to social justice. The participants uniformly indicated that race, disability, and English Language Learners (ELL) were not priorities in their administrative preparation programs. I have a concern as a Black academician that I am failing to instill in and/or support the essential and critical premise that prospective administrators can mitigate and reduce the effects of low social-economic status on at-risk subpopulations. In the Theoharis (2007) study the participants found their social justice empathies were not enhanced by their university preparation and they did not develop strategies to deal with racist teachers, entrenched racist school practices, and restrictive school climates. A review of research on the curriculum in educational leadership preparation programs by Osterman and Hafner (2009), indicates that social justice is an important espoused theme in an educational leadership curriculum. However, they identified studies showing that social justice themes are not incorporated widely into the enacted curriculum. The few studies that explored the effect of exposure to a social justice curriculum identified changes in students' espoused theory that corresponded to the curriculum, but the one study of a curriculum that was directly focused on social justice, was unable to find evidence that students were applying these principles in their work. The social justice strand, although having the potential to inform and direct the actions and decisions of administrators in African American schools is sadly minimized in the educational leadership curricula. Readings that offer a social justice perspective (Larson & Murtadha, 2002; Spillane, Hallett, & Diamond, 2003) should be a staple for administrative preparatory programs. It is necessary for the scholarship by Black, Asian, Hispanic/Latino and other typically marginalized scholars to be required preparatory course reading and reflection (Fenwick & Pierce, 2002b).

THE EPISTEMOLOGICAL RESTRAINTS TO ACKNOWLEDGING BLACK SCHOOL EXPERIENCES

In addition to my challenge of expanding the context of my pedagogy to the Black school setting, I find the underpinnings of the administrative leadership literature to be contrary to my experiential and racial knowledge base. As a practitioner I could ignore this literature and focus on documents appropriate to my district. However, as an academician I have more restricted choices in the selection of documents if I am to expose students to the full scope of leader skills, responsibilities, and understandings. Bernal and Villalpando (2002) explain the dilemma for faculty of color as "the Eurocentric epistemological perspective creating racialized double standards that contribute to an apartheid of knowledge separating from mainstream scholarship the type of research and teaching that faculty of color often produce" (p. 171). They explained apartheid of knowledge as ignoring and excluding the "cultural resources" that are based on the epistemologies that many faculty of color bring to academia (p. 172). The syllabi as constructed are not inclusive of all ethnic stakeholders and, when ethnic groups are acknowledged, they are portrayed in a stereotypical manner. In order to understand the effects of this dimension of teaching I will look at the assumptions of the written curriculum.

The course syllabi in educational leadership courses mirror the exclusionary current best thinking of scholars in the limited scope of educational leadership. It is therefore legitimate for me to inquire into the philosophical roots of the educational leadership curriculum and the cultural scope of that curriculum to determine the relevance of the educational administration curriculum for potential school administrators in Black schools. I believe the epistemological underpinnings of the educational leadership field, the intra-disciplinary matrix or the discussibles that direct the syllabi of courses have limited my ability to make ethnic issues and concerns central to instructional delivery. In addition, the hidden curricular messages and the social justice curriculum strand, important to my success and value as a Black administrator, are largely ignored in syllabi.

The framework of purported sound and important research that frames our curriculum content may in fact be an institutional racist structure that highlights and legitimizes African Americans as below the level of other groups on a number of reported and therefore important scales. The insidiousness of institutional racism is revealed through how we view African American communities and their constituents. If it is found that our research epistemologies are themselves racially biased as suggested by Scheurich and Young (1997), disconnection will occur through marginalization of African American schools. They argue that epistemological racism is based on broad civilizational assumptions that are seen as norms rather than as historically evolved social constructions. For African American schools this means that they are excluded from the epistemologies legitimated by a dominant White race with a specific and non inclusive social history. The notion that the very underpinning of the academy's research agenda is mired in epistemological racism must be addressed. The nature, methods, limitations, and validity of the content knowledge and beliefs in educational research create a misunderstanding of the significance of race as a problem in educational research. The basis for the construct of epistemological racism is embedded in the syllogism that if all of our epistemologies in education are products of a dominant White racial social history, then subcultures such as African Americans will have different epistemologies based on their divergent social positions.

An example of the results of epistemological racism is the persistence and perseverance on the issue of parental involvement. Administrative programs consistently emphasize the necessity for parents to be involved in schools illustrating what parent involvement should look like in schools and teaching strategies for effective parental involvement. There is minimal acknowledgment that parent involvement often operates differently in high-poverty African American schools. My contribution to the discussion based on my success in enlisting Black parent support to maximize student performance is excluded because it is an epistemology based on Black social position.

During my practice in schools I drew upon non-leadership research studies and my experience to develop an alternate view of the parental engagement aspects of No Child Left Behind (NCLB) for Black schools (Thompson, 2007). While I recognized parent involvement as critical for student achievement, I found only specific strategies seem to have a direct influence on the academic performance of my students. Administrators in low-income and high needs African American schools frequently confront the obstacle of minimal parental involvement not faced by their colleagues in White schools. Many have ignored the NCLB mandates for parental involvement minimizing the importance and focusing on internal school structures to fill the parental gap. Others move from one NCLB parental strategy to another hoping to effect changes in parent motivation and student achievement. Still others rely on top-down approaches to giving information, while failing to encourage dialogue and provide feedback mechanisms for parents. Unfortunately, the legal frameworks of NCLB do not encourage or support alternative strategies to parental involvement. As an administrator in a Black district, I did not have the luxury of implementing the NCLB requirements for parental involvement with the same lens as administrators in a White middle-class school. The manner in which I re-conceptualized my approach, integrating informational, governance and engagement strategies, and aligned them to specific instructional goals that engaged my parents in the support of their children would be necessary for the success of an administrator in a Black school. However, the epistemology of educational leadership fails to make this distinction for praxis and not only minimizes my academic voice, but also places my voice at the outskirts of the discussion of parental involvement framed by curriculum. My challenge in the face of epistemologies that define the field is to convince my students that because of race and social class, Black parents have a status that places them in a disadvantaged social location compared to the advantaged social location of white parents. This teaching agenda frequently makes students uncomfortable, resistant or combative creating negative feelings that are reflected in the students' evaluations of the instructor. My experiences necessitate teaching my courses through a social justice lens. However, initially I was confronted with reduced student participation that Ladson-Billings (1996) termed "silences as weapons" (p. 79). In her article she indicated that teacher race, class and/or gender could precipitate student silence especially if students perceive the promulgation of a specific agenda. Black professors who believe that leadership of Black schools is critical to academic and social success do not have the luxury of sanitizing the leadership curriculum to assuage student sensitivities. However, with the knowledge that my students may find themselves in Black schools, I must be accountable for provoking dialogue through alternative pedagogically sound strategies to reflect and examine their belief systems.

African American School Administrators in Internship Experiences

An unintended consequence of the internship experience for students is reinforcement of the belief that high performing districts have the more effective administrators. The internship component of educational administration programs has the potential to broaden the experiences of potential administrators in a number of settings. Schein (1993) maintains that if leaders do not understand the cultures of their schools they will not be successful. Therefore, my role of instructor is to use internship experiences of students to expand and enlighten their views of all schools, but especially environments unfamiliar to them such Black schools, teachers and administrators. However, while the research literature does address the importance of internship site placements, there is little research on the quality of placements, let alone the diversity of placements. In our program, students complete their building level internship at their schools primarily because there are not full-time internships available due to the time limitations of working teachers. We urge students to select a district level internship in another setting that the program arranges for them, but do not use diversity as selection criteria. The perception of the administrator as successful is the major criterion and frequently eliminates Black administrators from being pursued as mentors if success is measured by student achievement scores. Most students view African American schools as inferior or undesirable placements because of achievement gaps between predominantly White and Black districts. They typically do not see themselves as working in Black districts and Preparation programs are reluctant to send administrative interns to lower scoring, high density Black districts. This further reinforces the belief that high performing districts have the more effective administrators.

Although in several states there is a requirement for student teachers to have experiences in both high and low needs schools, this requirement has not been extended to administrative certification in my state and perhaps others. Since students lack valid experiences in Black districts, I find it is my responsibility to teach the norms, values, competencies, practices, and subjectivities of the Black experience. The challenge when using my experiences as data in the classroom is to avoid being viewed as an exception or my school as not representative of Black schools. O'Connor, Lewis, and Mueller (2007) maintain the heterogeneity of the Black experience is masked because of focus on the Black poor as a homogenous social category. This creates the tendency to "overlook the ways in which space, time, and social class moderate the experience of being Black" (p. 543) and for White students to view my experiential data as outliers. I find I am in the unenviable position of serving as a sole voice presenting, speaking for and defending Black schools, a position that creates dissatisfaction by requiring me to continually renegotiate my imposed roles as activist, teacher, and colleague.

THE HIDDEN CURRICULUM—
AFRICAN AMERICAN SCHOOL MARGINALIZATION

The hidden curriculum is the discrepancy between the intent of the academy's written curriculum and the actual attitudes and values students leave their programs with. This aspect of curriculum is most pronounced in my courses during class discussions when students are asked to apply concepts and understanding to their work experiences. It is specifically during these verbal exchanges that negative attitudes and values toward African American schools can be identified. My role as instructor is to challenge the negative stereotypes students have of Black schools. However, I am acutely aware that my experiences can have the reverse effect of reinforcing stereotypes. This understanding is particularly important because these students are redefining their social class status as they complete the leadership program. Anyon (1980) attributes this change to students viewing themselves as managerial and in greater control of their work environments. She maintains that based on the types of schools they find themselves administering, they will create stereotypic structures that can serve as barriers to students they view as of lower social status. I recall that when I was a student in an administrative certification program the instructor solicited my urban experiences and, at that time, I believed valued as authentic my contributions to class discussion. However, the experiences I related in contrast to my peers in White middle-class schools reinforced their Black school perceptions of lack of resources, general concern for classroom and school management, and issues of safety. At that time I became less self-disclosing because of my naiveté and ignorance of White schools (Ladson-Billings, 1996). My discussions of the merits of my school, such as four of my students being accepted to Ivy League schools or my percentage of students in the highly praised countywide vocal and instrumental music competitions were greeted with obvious surprise and respect for my personal skill in creating the platforms for such achievements "against great odds." However, these positives from my African American school were more often than not paltry compared to the percentages of Ivy League acceptances of students in my classmates' schools, or the requirement of all students in some schools to participate at some level of music competitions. Therefore, as an instructor I find an added responsibility when critiquing discussions and assignments that demand student experiential input to be vigilant of stereotypical view of urban African American schools.

As a professor with a small percentage of students working in urban or urban-like schools, I must be continually aware of my inclination to draw on and highlight the distinctions between urban and other school environments. Several Black students in low performing Black schools in one of my certificate programs privately expressed how the educational leadership program had made their present teaching assignments intolerable. They indicated that the program had for the first time really heightened their awareness of the differences between schools in urban and other settings and gave impetus for what may have been thoughts to find positions in non-urban settings as teachers. However, more significantly, they indicated that upon completion of their programs they would be applying for non-urban or exclusively high performing schools or school districts. If the medium is the message (Am I the messenger?) this and perhaps other educational leadership programs are merely not preparing students for educational leadership in urban schools but actively if not consciously discouraging their application to these districts.

Service

The shift in my roles from being potentially served by the academy, to one in the position to serve Black schools has created conflict. There are no formal partnership arrangements in leadership programs for faculty to connect with Black schools. This missing structure reflects the attitude of the academy for external service. My natural inclination to provide service to Black schools is thwarted by the low esteem to which external service is held in the academy, and pervasive attitudes of superiority of academicians toward Black administrators. This view is supported by the findings of Williams and Williams (2006) in their study of perceptions of African American junior faculty. The study states,

> African American faculty at my institution tend to be in demand within the local Black community … from speaking at churches and schools to helping design a survey or providing feedback and direction for a community project. However, the service we provide isn't recognized and definitely not rewarded in our institution. (p. 10)

Assessing faculty contribution in the area of service is more amorphous than scholarly research and teaching. Faculty in turn give less attention to external service because it is less rewarded (Ward, 2003). The works of Butin (2007) and Adams, Ajirontutu, and Jay (2007) suggest that service learning within social justice contexts can reduce the notions of power and privilege that scholars have when approaching Black schools. However, service learning remains relatively unimportant as an area of the academy service agenda. As an untenured faculty member I am cautioned that presentations and in-service activities including mentoring have less weight than internal university service. Therefore, as a former practitioner with deep professional and emotional roots in a number of Black school districts, I find I am challenged to provide service to Black districts. In addition, in discussions with colleagues, I find their approach to Black schools to vary from charity to autocracy. They blame administrators for the conditions of Black schools and they design an agenda for "fixing" the administrators, teachers, and/or students. Most instructors ignore Milner (2007) who maintains that academicians must be more culturally respectful and responsive to communities of color.

In this volume, Raquel Farmer-Hinton's discussion of service scholarship indicates that the service experience she engaged in significantly informed her research, changed her research agenda and enabled her to dissect the research literature in a more productive manner. The minimization of service limits my ability to continue to continue to expand my experiential base regarding ever-changing Black schools and to pursue areas of research that I feel are important.

CONCLUSION: ADDRESSING THE DISCONNECTION BETWEEN THE ACADEMY AND AFRICAN AMERICAN SCHOOLS

The issues of race, social class, and gender as a Black male in American society are omnipresent. However, in my former role as an administrator in a predominantly Black district the distinctions between these identities were merged. The Black schools where I served in did not conflict with or present challenges to how I perceived my role in the workplace. My transition to the academy's leadership program faculty has activated issues of racial identity, organizational standing, and gender. It is clear from this discussion of the academy's scholarship, teaching, and service agenda that race, social class, and gender moderate the roles and responsibilities of faculty. In addition, these factors must be integrated. When race, social class, and gender are viewed as homogenous, we fail to understand the complexity of their combined impact on faculty and students thus making us prone to over simplification of problems and concerns. What I find is that there is a misalignment of how I experienced these constructs in my work as a practitioner with how these constructs are embedded in the core of leadership programs. The concern for the academy is twofold: (1) practitioners such as me will leave leadership programs where they feel marginalized and/or, (2) the programs will be denied perspectives of Black schools, teachers, and students that will be critical to their success in any setting.

Micro approaches to ameliorating this concern must be addressed on several levels including the individual Black faculty and the entire leadership program faculty. As a Black faculty member I found in the foundations literature sources of historical, sociological, and philosophic perspectives that expanded my pedagogy by challenging the pervasive colorblind framework. I found I was able to expand my syllabi including required readings from a variety of perspectives that supported students in understanding the relationship of their administrative roles in the context of a variety of school contexts. In addition, I was able to utilize the national trend for the passing of tests for administrative certification to demonstrate the need to have a cohesive programmatic focus. The curriculum mapping that took place in response to these new assessments enabled the inclusion of social justices and reflective leadership strands across courses.

The challenges to service by Black academicians are ameliorated by the adoption and perpetuation of new models of external service. Raquel Farmer-Hinton's chapter demonstrates how service experiences legitimately link research agendas to school and community service. Her description of her personal reflections of growth from her service experience serves as a powerful demonstration of how practitioner experience and academician foci can be blended to enhance racial, social, and gender identity of Blacks. New junior faculty in educational leadership programs have several important and effective models to emulate as they combine their service and research agendas. The contributions of Scott (2003, 2004; Scott, Avolin, & McVea, 2003; Scott & Fisher, 2004; Scott, Lew, & Silver, 2003) to an understanding of Black girls were based on a school-based program she established in a low performing racially segregated suburban district. Her qualitative longitudinal study of these girls provided significant insights to school administrators for developing new structures through policy and procedures for meeting the changing needs of girls as they progress through a challenged school system.

Redefining the Servers and the Served

On a macro level, the work of Fenwick and Pierce (2002a) offered a hopeful future for the academy's relationship with African American schools. They noted a trend in doctoral educational leadership programs toward changes in course content as becoming more relevant to preparation for effective leadership. They also noted the growth in regionally available programs and their potential influence on African American school leadership. This direction refocuses the academy's raison d'etre on people in the context of their environments. In my role as faculty I now see myself as the server to potential administrators in very distinct schools and school districts. My scholarship must be inclusive and deep enough to address the needs of the least served schools, which are primarily urban and African American. Perhaps as researchers, as servers we tend to confuse the served with servants. African American schools are not servants to the academy but the served of the academy. This distinction permits the development of a mutualistic symbiotic relationship between the academy and African American schools.

REFERENCES

Adams, S., Ajirotutu, C., & Jay, G. (2007). Service learning, multicultural education, and the core curriculum: A model for institutional change. *Diversity Digest, 10*(2), 9–11.

Anyon, J. (1980). Social class and the hidden curriculum. *Journal of Education, 162,* 67–92.

Bell, D. A. (2004). *Silent covenants: Brown v. Board of Education and the unfulfilled hopes for racial reform.* New York: Oxford University Press.

Bernal, D. B., & Villalpando, O. (2002). An apartheid of knowledge in academia: The struggle over the Alegitimate knowledge of faculty of color. *Equity & Excellence in Education, 35*(2), 169–180.

Bonilla-Silva, E. (2003). *Racism without racists: Color-blind racism and the persistence of racial inequality in the United States.* Lanham, MD: Rowman and Littlefield.

Boyer, E. L. (1990). *Scholarship reconsidered: Priorities of the professoriate.* Lawrenceville, NJ: Princeton University Press,

Butin, D. (2007). Justice-Learning: Service-learning as justice-oriented education. *Equity and Excellence in Education. 40*(2), 1–7.

Cooper, H. (1996). Speaking power to truth: Reflections of an educational researcher after 4 years of school board service. *Educational Researcher, 25*(1), 29–33.

Delgado, R., & Stefancic, J. (2001). *Critical race theory: An introduction.* New York: New York University Press.

Donmoyer, R. (1995). A knowledge base for educational administration: Notes from the field. In R. Donmoyer, M. Imber, & J. J. Scheurich (Eds.), *The knowledge base in educational administration: Multiple perspectives* (pp. 74–95). Albany: SUNY Press.

Edelman, M. (1977). *Political language: Words that succeed and politics that fail.* New York: Academic Press.

Fenwick, L. T., & Pierce, M. C. (2002a). *Professional development of principals.* Washington, DC, ERIC Clearinghouse on Teaching and Teacher Education. (ERIC Document Reproduction Service No. ED 477 731).

Fenwick, L. T., & Pierce, M. C. (2002b). To train or educate: How should the next generation of principals be prepared? *The Principal Advisor, 2*(1), 1–2.

Fordham, S. (1996). *Blacked out: Dilemmas of race, identify, and success at Capital High* (p. 423). (Eric Document Reproduction Service No. ED 398 349).

Giroux, H. (1989). Schooling as a form of cultural politics: Towards a pedagogy of and for difference. In H.A. Giroux & P. McLaren (Eds.), *Critical pedagogy, the state and cultural struggle*. Albany: State University of New York Press.

Goldring, E., & Sims, P. (2005). Modeling creative and courageous school leadership through district-community-university partnerships. *Educational Policy, 19*(1), 223.

Griffin, K., Allen, W. R., & Kimura-Walsh, E. (2007). Those who left, those who stayed: Exploring the high-achieving Black and Latina/o students at magnet and nonmagnet Los Angeles high schools (2001–2002). *Educational Studies: Journal of the American Educational Studies Association, 42*(3) 229–247.

Hilliard, A. G., III (1995, November 12). *Teacher education from an African American perspective*. Paper presented at an Invitational Conference on Defining the Knowledge Base for Urban Teacher Education, Atlanta, GA.

hooks, b. (1995). "This is the oppressor's language/yet I need it to talk to you": Language a place of struggles. In A. Dingwaney & C. Maier (Eds.), *Between language and cultures*. Pittsburgh, PA: University of Pittsburgh Press.

Hostetler, K. (2005). Research news and comment: What is "good" educational research? *Educational Researcher, 34*(6), 16–21.

Ladson-Billings, G. (1995). But that's just good teaching! The case for culturally relevant pedagogy. *Theory Into Practice, 34*(3), 159–165.

Ladson-Billings G. (1996). Silences as weapons: Challenges of a black professor teaching white students. *Theory Into Practice, 35*(2), 79–86.

Ladson-Billings, G. J., & Tate, W. (2006). *Education research in the public interest: Social justice, action, and policy*. New York: Teachers College Press.

Larson, C. L., & Murtadha, K. (2002). Leadership for social justice. In J. Murphy (Ed.), *The education leadership challenge: Redefining leadership for the 21st century. NSSE yearbook* (pp. 134–161). Chicago: University of Chicago Press.

Leithwood, K., Louis, K. S., Anderson, S. & Wahlstrom, K. (2004). *How leadership influences student learning* (Learning for Leadership Project). New York: The Wallace Foundation.

Levine, A. (2005). *Educating school leaders* (The Education Schools Project). New York: Teachers College.

Mazzocco, P. (2006). *The dangers of not speaking about race*. Kirwan Institute for the Study of Race and Ethnicity. The Ohio State University. Retrieved from www.mazzocco.6@osu.edu

McClintock, R. (2007). Educational research. *Teachers College Record*. Retrieved December 10, 2007, Retrieved from http://www.tcrecord.org. ID Number: 13956.

Milner, H. R. (2007). Race, culture, and researcher positionality: Working through dangers seen, unseen, and unforeseen. *Educational Researcher, 36*(7), 388–400.

O'Connor, C., Lewis, A., & Mueller, J. (2007). Researching "black" educational experiences and outcomes: theoretical and methodological considerations. *Educational Researcher, 36*(9), 541–552.

Ogbu, J. U. (2003). *Black American students in an affluent suburb: A study of academic disengagement*. A volume in the Sociocultural, Political, and Historical Studies in Education Series 2003, pp. 340 (ERIC Document Reproduction Service No. ED 476 118)

Orr, M. T. (2007). *How preparation influences school leaders and their school improvement: Comparing exemplary and conventionally prepared principals*. Paper presented at the annual meeting of the American Educational Research Association, Chicago, IL.

Osterman, K., & Hafner, M. (2009). *Curriculum in leadership preparation: Understanding where we have been in order to know where we might go*. New York: Routledge.

Park, B., & Judd, C. M. (2005). Rethinking the link between categorization and prejudice within the social cognition perspective. *Personality and Social Psychology Review, 9*(2), 108–130.

Pattillo-McCoy, M. (1999). *Black picket fences: Privilege and peril among the black middle class*. Chicago, University of Chicago Press.

Schein, E. H. (1993). *Organizational culture and leadership* (2nd ed.). San Francisco: Jossey-Bass.

Scheurich, J. J., & Young, M. D. (May 1997). Coloring epistemologies: Are our research epistemologies racially biased? *Educational Researcher, 26*(4), 4–16.

Scott, K. A. (2004, August). *African-American girls' peer groups in a state-operated school district*. Refereed roundtable at the American Sociological Association, San Francisco, CA.

Scott, K. A. (2003, February). *Getting through: African-American girls' perceptions of a state operated district*. Paper presented at the Ethnography in Education Research Forum, Philadelphia, PA.

Scott, K. A., Avolin, C., & McVea, N. (2003, February). *Forty-minutes and counting: Ethnographic research in a State operated urban school district*. Paper presentation at the Ethnography in Education Research Forum, Philadelphia, PA.

Scott, K. A., & Fisher, M. (2004, April). *African-American girls' virtual selves in a state-operated school district*. Paper presented at the American Educational Research Association, San Diego, CA.

Scott, K. A. Lew, J., & Silver, M. (2003, August). *Teaching race relations*. Roundtable presentation at the American Sociological Association, Atlanta, GA.

Silberman, C. E. (1970). *Crisis in the classroom*. New York: Random House.

Spillane, J. P., Hallett, T., & Diamond, J. B. (2003). Forms of capital and the construction of leadership: Instructional leadership in urban elementary schools. *Sociology of Education, 76*(1), 1–17.

Theoharis, G. (2007). Social justice educational leaders and resistance: Toward a theory of social justice leadership. *Educational Administration Quarterly, 43*(2), 221–258.

Thompson, E. G. (2007). Reconceptualizing parent involvement in minority communities: Expanding NCLB to improve student achievement in African American schools. *Journal of School Public Relations, 27*(4), 420–444.

Ward, K. (2003). *Faculty service roles and the scholarship of engagement*. ERIC Digest. (ERIC) Document Reproduction Service No. ED 480 469). Retrieved March 10, 2008, from http://www.ericdigests.org/2004-3/faculty.html

Williams, B. N., & Williams, S. M. (2006). Perceptions of African American male junior faculty on promotion and tenure: Implications for community and social capital. *Teachers College Record, 108*(2), 287–315. Retrieved May 16, 2008, from http://www.tcrecord.org/PrintContent.asp?ContentID=12311

Zweigenhaft, R. L., & Domhoff, G. W. (2003). *Blacks in the White elite: Will the progress continue?* Lanham, MD: Rowman & Littlefield.

CHAPTER 11

GETTING BEYOND THE SCRIPT

Negotiating the Complexity of Urban Settings as Research Sites

**Amina Jones, Na'ilah Suad Nasir, and
Tryphenia B. Peele-Eady**

INTRODUCTION

How difficult can it be to donate a bed? After completing 18 months of ethnographic study at a residential shelter for young adults aged 18–24, it was time for Amina Jones to leave the "field" and focus on completing the written results of the project. Yet, leaving the field was difficult because of Jones' connections to the staff, neighborhood centers, and local schools that were beyond the scope of her study. When Jones announced her plan to relocate to another state, shelter staff asked if she had any home goods to donate. Jones offered to donate several items including a bed. At the time, three former shelter residents were transitioning to unfurnished apartments. Coordinating the pick-up of the bed was both a logistical and interpersonal challenge for Jones. For instance, the organization used its 15-passenger van to transport clients to the shelter and also to do late-

*Research in Urban Educational Settings: Lessons Learned and
Implications for Future Practice*, pp. 201–222
Copyright © 2011 by Information Age Publishing

night outreach to youth living on streets. It was difficult to establish a pick-up time that did not conflict with this schedule. Due to high staff turnover, there was only one outreach coordinator and he would need assistance to move the bed. The director of the organization called to inform Jones that two residents volunteered to come with the coordinator to help remove the bed from her apartment. With some hesitancy, Jones pointed out that both volunteers had participated in her study and asked if the client/staff code of conduct that prohibited home visits should be extended to include her. In this moment, as in many others, the absence of borders in Jones' role as a community member, volunteer, and researcher became obvious.

Many factors contributed to the blurring (or absence) of borders that defined Jones' researcher positionality. These factors included, but were not limited to race and ethnicity, gender, and age—factors that, as we later discuss, subsequently mediated our insider and outsider status in different ways across the various sites. Like Jones, Na'ilah Suad Nasir and Tryphenia B. Peele-Eady are African American women, teachers, and speakers of African American English, with knowledge of, and interest in, African American cultural norms and values. We all conducted studies in predominately African American urban settings we lived and worked in or near the communities we studied. In this chapter we draw on our interactions as researchers in three particular sites—an urban high school with a long history of failure, but in the midst of reform; a crisis shelter for homeless teens; and an African American Sunday school church community—to explore some of the features of urban settings that make them complex research sites within which to negotiate methodology and researcher positionality. Specifically, we focus on three layers of challenges: (1) practical constraints and affordances for conducting research in urban settings, including high turnover of staff, teachers, and students, issues of space, and finding ways to reciprocate in high-need settings, (2) understanding the difference between the reality of interactions and outcomes in these settings, and the existence of a "script" that participants selectively used to talk about their experiences, and (3) negotiating our own positionality in these settings—including both our own goals and sensitivities to the expectations and racial, gendered, and age roles in which we were cast by research participants. As participants in each site marked various aspects of our identities as salient, our research relationship with participants—that is, the nature of our conversations and vantage as participants and observers in the sites—was reshaped. Although challenging, these shifts in positionality allowed us to get beyond the script that participants may have commonly used in a research context, to gain access to information that otherwise would have been unavailable to us as researchers. The three layers of challenges we describe were negotiated in partnership with participants, and the nuances of these interactions are particularly relevant for analyzes of subjectivity and methodology in urban research settings.

We focus on the work Nasir and Jones conducted in the high school and shelter sites to highlight the constraints and resource limitations of urban settings as research contexts, and we draw on Peele-Eady's research of the Sunday school church community to further highlight the relational challenges of conducting research as cultural insiders. In all three instances, we found ourselves having to negotiate and renegotiate these constraints, while unpacking scripts often typical of urban contexts. In the next sections, we introduce the three contexts and discuss aspects of the sites that made them unique.

INTRODUCTION TO THE STUDIES

While different in scope, all three studies took place in large, predominately African American cities in Northern California. Jones and Nasir focused on Jackson High, the primary high school serving South Jackson residents, and a nearby crisis shelter for teens. In the year prior to Jones and Nasir's project, the 4-year graduation rate at Jackson High was 54%. Jackson High School was in the midst of reform, undergoing a district mandated curricular and structural redesign process facilitated by several outside education agencies, and administrators who identified improving the graduation rate as a top priority. Drawing on the existing literature on school engagement, school connection, and achievement (Finn, 1989; Furrer & Skinner, 2003; Klem & Connell, 2004; Libbey, 2004) among African-American youth, Nasir and Jones' research team designed a study to examine: (1) relevant aspects of connection and disconnection in an urban school setting, how these processes took shape, and how the context might differ for different students, (2) how these aspects of (dis)connection were related to one another, and (3) how these aspects of (dis)connection were related to learning and academic identity. Nasir and Jones conducted a 2-year ethnographic study that involved multiple methods of data collection, including student shadowing, participant observation, student focus groups, and interviews with students, teachers, and staff members as well as a "connectedness" survey (findings from this study can be found in Nasir, Jones, & McLaughlin, 2007, 2009).

We conducted observations in classrooms and during lunchtime as well as in unmonitored areas around the school site where students congregated during class-time at least twice weekly for the duration of the study. Twenty-five students took part in weekly focus groups for the first year. Seven students, across genders and achievement levels, were shadowed for at least 8 full school days during class sessions and during lunch.

Detailed field notes were taken for both general observations and for student shadowing. The team also conducted formal and informal interviews with students, teachers, and administrators. Interview questions focused on the nature of the school climate, experiences with choosing courses, relationships with teachers and staff, and orientations toward school. Interviews with teachers and staff also addressed school climate, discipline, and student motivation and behavior. Finally, we conducted a survey of 120 students, which measured connection and its multiple aspects, academic identity, family support for school, racial identity, and achievement.

During the course of the study, 8 of the 25 focus group students did not advance to graduation. Three students left before completing 4 years and did not re-enroll in another school program, two students enrolled in a GED program, and three students attended 4 years, but had not acquired enough units to graduate with their cohort. We continued interviews with this subset at locations throughout the neighborhood. Staff also connected with the GED program at the nearby community center that enrolled many former students of the high school. The community center also managed a crisis shelter that provided temporary residence to clients between 18–24 years old. Through an emergent research design, the crisis shelter subsequently became another core site for the research project and Jones' dissertation research, which focused on understanding the ways in which *disconnected* youth manage the transition to adulthood. To that end, 75 youth were surveyed, 10 service-providers were interviewed, and 10 residents participated in ongoing case-study profiles. Weekly observations were documented through field notes. Findings from this aspect of the work are forthcoming in Jones' doctoral dissertation.

Peele-Eady's work in the Sunday school church community was also part of a 2-year ethnographic study. Focusing on the language socialization of African American children in the Black church context, Peele-Eady observed and audiotaped the Sunday school lessons, interviewed members of the Sunday school church community, held ongoing conversations with the students' parents, and engaged in informal conversation with family and other church community members. Participants in Peele-Eady's study were the Sunday school students, ages 9 to 12, their two teachers (one of whom became the focal teacher of Peele-Eady's research), and the pastor of the church (whom members considered the master teacher in the site). Peele-Eady's goal for data collection was to gather any information that offered insight into the participants' cultural action and understanding of it, particularly with respect to communicative behavior. She conducted classroom observations of the Sunday school class, which met every Sunday morning for approximately 1 hour and 40 minutes. She entered the classroom when Sunday school began, sat in the back of the classroom, writing copious field notes (Emerson, Fretz, & Shaw, 1995), and refrained from interacting with students unless they or their teachers addressed her directly. Peele-Eady wrote notes about the action she observed—such as what the children and teachers did and talked about— and at various stages in the process, she began trying to understand the significance that the children and their Sunday school teachers seemed to attach to their actions.

Interview questions for the Sunday school teachers and the pastor covered the following topics: general background information, their ideas and attitudes about their work in the church, and their instructional goals for the children who attend church and Sunday school. In addition to scheduled interviews with Sunday school teachers and focus group interviews with the children, Peele-Eady maintained detailed records of her informal conversations, which often took place after class, in the classrooms, and in the hallways of the church and later, away from the church campus. Findings from this research can be found in Peele-Eady (2005, 2008).

PRACTICAL AND ETHICAL CONSTRAINTS: FROM THE STUDY TO THE FIELD

There are practical and ethical constraints in implementing any research study. Some of these constraints, such as staff turnover, resource limitations and competing student needs are more pronounced in urban settings. The lower levels of resources and higher levels of need in such settings raise important ethical considerations in the field. South Jackson was by almost any definition, resource-poor. According to the 2000 census data, 19,684 people lived in the South Jackson neighborhood. Almost half of the neighborhood residents ages 25 and over did not have a high school degree, and income levels in the neighborhood were the lowest in the county. South Jackson is the historically African American neighborhood in a county where Whites and Asian Americans comprise the majority. Jackson High School was the smallest in the district and had a long history of reproducing failure for students.

The Sunday school church community in Peele-Eady's study was located on the Southside of a predominately African American city similar to South Jackson. Although there were numerous small businesses, service stores, residential homes, and churches of varying denominations in the area, and over one-half (53.2%) of the residents were homeowners, the south side, which residents described as "reeking of gangs and drugs," had the reputation of being among if not the most crime-laden parts of the city.

Limited resources and issues of space and location presented both practical constraints, as we sought to find space and time to interview participants, and ethical constraints, as we observed and made decisions about portraying participants and teaching and learning interactions.

Practical Constraints

Nasir and Jones encountered the practical constraints of space allotment early in the research process. Originally administrators arranged for the student focus groups to meet in the community room that was located on the first floor near the main office and the front entrance to the school. This space was ideal because it was larger than the standard classroom and was furnished with small round tables and chairs that readily accommodated facilitating discussions. After a few sessions, we were informed that they needed to relocate because the community room was going to be used to process students who were caught hanging out in the neighborhood during truancy sweeps. The truancy sweep project was a joint police department and school district initiative to improve student attendance and decrease the number of youth congregating on public and private property near the school area.

During the course of the truancy sweeps, the focus groups were moved to a lecture style room on the second floor in a wing of the building that was not used for classes. The nearest restrooms, as well as the meeting room itself, were kept locked during the day. We arranged with the nearby book depository clerk to open the doors of the meeting room before each session, but she would not unlock the restrooms because a staff person was not available to monitor the area and she did not want the students to congregate there.

In addition to restricted physical space, the data collection process was also constrained by the limited free time of teachers and staff. The ongoing curricular and structural reforms required after-school and weekend staff development sessions. Teachers who were involved in these efforts had a more informed understanding of student performance data and areas of weakness in the curriculum and school policy, yet they were less available to be interviewed because of these obligations. We negotiated this constraint by attending these planning sessions, staff retreats and being flexible about conducting off-site interviews at times beyond regular school hours.

An additional practical constraint in the work at Jackson High involved sustaining the participation of students who were in the process of disconnecting from school. We anticipated that exploring the phenomenon of the lack of connection to an institution while using that same institution as the logistical base for the study, would be a challenge. Yet, the level at which students were comfortable leaving classrooms and the school campus during the day required us to foster a high level of trust with each student participant as well as to continually reassure teachers and staff that we were not evaluating their management skills. We interviewed and shadowed students congregating in the halls during class time, gambling in the stairways, skipping assigned classes to spend time in other classrooms with friends and leaving the school grounds during the school day.

For Peele-Eady, practical constraints surfaced when trying to connect with the children for individual interviews, which was hard to do because Sunday school attendance fluctuated, and there were limited opportunities to conduct interviews and conduct data outside of church and church-related functions. Another constraint Peele-Eady faced dealt with reconciling research needs with the participants' belief systems. For example, finding time to interview one of the Sunday school teachers proved difficult because she needed time to "pray on" it. Other constraints surfaced when Peele-Eady tried to enter the site. For instance, when Peele-Eady arrived at the church upon that first initial visit, she met a woman in the foyer wearing an outfit patterned after traditional African Kente cloth. Peele-Eady complemented the woman on her outfit. As she said thank you, the woman grabbed Peele-Eady's hand and hugged her as she kissed her on the cheek. After their "greeting," and now feeling comfortable and welcomed, Peele-Eady asked the woman where the Sunday school classes would meet. At that, the woman let go of Peele-Eady, and stared at her as if to ask for clarification. Reading the woman's gestural responses to the inquiry as somewhat suspicious or cautious at the very least, Peele-Eady let the woman know that she had spoken to Pastor and assured the woman that he knew of her plans to visit. Only after mention of this fact, did the woman begin to give Peele-Eady any information. Grabbing Peele-Eady by the arm and escorting her into the sanctuary, the woman finally introduced herself as Sister Battle[1] and she began describing how Sunday school at the church was organized.

As various persons entered the sanctuary and took their places at the front of the church, Sister Battle (whom at the time Peele-Eady later realized was one of the eight original charter members of the church) pointed out persons (mainly ministers and deacons) in leadership roles. Among them was the Pastor's biological son, Reverend Geman, who was an active minister at the church. At the conclusion of the general assembly meeting, Sister Battle escorted Peele-Eady to the front of the church to meet Reverend Geman, explaining that she was a student "doing research on Sunday school." Sister Battle told Reverend Geman that *he* (emphasis added) should escort Peele-Eady around the Sunday school and added that Peele-Eady would wait for him at her seat in the pews until he was ready to show her around the church. This exchange let Peele-Eady know that although Sister Battle had welcomed her with open arms and some "sugar" on the cheek, as a visitor and thus, an outsider, it would be inappropriate for her to roam the halls of the church alone. Peele-Eady negotiated this and other constraints by taking social, cultural, and linguistic cues from the participants for acceptable ways of speaking and relating.

Ethical Constraints

Among the ethical constraints Nasir and Jones encountered was how to describe—and understand—the variations in students' access to teaching and mentoring resources, what we came to call the "two-school" phenomenon. As Nasir and Jones observed classes, and talked to and shadowed students at Jackson High, they came to understand that while a small subset of students had access to effective teachers, challenging curriculum (including AP classes), and strong academic mentoring relationships with adults in the school, the large majority of students at Jackson did not.

The idea that large comprehensive high schools often house two schools that provide vastly different sets of experiences and opportunities for academic engagement has been present in the educational literature for at least 30 years. The classic research on tracking (Oakes, 1982) described schools across the country where certain groups of students— usually White—were enrolled in courses that prepared them for college and engaged them in critical thinking and high-level work, while other groups of students in the same schools--usually of color—were enrolled in low-level and remedial courses and given worksheet after worksheet with little to no academic challenge. These two groups of students hardly ever attended classes together, had different teachers, and essentially comprised two separate schools. More recently, Noguera and Wing (2006) reported findings from a study of a Northern California high school in which they described a similar phenomenon, also occurring along racial lines. Noguera and Wing report striking differences in the types of resources and access to the school environments that White and minority students were afforded.

As the majority of the students at Jackson were African American, the divisions there did not occur across racial lines. However, one school context there offered students higher than average academic standards, viewed students as capable and college bound, provided a prevalence of information about college, and incorporated students into the leadership of the school. Another school context provided students with little academic content, and no information about college or even their own academic standing and requirements to graduate. In this second context, students were put into courses without seeming attention to sequence or level, and class attendance was optional. By and large, students at Jackson realized that these two separate schools existed, though they rarely knew much about the day-to-day academic experiences of students in the "other" school. Collecting data in a school setting where attendance and participation norms were not consistent, required that we pay particular attention to issues of timing, setting, and audience when documenting observations and interviewing students.

For Peele-Eady, the "two school-phenomenon" surfaced in trying to understand the different trajectories that were in place for males and females at the church. While it was clear that men as well as women held leadership roles, it was also clear that these roles were very different. Boys were routinely referred to as "young preachers," and it was a good thing for a boy to be recognized as having the talent and skill to someday preach. As such, activities that adults structured for children overtly positioned boys as future "reachers" and girls as reaching their highest potential doing anything, "except preach."

This issue of two-schools also needed to be negotiated during data analysis. Those students at Jackson High who experienced the school as an environment with little academic content were dropping out and disconnected from a significantly different school context than those in other tracks. The reality of two-schools was also manifest in the way teachers described the use of school resources. At the same time that hopes were high for improving outcomes through structural redesign, veteran staff described systematic inefficiencies in appropriating funds for course materials, computers and supplemental services for under-performance on standardized tests. Nasir and Jones' analytic framework was designed to incorporate the perspectives of Jackson High School as both a place that improperly used resources and worked hard to create better experiences for students and increase the number of graduates who attend college. Similarly, Peele-Eady's task was to understand the Black church as a place that positioned and trained African American children to be leaders, but that also posited different expectations for the kinds of leadership roles girls and boys could occupy.

An additional ethical constraint was managing responsibilities as researchers to report what we observed while honoring the tremendous need, hope, and effort in the school and church communities. Not wanting to be a part of the ways in which university researchers often prey on underperforming schools and districts and students of color to collect exotic stories of failure, the researchers' willingness to adjust their research lens was critical in establishing trusting relationships with participants and in telling a story that was both honest and compassionate. In their book, *The Art and Science of Portraiture*, Jessica Hoffman Davis and

Sarah Lawrence-Lightfoot (1997) describe this dilemma, bringing to the fore, crucial questions about researcher positionality. How does one point out inequities and shortcomings and still remain sensitive to the tremendous challenges that exist for all members of the learning community in urban settings? And what is more, how do we, as both insiders and outsiders, negotiate these challenges with our participants? Through positioning ourselves as researchers invested in documenting how the participants made sense of the low graduation rate or gendered roles and by writing from the perspectives of multiple participants, we were able to include and analyze data on related factors that were not foreseen as significant in the design phase of each study.

ACCESSING AND GETTING UNDERNEATH THE SCRIPT

One aim of qualitative research is to unearth meanings participants attach to their words and experiences, apposing these against observed phenomena and interactions. For us, this unearthing posed particular challenges in the urban settings we studied for two reasons. First, it posed a challenge because participants were caught in a complex web of language (or broadcast) typically used to describe them and their settings, language that vacillated between analyses of institutional constraint, societal marginalization, and individual agency between particular students and young people. Second, it posed a challenge because issues of power and privilege were largely obscured in the scripts that participants were socialized into, yet young people often knew—either vaguely or precisely—that these issues were playing themselves out, but had trouble naming them.

Peele-Eady recalls a moment in her research when the script that adult participants used to talk about gender roles in the church shifted. During a dinner out with the "girls," which meant that men were not included, the Sunday school teachers and the other women who joined them began discussing what women do—and cannot do—in the Baptist church, particularly with the issue of women preaching. In her field journal, Peele-Eady noted that while one of the Sunday school teachers acknowledged understanding Pastor's views on the subject, she also acknowledged that some women, in her view, make good preachers. While it was obvious that the women around the table that evening recognized the central position they had in the church and by all accounts, knew some "dynamic women preachers," it was also obvious that this was not a topic they would offer up in a formal discussion or setting. Instead, to an outsider, their official script reflected acceptance and compliance of the gendered roles set forth. Others (Cole & Guy-Sheftall, 2003) have noted how, even when they disagree, African American women typically do not contest patriarchal ideas about women's roles and positioning in the church. This difference in script led Peele-Eady to pay particular attention to the different activities arranged for girls and boys and youth in general and try to make sense of what adults aimed to teach the children about being male and female members of the church community. In South Jackson, scripts were commonly offered to researchers and evaluators as a standard mode of interaction between the researchers and the researched. Students at the school site and young adults at the crisis shelter were accustomed to visitors coming for evaluation purposes. We entered a school setting crowded with evaluators and new project-based service providers. Students and staff were regularly questioned about their practices. Teaching practices were being monitored and new administrative staff persons were being trained to lead the reorganization. During the same year, a private foundation sponsored an initiative to coordinate on-campus after-school programs to boost student health, personal development and academic performance. In collecting observation and interview data Nasir and Jones had to continually identify themselves as researchers rather than assessors of student and teacher performance. Yet, teaching staff regularly expressed frustrations about the lack of large-scale student outcome improvements despite ongoing reform efforts. Some of the more veteran staff focused on the positive interactions they had with a small number of students and attributed the school's overall low-performing status to other conditions beyond their control. In both instances, teaching staff pointed out the differences between the reality of interactions and the reality of outcomes at the school.

Even with the prevailing sentiment of a small, "family-like" school community and an abundance of positive interactions noted by teachers and students alike, only about half the Jackson student body was graduating. Lower performing students were acutely aware of this and developed a standard script to describe what was happening. During initial interviews, students who were struggling academically adamantly defended Jackson as a "good school," "a place that had a lot of programs," and as "a place where you can do whatever you want." When asked to expand upon these perceptions, students qualified the school's goodness with examples of the social opportunities offered on the campus. All in this initial group had failed at least one course and were observed regularly skipping classes. Nasir and Jones noted that most students spoke often about feeling safe and personally cared about by staff, but not everyone received a consistent academic press to attend class and complete schoolwork. With this insight we were able to probe further about instances where what students were saying about their orientation to school was not supported by their own actions and/or may have been in conflict with the observed actions of school staff. During follow-up interviews with students, we were able to navigate conversations that went beyond the "scripted" responses about positive interactions and disappointing outcomes to better understand the process of how access to academic supports was distributed and the daily experiences of students who were among those identified by administrative staff as not likely to graduate.

A similar atmosphere of evaluation existed at the crisis shelter site. There were fliers posted on the wall near the front entrance to the shelter soliciting former foster care youth for a paid interview session as part of a local school of social work sponsored "outcomes study." When one of the shelter residents pulled a copy from the board, Jones asked her if she had participated in this kind of study before. She nonchalantly replied, "Yeah, it is easy. They always ask the same questions so I just give the same answers." This young woman was referring to exchanges with social workers and case managers that she and her peers described as so routine that their participation began to conform to a particular script. As recipients of several social services, residents at the shelter were well-rehearsed in sharing abbreviated versions of their mental health, household, education and employment histories. As a requirement for staying at the shelter, each client had to undergo a mental health evaluation, draft a transition plan and commit to seeking employment or enrolling in an education program. The operations handbook stipulated that those clients who did not comply would be asked to leave the program. However, staff was lenient about enforcing these case plan obligations. Clients were aware of the flexibility of these rules. One morning, two shelter residents were discussing the challenges that a peer was having with detailing a budget for her plan to move out of the shelter and share an apartment with a friend. The two older residents advised her to copy a budget that another resident submitted.

During the course of the 18-month ethnographic study, interviews with residents at the shelter became more substantive. Residents at the shelter were accustomed to single-survey style research studies and checklist evaluations of progress in meeting case plans. Their willingness to reflect on experiences in emerging adulthood and share details of their aspirations and fears about leaving the shelter increased when they realized that we maintained a consistent presence and did not assist shelter staff in monitoring case plans.

At Jackson, there were also times when the "researcher script" was profoundly different from the script students used to talk about their experiences. At the first focus group session, we asked students if anyone knew of someone who dropped out of the school. School staff members were puzzled when none of the students raised their hands. Staff followed by asking if anyone knew of someone who left the school before graduation. At that point several hands were raised. Comments were made about peers who "stopped coming for a while," "had to take care of a baby," "started working full time," and others who "thought they were seniors, but realized they didn't have enough course credits to graduate." In each case, the disconnection from school was described as a slow reactive process, not an isolated decision to "drop out." Those whose schooling experiences were interrupted by extended truancy, pregnancy, imprisonment, employment, relocation and/or transfer to a GED program were not considered by these students to have "actively" dropped out of school. These were considered among the many challenges that students faced on their path to graduation.

This difference in script about dropping out was more than just a difference of semantics. Students were pointing out to Nasir and Jones that dropping out or leaving school often had less to do with leaving the school and more to do with other challenges and obligations that young people faced as they negotiated the multiple aspects of their lives—of which school was only a part. This difference in script led Nasir and Jones to reconceptualize how they thought about the dropout dilemma to include a careful consideration of limited resources within the community. This reconceptualization was critical in Nasir and Jones' decision to embark upon the work at the community center drop-in teen shelter, which directly explored available community resources for late adolescents. We also reframed our work at Jackson to think more broadly about the interaction between community resources and school engagement in students decisions to discontinue school attendance. School administrative staff embraced the broadened frame of the dropout study; offered us increased opportunities to gathering observation, interview and survey data; and considered the findings to be relevant to ongoing school improvement initiatives. This shared sense of purpose regarding the study at the administrative level was critical in permitting us to collect data in spite of turnovers among teaching staff. As researchers, being open to a new casting of the drop out dilemma, allowed us to understand the manifestations of the issue that were unique to students in the South Jackson school context. As Passari (1997) argues in her study of anthropological locations, "disciplinary imperatives, funding requirements, and the received truths of existing literatures all combine to over-direct our research along avenues of what we already know, expect or assume." Our experience at Jackson confirmed for us that a critical aspect of breaking out of such over-direction is listening deeply to the experiences of our participants.

Volunteer, Neighbor and Ethnographer

Disciplinary convention has identified the "field" as a place where social science researchers go to and return from. However, as Clifford

(1997) argues, there is nothing given about a field and notions of community insides and outsides, homes and abroads, fields and metropoles are increasingly challenged. All three of us maintained ties that challenged such generic boundaries within the communities we studied. At times, the absence of these boundaries was critical to gaining access and developing insight. At other times, as we described earlier, the absence of conventional boundaries gave rise to misunderstandings and challenges to the research as well as new relationships and redefined positionality.

In contrast to Nasir and Jones' work as Jackson and the Shelter as well as most urban classroom settings, state bureaucratic mandates and research process restrictions had no influence on Peele-Eady's work at the church. Unlike school districts, the church did not have a formal review procedure in place for research projects. Ultimately, members trusted that since Peele-Eady had Pastor's approval, she had a similar church upbringing, a southern background, and was a member of the African American community, she would not do any harm. While these beliefs reduced suspicions of Peele-Eady and her intentions and increased participants' interest and willingness to take part in her study, they also placed a heavy burden of responsibility on Peele-Eady—she felt a tremendous sense of personal accountability and responsibility to the work as well as to the participants.

Much of this feeling stemmed from shifting roles as participant observer. Peele-Eady's role as participant observer ranged across a continuum of mostly observation to mostly participation throughout the data collection process (Glesne & Peshkin, 1992). That is, at different periods during data collection, she observed activities and events with little or no interaction with the participants while at other periods she interacted with less observation and more participation. For instance, when she began formal data collection, Peele-Eady had minimal interaction with the participants during the Sunday school lessons, and to avoid too much intrusion, she purposefully sat in the back of the classroom when recording observations.

Approximately 6 months into her project, however, after teachers invited her to participate in the opening and closing prayer rituals, Peele-Eady's role during the Sunday school lessons began to shift from observer as participant to participant as observer (Glesne & Peshkin, 1992). Marking this shift were invitations for Peele-Eady to join teachers and students in prayer and to comment on the lesson whenever the teachers solicited her input. Peele-Eady was overtly positioned as a member of the church when certain church members invited her to participate in extra-church activities and social events outside of church. For instance, some adult members invited Peele-Eady to their homes for social gatherings such as parties featuring the sell of home décor or specialty wares such as candles, beauty products, and food storage systems. Church members also invited Peele-Eady to birthday celebrations and the like, and she even tutored one member's two grandchildren twice a week after school. Consequentially, Peele-Eady became privy to the participants' candid conversations and unofficial scripts.

Thus, establishing and maintaining relationships figured prominently at each phase of Peele-Eady's research process. Her exit from the field illustrates the deeply rooted connections that defined her positionality. As she completed the study and exited the field, Peele-Eady began attending the church less frequently. In response to this change in behavior, members telephoned Peele-Eady to inquire about her slack in attendance, letting her know, they "missed" her, and to make sure that nothing was "wrong."

Peele-Eady's attempts to disconnect from participants' lives while maintaining the positive relationships she had established proved difficult for a number of reasons. For example, by the end of this study, she had become a regular part of the congregation and a part of the members' lives outside of the church context. The pastor sometimes referred to her as their "adopted member," while the focal Sunday school teacher came to consider herself Peele-Eady's "mom away from mom." Peele-Eady experienced feelings of loss and guilt for leaving the site because she had developed meaningful relationships with the participants and she enjoyed attending the church. And just as Peele-Eady became a part of the members' lives, they too became an integral part of her life, which made exiting the field emotionally difficult and draining.

In South Jackson, both Jones and Nasir developed intricate networks with the community and took up multiple complex roles. Due to both practical issues of access and ethical issues of reciprocity, the work in South Jackson began with a series of ongoing "focus groups" in which Jones and Nasir worked together with groups of 9–12 students that met weekly to discuss a variety of topics and to do activities, such as creating maps of their neighborhoods and creating a photographic journal of important places in their school. These focus groups positioned Nasir and Jones as pseudo-teachers in the eyes of students. Jackson High staff perceived these groups as a service intervention by mental health counselors (in part because many of the students were referred to us by the counselor who worked with the most "disconnected" students in the school). Either way, our willingness to commit time and to authentically engage reassured the school community that we were not simply outsiders needing research subjects to write about, but that we cared about the students and wanted to support their development.

As our work in the field developed, this pseudo-teacher role extended to a mentorship role, and we were challenged to make decisions about when we were simply observers, and when it was critical to act as agents of change. Given Jones' status as a graduate student, study participants often asked her questions about college readiness and campus life. One student, Lawrence, expressed an interest in computer programming and asked for advice about a particular local technical college that sent him a flier in the mail. Jones had not heard of the school and advised him to speak with a counselor. When Jones saw the counselor in passing, she mentioned Lawrence's interest and the counselor responded, "Who, Lawrence? He's not going to college. I don't know what he's thinking." That afternoon, Jones approached the attendance coordinator about the situation. He did not know Lawrence personally, but printed out his transcript and reviewed each class and accumulated course credits by year with our research team. He explained that because Lawrence did not retake all of his failed classes and did not enroll in core classes during summer school, he was short of graduation requirements by more than 60 units. During her next interaction with Lawrence, Jones again advised him to speak with his counselor about graduation requirements as well as his plans for college.

At the youth shelter, Jones took up a similar service role as staff asked her to offer a weekly class at the center. After a few months of collecting data at the Community Center, the shelter coordinator asked if Jones could "offer something to add to the nightly shelter activities program." The staff wanted to offer a series of workshops that would be fun, engaging and substantive. She and the staff agreed that Jones would offer an hourly creative writing class on Tuesday evenings. Exercises ranged from personal journaling to group story writing and creating a fictional shelter newspaper. Teaching this workshop proved to complicate Jones' relationships with youth, at times giving her insight into their thoughts and experiences, at other times positioning her as an authority figure to whom they may not want to reveal too much.

These mentoring and teacher roles were sometimes at odds with the role of the researcher, and we often made ethical decisions to allow the mentorship role to supersede the researcher role. With the support of shelter staff, moments arose when we chose to step out of the researcher's role to genuinely support the people in moments. Such was the case when a resident, Claire, revealed that she had a telephone conversation with the man who was her former pimp. As part of Claire's case management plan, she agreed to avoid contact with this person. After seeing him driving past her and her friends at the nearby gas station, she called to him to get details about where he was going and the other person in the car. Knowing that she violated her case plan contract and feeling emotionally upset about the conversation, Claire approached the shelter staff for advice. The shelter coordinator, who was male, turned to Jones and asked if she would speak with Claire, woman to woman, about ending the relationship.

In addition to the positionality as pseudo-teachers and mentors, Nasir and Jones both had additional ties to the community that reinforced their commitment to the youth and the school, but that also posed dilemmas and conflicts at times and complicated their relationship to students and to the community. Nasir was a resident of South Jackson and lived only three blocks from Jackson High. South Jackson was in a period of rapid growth, and like many other urban communities, was undergoing a process of gentrification in which middle-class families of a range of ethnicities were buying the property in the neighborhood due to its proximity to the city, low prices, and restorable houses from the turn of the century. Nasir bought a home in South Jackson, coincidentally, about six months before beginning the research in the community. Nasirs husband also worked in the community for a community-based organization that provided direct mentoring services and programs for youth. Being a resident of South Jackson meant that Nasir deeply understood the neighborhood context that the students were negotiating, and the ways in which members of the community were consistently marginalized, criminalized, and kept in fear through the presence of police, drug dealers and addicts, and prostitution. That marginalization and frustration were intensely felt when a crack-addict took up residence in Nasir's neighbor's backhouse while the neighbor was out of town, and when police responded to a call about loiterers outside only after several hours had passed.

Living in the community also made salient important insights about the drug trade in urban communities and the complexity of the relationship between drug dealers and community residents. From our work in the school, we knew that many of the youth, particularly young men, saw the sale of drugs as a viable means of making money and survival. However, living in the neighborhood helped us understand this choice for young people in new ways. On the block, the drug-dealers were not simply cold outcasts who made money at the expense of the safety of the community. In contrast, they were sons, brothers, nephews, and cousins who grew up in the neighborhood and cared deeply about its safety. Residents acknowledged that one of the reasons property crime was so low in the neighborhood was because the drug dealers had a constant presence on the corners, could see all activity on the block, and prevented outsiders from committing crimes there. The paradoxical protective function of the dealers and non-dealers who hung out on the corners was extended to Jones as she walked from Jackson High to Nasir's house on one occasion. As Jones prepared to cross the street, she passed a group of men, one of whom began to proposition her. Another of the men identified Jones as "with the people in the yellow house." Clearly, Nasir's family's status in the neighborhood as good citizens, and likely the community work that Nasir's husband was involved in at the time, prompted the man to want to protect Jones.

The complexity of the relationship with drug dealers was also apparent when a new drug dealer took up post just outside of Nasir's house, and stashed drugs under the fence adjacent to her yard. Her husband had a conversation with the man and asked him not to stash the drugs under the fence because they had young children who played in the yard. He agreed to remove the drugs and said, "I understand, I got kids, too." And yet, his continued presence in front of the house created additional traffic and made Nasir's family and guests anxious. Eventually, he was a major reason why Nasir decided to move from the neighborhood.

These community-linked roles were made more complex by positionality with respect to race and ethnicity, class, age, and gender. Being young, female, and African American while doing research in urban and predominantly African American communities made us insiders in a certain way, as it was easier for stakeholders to see that we had a vested interest the youth and in the community. We shared a set of cultural assumptions and practices with community members, as well as use of African American Vernacular English (AAVE) as a dialect, which eased communication and made access to in-group relations much smoother. For Nasir and Jones, the way in which school personnel at Jackson privileged African Americans was evident when a group of Nasir's undergraduate students from the university came to the school. The group was predominantly White, with a handful of students of color, including one African American student. When they went into the office to ask for instructions, the secretary spoke only to the African American student.

While our positions in our respective research sites were eased by a shared racial and ethnic heritage, Nasir and Jones found that their positioning as middle-class sometimes posed challenges. At times, for instance, the researchers' middle class values and background raised suspicions among participants. To illustrate, while collecting data at the crisis shelter, Jones met Sheila, a resident who was living with her boyfriend and earning money as a prostitute before coming to the shelter. Shelia asked Jones for assistance one night while sorting through clothes. Shelia needed a trash bag to dispose of the clothing she wore when she "worked the streets." She was very excited about making this life change and threw away several items that marked her past, including a pair of knee-length leather high-heeled boots. She was left with only a pair of slippers and wore them around the shelter and the neighborhood for the next week. Sheila declined offers to search through the donations bag for another pair of shoes. Sheila approached us and asked if Jones could bring in any unused sneakers. When Jones brought three pairs of slightly worn shoes,

Sheila declined them because she specifically wanted sneakers, not shoes. During the interaction, Jones was challenged to suspend judgment of Sheila's decision while continuing to engage her in the conversation about her desire to have sneakers that fit her style. This incident highlighted the class differences that prompted Sheila to not consider shoes (as opposed to sneakers) a viable choice, and Jones to have the opposite view. Sheila continued to wear slippers for another week until another shelter staff member donated a pair of sneakers that she liked.

Class privilege also meant that we were not subject to the same conditions as other community members, and thus were not complete insiders. For instance, while Nasir lived in the community, her children went to schools outside of the community; while many of the families with students attending Jackson were renters, Nasir owned her home. When Jones was out with homeless youth, police officers protected her from harassment perhaps because of the ways that her speech patterns and clothing separated her from the group. The issue of class privilege was not as salient in the church setting however, because members comprised a wide range of socioeconomic statues.

As African American women, gender positioning also had an impact on our access to information and the ways in which we navigated ourselves in the field. The majority of teachers at Jackson High School were female. Several of them who were of African American descent organized an after-school club for girls, which fostered sisterhood and provided decision-making support. Students and parents often invited lead teachers to attend family events. As female researchers, Nasir and Jones were welcomed into this atmosphere of female mentoring and invited to offer input on the program design. Jones related well both to the girls, because they saw her as a friendly confidant, and the boys, because they viewed her as physically attractive and assumed her to be closer to them in age than she actually was. Nasir was older and closer to the age of students' mothers, and she often felt a tension between simply understanding the youth's perspectives and offering motherly advice in the African American tradition. Nasir was in her early 30s at the time of the study and Jones was in her mid-20s. For Peele-Eady, being an African American woman from the south with a background in teaching children meant that church members expected her to participate in the young women's ministry group meeting and help plan and teach Vacation Bible School in the summers. While such participation provided Peele-Eady with insight into the kinds of activities available to various age and gender groups in the church context, at other times, it caused tension between her pedagogical knowledge and skill and her quest to document these activities and the ways members of the community went about teaching children what they needed to know.

At other moments, most often at the shelter in South Jackson, being female negatively impacted our access. After one of the Center's female staff was reprimanded for fraternizing socially with a former male client and a shelter security guard was fired for sexually propositioning multiple female clients, administrators set stringent protocol for client/staff codes of conduct. While at the shelter, we were permitted to enter both the male and female bed areas, but were intentional about conducting all interviews with young men in the common areas to prevent any accusations of impropriety. Nasir and Jones were also requested to accompany nightly outreach workers who canvassed the areas where street kids were known to gather. Workers disseminated snacks as well as information about the shelter and community center resources. Shelter coordinators raised concerns about Jones being unable to manage the sexual advances she might encounter and general issues of her safety due to gender. Consequently, Jones was unable to get permission to observe the nightly street outreach.

CONCLUDING THOUGHTS

By describing the challenges we faced as insiders and outsiders of the communities we studied and how we negotiated these challenges, we have highlighted several critical ways the nature of the urban environments we studied and the ways we were both positioned by others and positioned ourselves, influenced our data collection and analyses. Gathering data as African American women who lived and worked in the communities where we conducted our work, allowed us to observe and relate to participants in official as well as unofficial spaces. Beyond race, gender, and class positioning, our familiarity with African American cultural norms, values, and language figured prominently in the ways we addressed and interacted with members of the community. These factors not only mediated the methodological decisions we made while in the field, but also determined our inductive reasoning throughout the research process. At times, our status as cultural insiders enhanced the relationship we had with the participants, and subsequently, fortified the kinds of data we were able to collect in our sites. At other times, the paucity of resources in our sites, and our own racial, gender, and class positioning limited our access to aspects of participants' experiences and caused us to struggle to maintain (or release) our relationships in the field. But in each case, having borders at times, and allowing for the absence of borders at other times, were necessary parts of the research process.

In addition to practical constraints, we have also touched on the ways that the vulnerability of the people and communities we encountered in our work posed ethical dilemmas with the ways that we understood and portrayed participants, as well as the choices that we made as we met the requirements of our research projects, our ethical obligations as community members, and our responsibilities as humans to contribute to the well-being of others.

Specifically, we believe our account has implications for qualitative researchers conducting research in urban settings specifically, as well as lessons for those who are conducting research in communities similar to their home communities. Below, we offer a list of suggestions that stem from our experiences.

- Build relationships with key personnel and stakeholders (this will support access to limited time and space). As researchers, we have the responsibility to follow cues from our participants about the norms, rules, and expectations of the setting.
- Reciprocate in ways that the community finds valuable. Find ways to manage reciprocity so it does not interfere with the integrity of the research.
- Be flexible; both with respect to time and space, but also in terms of the roles you take on and are asked to take on. Know what promises you are willing to make and do not make promises you cannot keep.
- Be mindful of the social capital (and limitations) that positionality with respect to gender, race, and age offer in a particular site at particular times.
- Understand and attend to the nuances, tensions, and contradictions in urban school spaces, as well as the complexity of the broader social contexts within which they are set.
- Be aware of power and privilege (with respect to class, race, etc.) and how these function in interactions with participants.
- Work hard to establish high levels of trust with participants, through authentic engagement in the setting.

We think that these suggestions offer other researchers important issues to consider in conducting qualitative and ethnographic research. More generally, we hope our account not only gives justice to the complexity of negotiating researcher positionality in urban contexts, but also help others make qualitative research in urban school and community settings a productive and humanistic endeavor.

NOTE

1.   Pseudonyms replace the names of all people and places.

REFERENCES

Clifford, J. (2007). Spatial practices: Fieldwork, travel, and the disciplining of anthropology. In A. Gupta & J. Ferguson (Eds.), *Anthropological locations: Boundaries and grounds of a field science* (pp. 147–162). Berkeley: University of California Press.

Cole, J. B., & Guy-Sheftall, B. (2003). The Black church: What's the word? In J. B. Cole & B. Guy-Sheftall (Eds.), *Gender talk: The struggle for women's equality in African American communities*. New York: One World.

Emerson, R., Fretz, R., & Shaw, L. (1995). *Writing ethnographic fieldnotes*. Chicago: University of Chicago.

Finn, J. (1989). Withdrawing from school. *Review of Educational Research, 59*(2), 117–142.

Furrer, C., & Skinner, E. (2003). Sense of relatedness as a factor in children's academic engagement and performance. *Journal of Educational Psychology, 95*(1), 148–162.

Glesne, C., & Peshkin, A. (1992). *Becoming qualitative researchers*. White Plains, NY: Longman Publishing Group.

Klem, A. M., & Connell, J. P. (2004). Relationships matter: Linking teacher support to student engagement and achievement. *Journal of School Health, 74*(7), 262–273.

Lawrence-Lightfoot, S., & Davis, J. H. (1997). *The art and science of portraiture*. San Francisco: Jossey-Bass.

Libbey, H. P. (2004) Measuring student relationships to school: Attachment, bonding, connectedness and engagement. *Journal of School Health, 74*(7), 274–283.

Nasir, N., Jones, A., & McLaughlin, M. (2007). *School Connectedness for students in low-income urban high schools*. Unpublished manuscript, Stanford University.

Nasir, N., Jones, A., & McLaughlin, M. (2009). What does it mean to be African American?: Constructions of racial/ethnic identity and school performance in an urban public high school. *American Educational Research Journal, 46*(1), 73–114

Noguera, P., & Wing, J. (2006). *Unfinished business: Closing the racial achievement gap in our schools*. San Francisco: Jossey-Bass.

Oakes, J. (1982). *Keeping track: How schools structure inequality*. New Haven, CT: Yale University.

Passari, J. (1997). You can't take the subway to the field!: Village epistemologies in the global village. In A. Gupta & J. Ferguson (Eds.), *Anthropological locations: Boundaries and grounds of a field science* (pp. 147–162). Berkeley: University of California Press.

Peele-Eady, T. (2005). *God don't like ugly: The socialization of African American children in Sunday school at a Missionary Baptist Church*. Unpublished doctoral dissertation, Claremont Graduate University, Claremont, CA.

Peele-Eady, T. (2008). *Constructing a membership identity through language and social interaction: The case of African American children at Faith Missionary Baptist Church*. Unpublished manuscript, University of New Mexico.

ABOUT THE AUTHORS

Wanda J. Blanchett is the dean and Ewing Marion Kauffman/Missouri Endowed Chair in Teacher Education at the University of Missouri-Kansas City. Dr. Blanchett's research focuses on issues of inequity including urban teacher preparation, issues of race, class, culture, and gender, disproportionate representation of students of color in special education, severe disabilities, and issues of sexuality for students with disabilities.

Andrew Brantlinger is a third-year assistant professor in mathematics education at the University of Maryland, College Park. Andrew's research interests are in the areas of secondary mathematics education, urban schooling, alternative routes to teaching, and the sociology of education.

Beverly Cross is the Moss Chair of Excellence in Urban Education at the University of Memphis. She is nationally recognized for her record of teaching, scholarship, and service in urban education. She has conducted research in the areas of teacher diversity, urban education, multicultural and anti-racist education, and curriculum theory.

Raquel Farmer-Hinton is an associate professor in the Educational Policy and Community Studies department at the University of Wisconsin-Milwaukee. Her research, teaching, and service agenda focuses on educational inequities, the urban context in which many of these inequities exist, and the school communities who educate within these inequitable contexts.

Delsue Frankson is a doctoral candidate at Florida International University in Miami, Florida. She is currently a response to intervention and inclusion education learning facilitator for the School District of Palm Beach County, Florida. She previously worked as an adjunct professor at Florida International University College of Exceptional Student Education.

Liana Gonzalez is a graduate of Florida International University where she is currently a visiting instructor for the College of Education. Inspired by her experiences as a teacher, Dr. Gonzalez' current line of research focuses on the inclusion of students with disabilities in urban settings.

carol d. lee is the edwina s. tarry professor of education and social policy and professor of African American education at Northwstern University. She is a past president of the American Educational Research Association and of the National Conference of Research on Language and Literacy, and a member of the National Academy of Education. She is a founder of four schools in Chicago.

Jamie Lew is associate professor of sociology at Rutgers University, Newark, New Jersey. Her research area includes sociology of education, immigration and education, race and ethnicity. She specializes in school achievement and racial identities of children of immigrants.

Na'ilah Suad Nasir is an associate professor of education and African American Studies at the University of California, Berkeley. Her research centers on how issues of culture and race influence the learning, achievement, and educational trajectories of African American students in urban school and community settings.

Jody Polleck is currently a full-time assistant professor in adolescent literacy at Hunter College and a part-time 10th grade English teacher in New York City. Her research focuses on differentiated instruction and culturally responsive instruction and curriculum for urban youth.

Kimberly A. Scott is an associate professor in Arizona State University's School of Social Transformation. Kimberly has developed a research agenda focused on gender, age, race, and digital equity. Trained as a sociologist of education, she is currently serving as the principal investigator of a National Science Foundation-funded program, COMPUGIRLS (www.compugirls.asu.edu). This manuscript represents her third book and continued commitment to community.

Monika Williams Shealey is associate dean for teacher education and associate professor of special education at the University of Missouri, Kansas City. Dr. Shealey's research interests examine the intersection of urban and special education, experiences of traditionally marginalized groups in special education, and the leadership development of students and faculty of color.

Jessica A. Solyom is pursuing her PhD in justice studies at ASU Jessi has worked with several social justice oriented programs including Upward Bound, the Utah Opportunity Scholarship and COMPUGIRLS. While with COMPUGIRLS, in collaboration with the Gila River Indian Community, she helped start the program's first branch in Indian country.

Eustace G. Thompson is currently associate professor and assistant chair of the Department of Teaching, Literacy and Leadership at Hofstra University. He was formerly the deputy superintendent of the Uniondale Public Schools, located on Long Island, New York. He has 37 years of experience in urban and suburban public schools settings.

Kimberley Woo's research interests include Asian American students, multiculturalism, and teacher preparation. The foci of her work include decreasing the chasm between theory and practice, promoting multicultural awareness, and facilitating discussions of diversity. Currently, Woo is currently working as an independent educational consultant.

Shelley Zion is an assistant research professor at the University of Colorado Denver. She works on three levels: with school leaders to improve and inform the ways that schools are constructed; with doctoral students to understand the influence of power and privilege; and with high school students to effect change.